Ethics, Aesthetics, and the Beyond of Language

SUNY series, Insinuations: Philosophy, Psychoanalysis, Literature

---

Charles Shepherdson, editor

Ethics, Aesthetics, and the Beyond of Language

Robert Hughes

SUNY PRESS

Published by State University of New York Press, Albany

Printed in the United States of America

For information, contact State University of New York Press, Albany, NY
www.sunypress.edu

Production by Eileen Meehan
Marketing by Anne M. Valentine

Library of Congress Cataloging-in-Publication Data

Hughes, Robert, 1968–
Ethics, aesthetics, and the beyond of language / Robert Hughes.
p. cm.
Includes bibliographical references and index.
ISBN 978-1-4384-3193-2 (hardcover: alk. paper)
ISBN 978-1-4384-3194-9 (pbk. : alk. paper)
1. American fiction—18th century—History and criticism. 2. American fiction—19th century—History and criticism. 3. Ethics in literature. 4. Aesthetics in literature. 5. Psychology and literature. I. Title.

PS374.E86H84 2010
813.001—dc22 2009051690

10 9 8 7 6 5 4 3 2 1

Contents

List of Illustrations

Acknowledgments

Cover image: Gustave Moreau (1826–1898), *Orpheus*, Musée d'Orsay, Paris, France. Photo credit: Réunion des Musées Nationaux/Art Resource, NY.

A shorter, earlier version of chapter one was published under the same title in *Arizona Quarterly* 61, no. 3 (Fall 2005).

The image of the portrait associated with Beatrice Cenci, in chapter 2, has been granted courtesy of the Archivio Fotografico Soprintendenza Speciale per il Patrimonio Storico Artistico e Etnoantropologico e per il Polo Museale della città di Roma. Photo credit: Scala/Ministero per i Beni e le Attività culturali/ Art Resource, NY.

The image of Vincent van Gogh's *Shoes*, in chapter 4, has been granted courtesy of the Van Gogh Museum Amsterdam (Vincent van Gogh Foundation).

The image from Iannis Xenakis' score for *Nomos Alpha*, in chapter 5, is reprinted by permission of Boosey & Hawkes, Inc. © Copyright 1967 by Boosey & Hawkes Music Publishers Limited.

A shorter, earlier version of chapter 7 was published under the same title in *Postmodern Culture* 17, no. 3 (May 2007).

Introduction

Opening Questions: Ethics, Literature, and the Beyond of Language

Since at least the time of the classical Roman poet, Horace, it has been a commonplace of how we speak about literature to say that it must not only delight and give pleasure—it must also instruct and be useful (*Ars Poetica*, lines 333–34, 343–44). True, we do not ordinarily expect a poem to teach us how to make a couch or train a horse, but when children are required to read literature in school, perhaps more than anything else we expect it to educate their moral sensibilities. Ubiquitous as the Horatian platitude remains, it has hardly gone uncontested in recent centuries—even among critics and writers seeking merely to refine its scope. Nathaniel Hawthorne, for example, who so often proposed an explicit moral to his tales, nevertheless did not flatter himself that such apothegms, or the romances that support them, operate with anything like direct influence. As he puts it in the preface to *The House of the Seven Gables*:

> When romances do really teach anything, or produce any effective operation, it is usually through a far more subtile process than the ostensible one. The Author has considered it hardly worth his while, therefore, relentlessly to impale the story with its moral . . . — . . . as by sticking a pin through a butterfly—thus at once depriving it of life, and causing it to stiffen in an ungainly and unnatural attitude. (352)

Thus, Hawthorne suggests—and perhaps the old Roman would agree with him[1]—that the living ethical force of a work of literature, the good that it may effect, is reducible neither to the content of any didactic advice it may offer, nor even to its moral theme. Indeed, to insist relentlessly upon a direct exposition of the moral is to do violence to both the aesthetic and the ethical potential operative in the work, since this potential derives from some indirect, "far more subtile" process amenable to beauty, pleasure, and life.

Such indirection seems counterintuitive in many respects, not least of which is our everyday notion of language. In the ordinary consideration of the matter, language is a tool. One has a thought, perhaps a moral injunction, and wishes to make it someone else's thought too, so one speaks, or writes, and the thought is thereby carried on the wings of language from one's own mind to that of the other. And yet, upon further reflection, most people will also recognize that language can reach beyond its function as a tool for the communication of ideas. In language, writes Johann Gottfried Herder, the great eighteenth-century critic and philosopher,

> [a] breath of our mouth becomes the portrait of the world, the type of our thoughts and feelings in the other's soul. On a bit of moving air depends everything human that men on earth have ever thought, willed, done, and ever will do; for we would all still be roaming the forests if this divine breath had not blown around us, and did not hover on our lips like a magic tome.[2]

Language is more than just the first, most fundamental technology and does more than just carry ideas from one head to another. It is also, as Herder suggests, the foundational fact of our humanity. In the most thoroughgoing way, language structures our thought, guides our perception, and gives the very raw material of our dreams and imaginings. Even beyond its celebrated power for representation, language reaches into our souls, enlivens the world and the things around us, and structures the most basic relationship between ourselves and the other. It is the most essential work of literature—as the present book will argue—to renew our sense for this dimension of language beyond representation. But if this is so, how then are we to understand the common intuitive sense, recognized from Horace to Hawthorne, that literature also bears upon the ethical? What does this insight imply for an ethics beyond representation and representational thought? How would we understand an ethics in these terms? And how, finally, are we to think about the relationships among literature, ethics, and this "beyond of language"?

So here, on the terrain of this "beyond" of language, the present study addresses itself to the intersection of two problems: the problem of literature and the problem of ethics. The problem of *literature* regards the question of what literature is—for present purposes, this regards especially the question of how literature works to engage the reader's interest and passion, what kind of work it performs upon the reader, and how it manages to afflict the reader with the urgent sense that something in the text is calling for a response. The problem of *ethics* regards the question of whether anything even remains of ethics after one concedes the point that virtually everything one may consciously think perhaps falls more properly under the heading of *politics*—that is, under the historically contingent and the ideologically freighted. At the intersection of these two problems, then, one finds the two more precise questions of this book: how might one think of a properly ethical dimension to literature, and how might one think of an aesthetic dimension to ethics. These key questions are posed in tandem by the core literary texts of the present work, three works of Romantic American fiction: Charles Brockden Brown's *Wieland* (1798), Washington Irving's "Legend of Sleepy Hollow" (1820), and Nathaniel Hawthorne's *The Marble Faun* (1860).

Each of these texts, as we shall see, strikes a complex relation between the ethical and the literary, a productive tension between an intellectual effort to describe or to present the ethical and the necessarily indirect, aesthetic workings of literary fiction. In the postscript to "The Legend of Sleepy Hollow," for example, the text begs the question of the moral of the preceding tale, but then seems to assert that no reasonable moral may be derived from the remarkable legend. In *Wieland*, the prefatory advertisement claims as the novel's purpose the illustration of the moral constitution of man, but then the novel proceeds to destabilize both an ethics of faith as well as an ethics of reason. In *The Marble Faun*, the preface announces the novel's ambition to evolve a thoughtful moral, but then weaves a text of the most fragile uncertainty and profoundest perplexity, as if to suspend its readers in relation to a void of thought, a place where ethics confronts some impossibility of thinking.

The present study reads these works of early American fiction and takes them in earnest both for their moral ambitions and for the impossibility they seem to announce in the way one can think about ethics. What this book finds is that each text locates an ethical demand precisely at the place where language and understanding fail and reason arrives at an impasse. Literature, as we shall see, highlights and imposes a psychological, existential, and ethical necessity to respond to this crisis in language. Thus, for instance, in the strangely contagious tale of Sleepy Hollow and in the nightly rhythms of its uncanny horseman, this book finds the force of an enigmatic ethical imperative: an obligation to bear witness to an event from the Revolutionary War—and to do this despite the confounding impossibility of determining the precise nature of that event. Something analogous is at work in the other two texts as well: *Wieland* presents a heroine who, haunted by the unaccountable and unforgettable image of her brother's suicide, must not only write to live but live to write. And through its strange suspension before the alterity of time, death, and radical enigma, *The Marble Faun* calls upon its readers to assume an ethical relation to the text and to bear without relief the weight of its mysteries. Thus, in all of these texts, out of an overwhelming encounter with death, where being and subjectivity themselves come under question, we find not only a certain impasse of expression and understanding, but also a powerful ethical obligation to speak and to tell a tale. What we see opened up aesthetically, here in the desperate struggle to put the mysterious event properly into language, is an ethical space where human nature can come into its own.

To further develop the theoretical stakes of these literary readings, the present book also reads four twentieth-century continental thinkers, Jacques Lacan, Martin Heidegger, Emmanuel Levinas, and Alain Badiou, who in psychoanalysis and philosophy renewed the effort to think about an ethics beyond cognition and its contingent values. It is a remarkable fact that, in their efforts to speak about foundational ethics, they each in turn find themselves impelled to speak also about art and literature, as if aesthetics and art had some special capacity to bring this obscure and abstract ethical space into view. Thus, in tandem with writing and speaking about ethics, Lacan speaks about Cézanne's apples, gothic cathedrals, and *Antigone*, Heidegger writes of Hölderlin's poetry, Van Gogh's painting of a pair of peasant shoes, and (again) *Antigone*, Levinas writes of Xenakis' "Nomos Alpha for Cello Solo," *Macbeth*, and the Vatican's statue of the Laocoon group, and Badiou writes of *Hamlet*, Beckett's prose, and Schoenberg's serialist music. Through these more theoretical readings, it will be seen that, as a mode of expression that draws its power from a certain relation to the incomprehensible, the unknown, or the unconscious, literature is able to communicate a part of ethics that resists traditional philosophy.

We are not concerned, then, in the present project on ethics, to venture into any question of values or systems of values—although indeed Lacan, Heidegger, Levinas, and Badiou each adopt something very much like a value, a single value, as the foundation for their ethics, a kind of truth they hold to be self-evident and thus subject to no further justification. The psychoanalyst, perhaps unsurprisingly, picks the value of desire, the philosophers pick the value of the truth of being, and the postwar Jewish thinker of ethics asserts the prohibition against murder. But they all, as this book will note, situate these dicta in terms of the human relation to language. Moreover, Heidegger, Lacan, and

Badiou (all explicitly) and (less necessarily) Levinas all link this relation to language to the workings of art.

Lacan, for example, observes in his clinical practice that the pathological guilt feelings patients arrive with correlate not so much with having violated some law or social more, but rather with having given up on desire. That is, in their denials and repressions, the guilty patient has betrayed not some object of desire; rather, they've betrayed the psychological and ethical imperative to desire as such. Psychoanalysis is an ethical practice, then, insofar as it aims to bring patients to a more sustained relation to their faculty of desire. One of the things this means, and here the ethics of psychoanalysis begins to intersect with literature, is that since desire and language are bound up together in the same problematics, human subjects must open themselves up to the desire that comes out of the absence or void inherent in language. Lacan's theory of aesthetics describes art and literature in these same terms: art, for Lacan, is an encounter with the absence at the heart of language and the signifier.

In a Heideggerian consideration, ethics bears upon the obligation to attain to a higher degree of *being*. What this entails, however, is a special kind of engagement with *language*, a responsibility to read and to listen with care to how language, in its nonrepresentational, poetic dimension, opens up the world. In Heidegger's remarkable reading of Van Gogh's shoes, we sense this ethical obligation to bear witness to being and language by attending carefully to art, and we see, moreover, that art and literature have a special capacity to bring us into relation to being. Language, says Heidegger, calls to us, summons us to being, and appeals to us to speak as poetically as possible and thereby to testify to our own humanity and its uncanny way of being.

Levinas, throughout his long career, describes the ethical in a number of different ways. In *Otherwise than Being* (1974), he describes it as an abandonment of ego-bound solipsism and a venturing forth toward the other—such as one might see in an event of language. Levinas calls the ethical dimension of language the "saying." The saying suggests the way that, before one opens one's mouth to speak or even knows what to say, one gives oneself over to the other, forsaking the inwardness of silence and offering oneself in an ethical act of language. Here one glimpses one way of thinking about the ethical dimension of art and literature for Levinas: art not only shares with other language events that ethical opening up to the other, but, as an aesthetic event, it goes still further, implying a vulnerability to being affected in a way that affirms that the sensate subject is for the other (and not for him- or herself). This is why, as Levinas argues, a poem constitutes a kind of ethical movement, a quest for the other. Additionally, by considering the event of art together with its call for exegesis, Levinas proposes an ethics of criticism directed at reawakening within the work of art the ethical saying that gave rise to it.

For Badiou, ethics concerns faithfulness to the emergence of a new truth within one of four registers: science, politics, love, and art. It is "ethical" insofar as, by faithfully participating in a truth, one is able to surpass one's animal finitude and accede to a fully human subjectivity. Ethics intersects with the literary both in that art is one of the four procedures that produces a truth and also in a more specific way: to be faithful to a truth requires that one continue the truth process beyond its initiating event in part by striving to bring this truth into the language of the situation in which that truth happens. Because the existing situation itself cannot provide the language for a truth that is radically alterior to that situation, the ethical subject must, as Badiou puts it, "poeticize" in order to name and be faithful to the truth.

So, finally, what we might say of all these literary and theoretical readings—and this is really the thesis of the present book—is that language, especially in its nonrepresentational dimension, such as we see it in literature, opens upon the ethical for human beings. This other dimension of language involves matters of address, of response and responsibility, of entering into the world of language and the relationships and limitations it entails. To enter more fully into language is ethical, as will be seen, because it casts us into relation with death or mortality or the void, but does so in order to rearticulate that relation with death into the relation with life.

Hence, this book, like the psychoanalysts and philosophers it discusses, and as will emerge in the literary texts it reads, describes a foundational ethics, and does so, it will be admitted, within very narrow terms. Let it be said here, however, that to speak of an ethics or of literature beyond logic or reason or cognition is not to promote illogical irrationalism, and to speak of an ethics beyond values is not to declare that all values are to be rejected. This study does not contest the indispensable social and psychological importance of moral-political-ideological values. Nor could it possibly contest the power of reason. The present book does not set itself in opposition to reason and values, but takes as its theme the beyond of these things, and attempts to treat this beyond with rigor and critical responsibility. Values are not, as we shall see, the only terms under which one may think about ethics, and reason is not the only term under which one may think and conduct critical practice.

In Lieu of a Historical Introduction

So, the texts at the heart of this book, literary, philosophical, and psychoanalytic, are united in posing, more or less explicitly, the question of the intersection of aesthetics and foundational ethics and in thinking through that intersection as it appears for the split subject, in and through literary or "poetic" language.

This is, in fact, a tradition in thinking about art and literature that originates with the early Romantics in Germany: with Friedrich Schiller and Friedrich Schlegel especially, but also with the broader circle of Jena Romantics, including Novalis, Friedrich Hölderlin, and Friedrich Schelling. From this German tradition we find the claim that humanity is essentially, existentially, lacking and that poetry and art offer a renewal of our relation to *being* by way of poetry's extraordinary use of *language*. These Romantic claims would be brought to a fuller first articulation in America in the essays of Ralph Waldo Emerson (and then retransmitted back to German philosophy by way of Nietzsche's reading of Emerson), but it was only in the twentieth century, with Heidegger and Lacan and their intense interest in the relation between language, on the one hand, and being or subjectivity, on the other, that these ideas could arrive at something like a mature theory of art and literature. The contribution of psychoanalysis is especially significant here, for while psychoanalysis does not generally have a professional interest in art and literature, psychoanalysis—as the *talking* cure, after all—must strive, for its own practical reasons, toward a theory that relates language to what we might call the aesthetic body, the body that manifests symptoms, but that also, as Lacan notes, responds in uncanny pleasure and interest to the workings of art based on nothing other than the word and the workings of the signifier.

Reading American Romantics together with twentieth-century and contemporary continental aesthetics is not so strange, then. Despite the ocean and the century between the two, and despite the academic divisions that have since arisen to defend their separateness, they share a developing Romantic and post-Romantic tradition of thinking about the work of art.

The present book is not primarily a historical study. A true historical study would have to give more fully developed pieces devoted to the German Romantics and Idealists, of course, but also to other American thinkers of art—to Emerson, naturally, but also to Poe and Melville and to Hawthorne in a more programmatic mood (as in his tale "The Artist of the Beautiful" and sections of *The Marble Faun* we leave aside in the chapter here). It would have to consider other key continental figures in the twentieth century who developed their ideas on art in a now post-Romantic tradition that was also distinctly Heideggerian: Maurice Blanchot, Jean-François Lyotard, Jacques Derrida, Jean-Luc Nancy and Philippe Lacoue-Labarthe. And it would have to pay particular attention to key transition figures—for example to Samuel Coleridge and Thomas Carlyle, as conduits between the German and the American Romantics, and to Friedrich Nietzsche,[3] as the key transition figure between Emerson and Heidegger.

Nonetheless, we might briefly observe that Charles Brockden Brown was quite directly familiar with the Germans, reading them as they appeared in journals in English translation, studying German himself, and participating in an intellectual circle that was distinctly Germanophile—translating Kotzebue (as William Dunlap did) and adapting Schiller for an operetta (as Elihu Hubbard Smith did). Indeed, Brown's own debt to Schiller, the real Professor of History at Jena (and the historian and playwright of Wallenstein), is generally underappreciated, especially as it appears in Brown's own major essay on aesthetics, "Walstein's School of History." As for Washington Irving, the seeming Germanisms of his well-known tale "Rip Van Winkle" are explicitly remarked upon in a postscriptive note by the narrator himself. Often overlooked, however, is the fact that Irving wrote his legend about the headless German soldier terrorizing Sleepy Hollow while in the company of Walter Scott who, to be sure, was remarkable for inventing a national literature for the Scots (as Irving is credited with doing for the Americans), but who was also, in the 1790s, the translator of Goethe's *Götz von Berlichingen* and other German works. Nathaniel Hawthorne arrives rather later in literary history, when American literary culture had been already Romanticized, German literary culture to some degree assimilated, and the German cult of Shakespeare broadly established. Still, his neighbor and walking companion, Ralph Waldo Emerson, owned a library full of German titles, in the original and in translation: Schiller and Goethe, of course, but also Jean-Paul, Novalis, Schelling, the Schlegels, and others.[4] Additionally, we might say of contemporary continental aesthetics that there are two principal, sometimes interrelated strains of thought: the Marxist and the Heideggerian. The Heideggerian strain, treated in the present book, descends directly from Martin Heidegger's engagement with the thought of the German Romantic poets Novalis and Friedrich Hölderlin, and to some extent from his reading of Nietzsche, whose debt to the German Romantics, through Emerson, has already been remarked. Finally, although the German Romantics themselves had only a peripheral importance in the development of psychoanalytic thought, ever since Freud's first articulation of the Oedipus complex, psychoanalytic thought has turned repeatedly to the work of two pre-Romantic literary figures—Sophocles and Shakespeare—who were taken over and "Romanticized" as a constant touchstone (and object of translation)[5] for the early German Romantics themselves. Indeed one might well argue that when Sigmund Freud, or Ernest Jones, or Jacques Lacan consider art through the lens of Sophocles and Shakespeare, they are really reading "the Romantic Sophocles" and "the Romantic Shakespeare," rather than the Attic Sophocles or the Elizabethan Shakespeare. So, while the present book is driven more by questions of aesthetics and ethics than by questions of history, nonetheless, the essays here closely concern the development of a coherent historical entity deriving from the German Romantics: a shared tradition, generally overlooked within the bounds of contemporary disciplines, of American Romantic and continental post-Romantic thinking about art and ethics as together bearing essentially upon a certain relation to language and existential lack.

One might suppose, then, that the literary texts for this project could have been chosen from any period and any national literature whatever, so long as they were instances of "literary" texts, in the sense of braiding together language, ethics, and a radical subjective void, in ways that will be described later in this book. Perhaps so. Nonetheless, had the literary texts selected been written by Sophocles, William Shakespeare, and Friedrich Schiller, or by Wallace Stevens, Ralph Ellison, and Vladimir Nabokov, or by Franz Kafka, Mikhail Bulgakov, and J. M. Coetzee, or by Paul Auster, Don Delillo, and Cormac McCarthy, it would have obscured one historical claim that this study would happily assert: namely, that these early American fictions were then—and are still—participants in a larger, Western discourse about ethics and art and that to treat them in unnatural national isolation is to ignore the social connections and the actual reading habits of the writers themselves, which were rather more cosmopolitan than is usually remembered.

One final remark regarding the composition of the present book: it is an additional legacy of German Romanticism to suggest that literature is itself a way of thinking. Friedrich Schlegel, for example, in his *Athenaeum Fragments*, suggests that, as poetry becomes art and surpasses mere craft, it fuses inspiration *and* criticism (§116) to become simultaneously a work of art and a reflection on its own status as a work of art (§255). In other words, *literature*, Romantically defined, *thinks*—and what it thinks, what it puzzles over, is itself. Certainly, a literary text—like any text or any object at all—can serve to provide illustrations for nonartistic ways of thinking—and historians, philosophers, clinicians, and other writers and teachers have often turned to literary texts to fulfill just this handmaidenly task. In fact, at several points, the present book will itself exploit literary and artistic examples in just this way. But literature, as Schlegel suggests, can do something more—something specifically related to its essence as art and quite apart from whatever philosophy or science would make of it. If literature is indeed a mode of thinking, then literature must proceed according to its own logic, distinct from the logic of philosophy, even the logic of the philosophy of art, and distinct from any clinically based, psychoanalytic consideration of art. The logic of *literature*, we might say, is responsible to the work of art: it must seize hold of itself as a work that, in some uncanny way, moves the subject, manipulating the subject's relation to what this book will describe variously as trauma, the real, the thing, nothingness, absence, death, and/or the void. For present purposes, we might say that the logic of *philosophy*, in contrast to that of literature, is responsible primarily to reason and to some degree of systematicity, to truth and to what *is*; the logic of *psychoanalysis*, in yet another contrast, must be responsible to what appears empirically in the clinic and, ultimately, practically, to clinical efficacy. In short, literature, psychoanalysis, and philosophy are each modes of thinking with varying commitments and values and with different definitions of what constitutes legitimate thought. It is the wish of the present book to capture some of what each of these modes of thinking—literary, philosophical, and psychoanalytic—properly has to offer in considering the intersection of art and ethics.

Such an ambition faces an immediate practical obstacle in a certain "powerlessness" essential to artistic thought. As plenty of well-intentioned and otherwise interesting critical studies demonstrate, the evanescent encounter with the thought of literature is all too easily overwhelmed by the forceful claims that philosophy and clinical practice assert. A precious and fragile thing emerges in the work of art, and an "ethical" criticism must respect that thing and must resist as much as possible the impulse to imperialize the literary moment by imposing the dogma of literary theory or the claims of philosophy and psychoanalysis. At the same time, the power of expository writing to lay out and develop ideas clearly and systematically seems indispensable for critical work. So what is one to do? To allow for these differing modes of thinking, the present book has been chaptered to allow the main literary works a space of their own, while in other chapters offering more expository readings of philosophical and psychoanalytic texts that explore and develop and complicate the scope and the stakes of the thought posed by the literary texts themselves. The author hopes that this alternation of literary and philosophical/psychoanalytic chapters will lead the reader along a pleasing, thought-provoking, and ever-deepening course of thought. Readers who find this solution inconvenient and wish that the theoretical reflections had been grouped together at the start or at the end of the book may, of course, avail themselves of the table of contents and read the chapters in whatever order they please.

Before turning to the essays themselves, the reader will kindly indulge the author as he mentions a few names in sincerest gratitude. This project, as a whole, found its first articulation in a dissertation seminar with Professor Jean-François Lyotard at Emory University; most of these chapters were first drafted under the direction of Professor Cathy Caruth, also at Emory. Without Professor Lyotard's excitement and Professor Caruth's patient care, that dissertation and this book would never have been written. The book also owes very deep debts of gratitude to three other readers: to Jennifer Ballengee, now at Towson University, to Charles Shepherdson, editor of this book series, and to Epp Annus, a novelist and scholar now with the Estonian Literary Museum. These three readers saved the author's life in more ways than one and gave this book their time, care, and interest at exactly the times it needed these things most. In such cases, mere gratitude must suffer the pangs of its own inadequacy and yet it must give itself out nonetheless. And: more names, more pangs, more thanks to be given to: Professor Ellie Ragland at the University of Missouri—Columbia; Professors Mark Bauerlein, Elissa Marder, Claire Nouvet, Jill Robbins, and Cynthia Willett, all at Emory University; Professor Kareen Malone at the State University of West Georgia; analysts Willy Apollon, Danielle Bergeron, and Lucie Cantin, all with the Gifric group in Québec; Professor Michael Schwartz at Augusta State University in Georgia; Professors Susan Williams, Elizabeth Renker, David Herman, James Phelan, and Ethan Knapp, all at Ohio State University; my student research assistants, Ashley Matney and Jon Holmes, at (or formerly at) Ohio State University; the editor and readers at *Postmodern Culture*; the editor and readers at *Arizona Quarterly*; and the often very, very generous institutions that have supported the writing of this book: the Department of Comparative Literature at Emory University, the Department of Languages and Literature at Augusta State University, and the Department of English at Ohio State University. *Ja veel üks kord Epule: sa oled ikka ja alati mu kõigeparem lugeja ja kõigekallim armastus.*

CHAPTER 1

Sleepy Hollow

Fearful Pleasures and the Nightmare of History

Rhythmic Beauty and Dreamy Charm: Memory, History, and the Pleasurable Tale

Some of the most sophisticated writings that recent decades have witnessed at the nexus of literature and history have been in the field of what has come to be called trauma theory.[1] One suspects that trauma theory has been especially fertile for literary studies at least in part because the telling of difficult histories gives rise to some of the most fundamental questions posed also by literature itself: questions about the nature of indirect reference, about the ethical stakes of putting events into language, and about the complex relations that may subsist between a spoken or written text and the world of history where social forces clash and real people live and die. The traumatized survivor—such as, for example, the soldier who suffers nightmares and flashbacks after returning from the scene of battle, or like a community ravaged by the chaos and violence of civil war—is haunted by a terrible and profound problem of memory, narrative, and ethics. How, for example, is one to *think* of—let alone *tell* of—an encounter with death, an event that by its very nature eludes human comprehension? How, for that matter, is one to account for the enigma of one's own survival in the face of death? As one influential critic has described the curious problem of history posed by traumatic events,

> The history that a flashback tells—as psychiatry, psychoanalysis, and neurobiology equally suggest—is . . . a history that literally *has no place*, neither in the past, in which it was not fully experienced, nor in the present in which its precise images

> and enactments are not fully understood. In its repeated imposition as both image and amnesia, the trauma thus seems to evoke the difficult truth of a history that is constituted by the very incomprehensibility of its occurrence.
>
> For the survivor of trauma, then, the truth of the event may reside not only in its brutal facts, but also in the way that their occurrence defies simple comprehension. The flashback or traumatic reenactment conveys, that is, both *the truth of an event*, and *the truth of its incomprehensibility*.[2]

Thus, on the one hand, it seems *impossible* to tell of such events that overwhelm any straightforward comprehension or narrative memory; yet on the other hand, to tell the tale, to bear witness, to testify to these events acquires for the traumatized subject a psychological and ethical *necessity*. To the question of how one is to reconcile this paradox of impossible discursive necessity, literature has seemed to promise an answer, as if literature perhaps had some privileged capacity for communicating the nightmares of history.

And indeed, one might argue that a relationship between literary writing and traumatic history was intuited as early as Sigmund Freud who, in his well-known essay on "The Uncanny" (1919), turned to the question of literature just as he was then also renewing his theoretical interest in trauma (in *Beyond the Pleasure Principle*), following the explosion of "war neuroses" in World War I. Freud was fascinated by the way severed heads and the return of the dead, for example, especially when presented to us through the "peculiarly directive power" of the storyteller (Freud, 266g, 251e), can call forth an unsettling, "uncanny" feeling that hearkens to what is at once intimately familiar and seemingly alien and strange—a feeling he described as referring ultimately to the "daemonic" automatisms of the death drive at the traumatic heart of human subjectivity (Freud 251g, 238e). Yet it seems plain too that direct testimonies of trauma—for example, testimonies from Holocaust survivors—are not themselves events of "literature," at least not as we have ordinarily used the term in university English or Comparative Literature departments. How, then, are we to understand the relations among history, trauma, and the properly literary? If we take Freud's hint and wish to consider the uncanny as the special province of trauma in literature, what are we to make of the indirection by which such fictional tales necessarily proceed—that they tell the truth, so to speak, by telling a lie? As the present essay will demonstrate, this shift from the traumatic register into the uncanny is precisely what allows the tale of a trauma to be told and heard and passed on again. Thus, a traumatic history—which of itself would be painful—is communicated instead as an uncanny tale that produces a strange variety of unsettling pleasure while still preserving a certain degree of traumatic force from the original historical event. The present essay will read "The Legend of Sleepy Hollow" (1820), the classic nightmare by Washington Irving (1783–1859), to trace out, in this one story, the transformation of a traumatic history from the Revolutionary War into a rather different sort of tale, a comic pastoral romance involving the disappearance of a schoolteacher.

Irving's legend revolves around Ichabod Crane, a New England schoolmaster with the comic figure of a scarecrow and an insatiable appetite for marvelous anecdotes, who arrives in the tiny Dutch hamlet of Sleepy Hollow, outside Tarry Town, New York, to establish a schoolhouse. Having accomplished this task with about as much success as one might hope for amid a rustic population suspicious alike of outsiders and book learning, Ichabod's attention turns to plump,[3] beautiful Katrina Van Tassel, the neighborhood's most eligible young woman and its most promising young heiress. Ichabod woos her like a champion, steals the field from his rival, the local rowdy, Brom Bones, and seems on the verge of bringing his suit to fruition, when an evening's festive quilting at the Van Tassels' brings an unforeseen reversal and a fall from fortune. At the party, toward the end of the evening, a "knot of sager folks" sits repeating frightful tales to each other in drowsy undertones (1077). Among them, Brom Bones, Ichabod's rival, tells of his own race against the region's most powerful spirit, a headless horseman, whose nightly rides on the byways of Sleepy Hollow are the terror of the countryside. As Ichabod heads home that fateful autumn evening, the pedagogue is ridden down by a headless horseman, and is never seen or heard from again by the people of Sleepy Hollow. The reader is left, at the end of the tale proper, with the coy question, Was Ichabod the casualty of fantastic legend or of real, mundane love? Was the horseman on the road that night indeed the spectral horror of legend? Or was the rider instead the prankish Brom Bones, sporting with the pedagogue's simple credence in tales of the marvelous, and ridding himself at the same time of a rival to the hand of the peerless Katrina? Brom Bones, Headless Horseman, we ask—What's the difference between the two? Or are they indeed identical? Is it even possible—or fruitful—to consider such nocturnal fantasies under the light of day, and if so, will the fantasy retain its otherworldly power as real, or will it be unmasked as a mere sport, a mundane counterfeit to excite and frighten the credulous?

The tale itself does not allow the reader to resolve the mystery of Ichabod Crane's disappearance nor the identity of the monstrous horseman. Some readers may find it reasonable to conclude that the horseman was Brom Bones, who takes such a hearty good humor in the tale of his rival's disappearance. Such readers might further give their confidence to an old farmer, who is one among a long chain of narrators of the tale, and who proposes (without citing evidence) that Ichabod survived and eventually found political appointment after retreating from the scene of Katrina's (alleged) amorous refusal. This is the reading that Disney, for example, gave in its comic pastoral romance, animated shortly after World War II, in 1949. But the fact remains that Irving was hardly averse to writing ghost tales,[4] and the problem of genre remains irreducible in Irving's own rendition of the legend. Indeed, the next in the chain of narrators, gives credence not to the farmer, but to the old country wives who are, he says, "the best judges of these matters," and who give a second reading, incompatible with the farmer's, maintaining that Ichabod was carried away by "supernatural means"—by the legendary headless horseman, one presumes (1086). One might look to Brom to settle the matter, but the boastful blade, uncharacteristically, says nothing at all on the matter of his rival's disappearance, making it impossible for the critical reader to determine whether the "knowing look" some observe on his face whenever the tale of Ichabod is told is indeed genuinely knowing, or else a consequence of the general neighborhood impulse to attribute anything like a prank to the rantipole hero (1069). Hence the two incompatible readings maintain an uneasy coexistence within the tale as Irving gives it to us. We shall see that the ambiguity assigned to the matter of *cause* in the tale (in the first instance, the difference between Brom Bones and the headless horseman) bears quite directly upon the peculiar relation between the uncanny quality of "The Legend of Sleepy Hollow" and the question of historical trauma. We shall see, moreover, that this question of the identity of the horseman, which lies at the center of even the most naïve reading of the legend, functions as a surprising but necessary proxy to still more profound questions that enable the transmission of a traumatic history in Irving's unsettling fiction.

Sleepy Hollow and the Nightmare of History

Near the start of Washington Irving's *Sketch Book of Geoffrey Crayon, Gent.* (1819–1820), the narrator explains his gravitation to Europe in terms familiar to readers of early American literary fiction. In a well-known passage, he writes, in "The Author's Account of Himself," that

> never need an American look beyond his own country for the sublime and beautiful of natural scenery.

> But Europe held forth the charms of storied and poetical association. There were to be seen the masterpieces of art, the refinements of highly cultivated society, the quaint peculiarity of ancient and local custom. My native country was full of youthful promise; Europe was rich in the accumulated treasures of age. Her very ruins told the history of times gone by, and every mouldering stone was a chronicle. I longed to wander over the scenes of renowned achievement—to tread as it were in the footsteps of antiquity—to loiter about the ruined castle—to meditate on the falling tower—to escape in short, from the commonplace realities of the present, and to lose myself among the shadowy grandeurs of the past. (744)

Sir Walter Scott's historical novels had garnered such enviable critical acclaim and popular success that Irving's Crayon, like Brown earlier and Hawthorne later,[5] must lament that America is a land without history. History and culture belonged, in the common view, to Europe. To America fell the sublimity of natural grandeur. Readers of Irving, however, will see a certain irony in such a division of human and worldly spoils. Even leaving aside the appearance in the 1820s of some outstanding American historical novels by Cooper, Child, and Sedgwick, Irving's own literary reputation had already been established with *A History of New York* (1809), his hugely successful (and gently satirical) history of the seventeenth-century Dutch settlement in New York. It may have been something of a burlesque, this history, but in important ways, it indicated a genuine and serious regard for the existence and necessity of an American history. It also foreshadowed Irving's more earnest researches in American history, some decades later, with his work on the early Spanish exploration of the Americas, the life of George Washington, and other topics. *A History of New York*, published under the pseudonym of Diedrich Knickerbocker, had gone through two editions (with a third under consideration) before Irving began writing on *The Sketch Book of Geoffrey Crayon, Gent.* To deny an American history is, therefore, to some degree specious, as the author certainly knows. Given the fact of an American history, then, what is at stake in his narrator's denial of such a history? To put the question more directly to the above quotation, what is it about the commonplace realities of the American present that beckon Crayon's escape into someone else's past? Why must the American past lack the European charms of "storied and poetical association?" What is it about American history that motivates the narrator's disavowal of its past and his escape from its present?

The opening paragraphs of "The Legend of Sleepy Hollow" echo the same yearning to escape from the cares of American life that we saw earlier in "The Author's Account of Himself," but amid Irving's charming language of pastoral romance, we already begin to get a sense for the bewitching fabric of his tale in the way it threads together a troubled life and a weary hint of death into a wished-for retreat into dream:

> If ever I should wish for a retreat, whither I might steal from the world and its distractions, and dream quietly away the remnant of a troubled life, I know of none more promising than this little valley. . . .
>
> A drowsy, dreamy influence seems to hang over the land, and to pervade the very atmosphere. Some say that the place was bewitched . . . and the night mare, with her whole nine fold, seems to make [Sleepy Hollow] the favourite scene of her gambols. (1058–59)

The oddity of the sentence is striking and opens for us the key question of Irving's legend: To what degree will the dreamy tale cancel out history and to what degree preserve it? On the one hand, the language issues a certain invitation to smile at the fanciful image of a mare and her fillies prancing playfully about an idyllic field; on the other hand, Sleepy Hollow has just been explicitly staged as the scene of a nightmare. Irving, again and again, dresses up his nightmares in the more becoming apparel of the pastoral or the comedic. Such generic transvestism is surely one of the contributing factors to the ambiguities of the tale (and the reading of its ending). It might also be taken as lending its terms to the two most famous film adaptations of Irving's legend: Disney's animated film gives a pastoral romance with a playfully comic tone (and the expected concluding fright); Tim Burton's beautiful film presents a gothic horror with an unambiguously menacing ghost and with an occasional touch of romance and light comedy. We shall return later to the complicated matter of the coexistent genres, after we have come to some preliminary understanding of the legend's relation to history. I would propose that what we have in "Sleepy Hollow" is a horrific *nightmare* that expresses itself essentially in masquerading as a pastoral *daydream*: neither just the one, nor the other, but rather some sort of complex interrelation between the two that allows both for the surprising appearance of a certain history, as we shall presently see, as well as for the fascinating beauty and captivating charm of the literary.

Directly following the "night mare" sentence quoted above, the specifically historical nature of the Sleepy Hollow dream starts to seep through the seams as we discover little eruptions of history into the seeming timelessness of the legend's enchanting Märchen guise. Irving writes:

> The dominant spirit, however, that haunts this enchanted region, and seems to be commander in chief of all the powers of the air, is the apparition of a figure on horseback without a head. It is said by some to be the ghost of a Hessian trooper, whose head had been carried away by a cannon ball, in some nameless battle during the revolutionary war, and who is ever and anon seen by the country folk, hurrying along in the gloom of night, as if on the wings of the wind. His haunts are not confined to the valley, but extend at times to the adjacent roads, and especially to the vicinity of a church at no great distance. Indeed, certain of the most authentic historians of those parts . . . allege, that the body of the trooper having been buried in the church yard, the ghost rides forth to the scene of battle in nightly quest of its head, and that the rushing speed with which he sometimes passes along the hollow, is owing to his being belated. . . . (1059–60)

The above passage is richly nuanced, but the unstable status of the historical allegations attracts immediate notice. The headless horseman "is said by some" (but perhaps not by others) to be the ghost of a Hessian trooper, and "certain of the most authentic historians" (though perhaps not all of them) "allege" without cited proof that "the ghost rides forth to the scene of the battle in nightly quest of its head." Readers of Irving will be familiar, from A *History of New York* and elsewhere,[6] with this Knickerbockerly fussiness concerning the authenticity of historians, but the play in evidence here goes beyond mere fussiness. Irving isn't just being coy about the reality or nonreality of ghosts in this narrative world. He is suggesting that the truth of the ghost of Sleepy Hollow rests properly not in the decisive judgments that one might wish to render, but instead in some more complex discursive place, in the sayings and in the allegings of those who live there. This isn't quite the same as taking a historicist or relativist stance on the truth of the ghost as "true for them"; nor yet is it to dismiss the question as a fool's game of undecidability or indeterminacy. Rather, it is to assert that the question of history in Irving's legend finds its force as a matter of speaking, of telling or transmitting a tale. In this respect, the persistent return to the instability of historical truth in the passage above echoes the authorial and narrative paradoxes this essay has already seen—when, for example, a historian of New York writes a collection of tales whose narrator remarks on the lack of American history, or when a tale of alleged dreamy forgetfulness is "found among the papers of the late Diedrich Knickerbocker," best known as the narrator of *A History of New York*, who there echoes Herodotus to urge the justice and the need to "rescue from oblivion the memory of former incidents" (377). History remains a crucial and unresolved problem, but it is *as* a problem that it transmits its force in Irving's legend.

Even leaving aside the instability of the allegations themselves, this essential ambiguity speaks likewise in the details adhering to the trooper. This headless horseman arrives not as some anonymous goblin imported unchanged from the Germanic folk tales of the local tradition. It is known, for instance, that he was a man, a Hessian mercenary, in the service of the British in the recent War of American Independence. It is known, moreover, that the Hessian's head was completely blown off by a cannon ball—"carried away," in Irving's infinitely suggestive phrase. And yet, what was the trooper's name? In which battle did he lose his head? More tellingly, who was there to witness the traumatic kiss? Where do the details of the legend originate? The tale reports that the Hessian lost his head "in some nameless battle." What does this mean? Why "nameless"? Any headless, foreign soldier buried in the churchyard of Sleepy Hollow presumably met his fate in the immediate neighborhood and wasn't just carried there from far away—can it be that the locals have given no name to the battle that took place in their own backyard? The nightmare image of the headless horseman would seem to present, to the people of Sleepy Hollow and to the reader of Irving's legend, the trace of an event that in some sense has failed to find its proper place in the symbolic world of Sleepy Hollow.

So what we have in Irving's legend is a tale that asserts and then all too swiftly buries its own history. Thus, the Disney film, for example, is able to drop altogether any specific sense of the history of the village (aside from a generally Dutch New York setting) and few would claim that historical sense is missed in that context. Indeed, when years later Irving wrote a nostalgic reminiscence of the Sleepy Hollow neighborhood, he described the hollow as if it were an eddy of timeless Dutch pastoral life, undisturbed by the mainstream of modern historical movement and insusceptible to its influence, until the steamboats of the nineteenth century brought New York City so much closer.[7] The strangeness is not that Sleepy Hollow may have been such an eddy of circular time, or at any rate that Irving presented it in such a way, but that the tale itself specifies that its most famous figure, the disruptive headless Hessian, comes from some other time, decades before the steam engine arrived on the Hudson, and yet he is clearly not a part of the mythical Dutch idyll. Where, one must wonder, does the historical trauma of the Revolutionary War figure into the seeming ahistoricity of the old Dutch hollow?

But while direct historical references in "The Legend of Sleepy Hollow" may be scant, they are not altogether absent, and there is, in fact, one scene quite devoted to the very particular history of the Sleepy Hollow community during the war. At the pivotal moment in Ichabod's fortunes—that is, toward the end of Van Tassel's party, after Ichabod's brilliant dancing with Katrina and immediately before conversations turn to the recent hauntings of the headless horseman—a knot of the sager folks is smoking and repeating in drowsy tones long tales of their experiences in the American War of Independence:

> This neighborhood, at the time of which I am speaking, was one of those highly favoured places which abound with chronicle and great men. The British and American line had run near it during the war; it had, therefore, been the scene of marauding, and had been infested with refugees, cow boys,[8] and all kinds of border chivalry. Just sufficient time had elapsed to enable each story teller to dress up his tale with a little becoming fiction, and in the indistinctness of his recollection, to make himself the hero of every exploit. (1077)

The unflagging charm of the narrative voice again almost invites a smile from the reader, this time at the heroism that survivors will use to dress their testimonies of war, without which dress the testimonies would be read more nakedly as tales of survival, of death fortuitously missed rather than heroically conquered. For example, of the two brief tales we are given, the first is of a Dutchman who survives the explosion of the cannon he is manning against a British frigate; the second tale is of an older gentleman who, though struck by a musket ball, had been saved by its deflection off the hilt of his sword; and both tales are dressed in the rhythmic beauty of Irving's most dapper literary prose. Following these tales of survival, the Sleepy Hollow people begin to dole out dismal, ghostly tales of funeral trains and of mournful wailings heard about the tree where the unfortunate Major André was captured during the war. However, the chief part of the stories turn, we are told, upon the patrols of the favorite specter of Sleepy Hollow, an insistent headless Hessian, far less fortunate than the surviving cannoneer or the older gentleman. Before the revel breaks up, the New England pedagogue shares his own tales, conned from Cotton Mather's *History of New England Witchcraft.*

We notice several important things about this instance of storytelling within "The Legend of Sleepy Hollow." Firstly, we see that the tales told by the Sleepy Hollow folk move from the historical events of the war to the ghostly afterlife of those events, a metonymy which underscores the association between the strictly historical (however dressed up) and the legendary supernatural of the neighborhood ghosts. If we understand that the ghostly tales of the restless dead (for which this region has a special appetite) enjoy some organic relationship with the community's experience of the war, that the tales of ghosts and apparitions follow from anecdotes of the war not just happenstantially but logically, we begin to suspect that these formally conventional ghost tales work as a sort of proxy for some other, more violent tale that remains to be properly told in its own terms. "But all these [stories of wartime chivalry]," we read, "were nothing to the tales of ghosts and apparitions that succeeded" (1078). It's an odd relationship: the heroically dressed anecdotes of escaping violent death give rise to ghost tales, tales which then retrospectively make "nothing" of the very stories that occasioned their own telling. This essay will argue that it is not an absolute negation that the latter tales effect, but rather a palpable, problematic "nothing" that carries an insistent weight even after these grounding historical anecdotes are submerged beneath the flashier and somewhat more conventional tales of the ghostly hauntings around Major André's tree and of the nightmarish returns of the headless Hessian.

The late night storytelling at the Van Tassels' also serves to remind us that Sleepy Hollow is in fact a real place and had a very particular history during the Revolution. As the longer passage cited above hints to us, the village had been right on the front lines of the war, between the British command center, down the Hudson River in New York City, and Benedict Arnold's American stronghold, up the Hudson River at West Point. The revolutionary history of the hollow, it turns out, was an anguished one of bitter civil war, controlled and protected by neither the British nor the American armies, but rather placed uneasily as the Neutral Ground between the two. Historian Robert E. Cray, drawing from firsthand accounts recorded by local residents, describes the radical disruption of Sleepy Hollow and the Westchester County countryside during the war—where, he says,

> irregular bands of loyalist Cowboys and patriotic Skinners, operating beyond the reach of military discipline, waged guerrilla warfare. Indiscriminate plundering was commonplace. Revenge spurred countless reprisals as people settled scores. Residents reeled from sorties by British and American units, probing for enemy weaknesses, faced repeated demands for

> supplies, torched farms, and stripped fields. Political loyalties often succumbed to the harsh reality of survival. Friends and neighbors fought each other, switched sides, turned neutral, or fled the county. Who was a patriot? Who was a loyalist? Simple questions about allegiances dissolved into a fog of ambiguity in the Neutral Ground. (Cray 376)

Henry Steiner, the modern day historian of the Village of Sleepy Hollow, reports that British-allied Hessian troops would range through the neighborhood, looting and foraging, raiding cattle, and taking prisoners from the resident Dutch Whigs. He also says that among the local tales of the war that survive (though not one that Irving reports) is the tale of Polly Buckhout, shot dead by a Hessian, who mistook her for a man because she was wearing a man's hat.[9] The history of this nightmare-ridden community has, then, been marked by battles nameless and otherwise, by marauding, famine, and "infestations" of refugees, by the confusion of identities and allegiances surrounding the treason of Benedict Arnold and the "unfortunate Major André" (as he is invariably called by Irving and by others), the British officer who arranged for Arnold's treason and had the misfortune to be caught behind lines, himself wearing the wrong set of clothes.[10] The movement of the line was fluid, however, and the residents of Sleepy Hollow had every reason to ask (as the unfortunate Major André might have asked) where they were. Donald Pease, whose particulars about Major André are erroneous in nearly every respect, nevertheless comes close to the matter when he writes that Major André was, for the people of Sleepy Hollow anyway, a figure of divided loyalties.[11] Probably it would be more appropriate to say—as was quite literally true of its geography—that Sleepy Hollow didn't know what side it was on. More precisely, then, Major John André serves as a figure suggesting the troubling ambiguity of identity in the context of the fluid front lines of a colonial rebellion against the motherland. A man calling himself John Anderson and dressed like a local civilian, turns out to be a British intelligence officer and is hanged for wearing the wrong clothes; the American major general, who ought to have been in charge of the affair, escapes to the British as a turncoat. Mather's accounts of the witch trials of 1692, which Ichabod relates that night at the Van Tassels', share certain structural similarities: here, too, the secret identities of those with whom one might identify turn out to be distressingly ambiguous legal affairs and liable to end, to no one's lasting satisfaction, at the end of a rope.

We can now see that the crucial question of Ichabod's disappearance concerns itself not just with the banalities of love and the pleasures of the imaginative tale, but also with the urgent question of historical trauma and survival—the question, so to speak, of the survival of one's own death. Or, to put it more pointedly: the hanged Major André or the hanged witches—how are they different from me? What accounts for the difference between the fortunate and the unfortunate, when to outward appearances they are identical? When so many die from exploded cannon or from musket balls less erring, how is it that *I* survived to tell the tale, leaving the scene of the event apparently uninjured? We earlier posed the key question of the legend in terms that now assume a more unsettling, less playful aspect. We asked then *Brom Bones, Headless Horseman, What's the difference?* When we consider Brom Bones as, precisely, a member of the Sleepy Hollow community—someone like me—and the headless horseman, that fragmented body, as, precisely, an image of surprising and enigmatic death, the question of Brom Bones and the headless horseman appears as an essential proxy to what one is tempted to call the *real* question of the legend and the literary tale: the surviving me, the violently, inexplicably, unexpectedly dead, *What's the difference?!* This, the terrible question of surviving one's own death, is of course the traumatic question par excellence. And how does it get posed in Irving's tale? The only way it can, given the spectral paradox of the question itself: by shifting into a different mode and masquerading as a different, more innocent question. It is important to note, however, that the traumatic historical enigma underlying the tale is not altogether lost, but rather persists, as we have just seen, between the very threads of Irving's complex tale, lending its texture to the warp and woof of his tapestry.

We get a sense, then, for the powerful motivation of these tales, one that is very much a matter of history: there is something so incomprehensible, so unaccountable about the historical event of survival in the face of overwhelming death, that one simply must, psychologically and ethically, take that unaccountability and, impossibly, *turn it to account*, in recounting the tale and bearing witness to the terms of insistent death and impossible survival. That necessity to speak the impossible word—that's why the locals must tell their tales of Major André's capture and of explosive deaths unexpectedly survived. That's why Ichabod tells the witchcraft tales of his native New England. That's why, above all, the survivors of Sleepy Hollow tell insistent tales of an unfortunate Hessian trooper. And if, like the spy, the traitor, or the witch, these frightful tales appear dressed up in a little becoming fiction, or in the vital, rhythmic charms of Irving's prose, so that they appear to be something more comfortingly familiar, the critic might justifiably suppose that the uncanny imposture only restages the essential, traumatic confusion of identity between the living and the dead. We shall return again to these matters. Let us here pause to pose yet again the problem of the event in Sleepy Hollow.

Hitherto, this essay has concerned itself with the historical event suggested in the figure of the headless horseman that the tale claims as "the dominant spirit . . . that haunts this enchanted region"—namely with the traumatic experience of the Sleepy Hollow community on the front lines of the war. In seeming contrast with the dressed-up tales of the survivors and the doleful tale of the wrongly dressed Major André, tales of the apparitions of the headless horseman would seem to present us with the real thing, the naked horror, so to speak, of the event of the war that still haunts the people of Sleepy Hollow. Nevertheless, given the persistent dual nature of Irving's tale, if we want to suggest that the tale of the headless horseman is *the* legend of Sleepy Hollow, we must also recognize that the legend is itself a doubled affair, *both* nightmare and daydream. It is not, after all, just the tale of the trooper that comes down to us—indeed two hundred years later, the details of the rider's battlefield demise are mostly eclipsed by the alleged predations of his ghost one dark and dismal autumn night, some years later. The reader might more precisely say that "The Legend of Sleepy Hollow," in all its richness, is the placing of another story into association with the story of the Hessian. It is, simultaneously with the tale of the headless horseman, the tale of the luckless Crane that the old wives (and the old farmer) now circulate. The event, then, appears to have a twofold nature: a traumatic, originary event in the war, and a secondary event, more contemporary,[12] and perhaps less violent (if the claims of the old farmer are to be believed over those of the old wives).

Indeed, even aside from their shared characteristics as outsiders vaguely associated by the simple community with sceptered despotic power (1072), the New England pedagogue and the Hessian trooper occasion tales of remarkably similar types. This becomes clear when we begin to ask those same critical questions of Ichabod's fatal ride as we did of the Hessian's. For example, the tale circulated between various of the narrators ("given, almost in the precise words in which I heard it related," 1087) gives some very particular allegations of Ichabod's last ride: the sounds heard nigh about Major André's tree, the misshapen apparition of the silent horseman, the panicked flight of an unskillful rider on an ornery steed, the gaining of the far side of the bridge, and Ichabod's final look back:

> [N]ow Ichabod cast a look behind to see if his pursuer should vanish, according to rule, in a flash of fire and brimstone. Just then, he saw the goblin rising in his stirrups, and in the very act of hurling his head at him. Ichabod endeavored to dodge the horrible missile, but it was too late. It encountered his cranium with a tremendous crash—he was tumbled headlong

> into the dust, and Gunpowder [Ichabod's mount], the black steed, and the goblin rider, passed by like a whirlwind. . . .
>
> The next morning . . . was found the hat of the unfortunate Ichabod, and close beside it a shattered pumpkin. (1085)

As with the events around the death of the Hessian trooper, one must ask (given the disappearance of the pedagogue and the speechless silence of the headless ghost), *Who* was there to witness these events we hear of in such particularity? Who again saw the fatal kiss? Who heard the crash of Ichabod's cranium? Who was there to witness his final fall, headlong (and maybe a head short) into the dust? On the evidence, the tale of Ichabod's ride would seem to have been spun out of an empty hat found by the brookside, and a shattered pumpkin nearby. But the details of the language are suggestive as to how the tale of Ichabod's mysterious departure comes to be threaded together with that of the Hessian: the empty hat, the coincidence of the name *Crane* with the word *cranium* and the associations of that word with the head(lessness) of the headhunting horseman. The violated pumpkin would seem the condensation of all of this, suggesting heads, their displacement, and their momentary substitution by head-shaped missiles, by cannonball or by cheerful orange gourd. The name of the horse (Gunpowder), citing Ichabod's final expectation of fire and sulphur, the use of "the unfortunate" in application to Ichabod, when Major André has all along—and without fail (1078, 1081)—claimed that dubious honorific. Such details suggest that whatever the historical truth of Ichabod's unaccountable departure, the tale draws its power from the weaving together of the two tales, from a narrative association between the uncanny tale of Ichabod and the traumatic tales of death and survival in the war—the tale of the Hessian, obviously, but also a more generalized experience of the war. Surely the frightful urgency, borrowed from the *earlier* event in the telling of the *later* event, is one reason why the reader, like at least one of the narrators, is likely to favor the old country wives who insist on the connection between the two, over the denial of history and the more mundane tale of love proposed by the old farmer.

Fearful Pleasures: From Trauma to the Uncanny

"The Legend of Sleepy Hollow," then, presents the critic with a remarkably intractable problem of history. We have seen that the legend is staged in a strong relation to history. This fact derives from the location of Sleepy

Hollow on the front lines of the War of Independence, and evinces itself generally in the propensity of its inhabitants for hallucinatory visions and nightmares—voices, (martial?) music, fireworks and flares shooting across the valley, the "angry echoes" that follow upon the report of a pleasure-shooter's gun (1059, 1058). We have also seen this strange history manifested more specifically both in the community's association of explicit tales of the war with tales of the supernatural, as well as in the details alleged of "the dominant spirit," the headless Hessian, said to haunt this enchanted region. Moreover, we have seen that the locals, the old country wives and the old farmer, have threaded this originary tale of battlefield trauma together with the secondary, perhaps more benign, tale of Ichabod's last ride, as *the* legend of Sleepy Hollow, weaving in with these, other ambiguities of their history: the unfortunate Major André, the witch trials in New England, the exploded cannon and deflected bullets of personal wartime anecdote. Irving's tale has thus proved itself to be irreducibly ambivalent. The tale is not just, on the one hand, about beauty, or daydreamy oblivion, or romantic rivalry, but neither is it just about history, or insistent nightmare, or traumatic horror. Rather, we can see that the terrible beauty and captivating charm of the tale owe their possessive power over Sleepy Hollow imaginations to the uneasy coexistence and ambiguous confusion of all these terms. Elements that ought to have had identities as distinct as life and death have been brought into some fateful convergence and the difference between the two fallen under question. Surely it is true, as Poe was fond of citing from Francis Bacon, that any exquisite beauty necessarily has some "strangeness in its proportion,"[13] but the strangeness of this legend—its enigmatic yet undeniable relation to the historical trauma of war—seems to place itself beyond critical reach. For what, one must still ask, is the critic to do in the face of an insistent history that seems to lack any directly specified referent? The most fundamental critical questions of any event—Who saw it? What did they see? How do they know the details they claim?—are missing here both in the case of the Hessian's last battle, as in the case of Ichabod's last ride in Sleepy Hollow. One might say that "The Legend of Sleepy Hollow" asserts, therefore, not so much an historical *event*, as a traumatic, historical *gap* that the tale and its narrators must fail to render in conscious, critical terms. And this gap, this hole within the Hollow, seems to define nearly every circumstance of the legend: the missing elaboration of the war, the missing Ichabod, the missing head of the Hessian, the missing witnesses, the missing comforts of normal self-identity—indeed, the missing answers to so many critical questions.

This isn't quite a gap like the absolute (and comparatively untroubled) one of Rip Van Winkle's twenty-year slumber, to cite the other well-known tale from Crayon's *Sketch Book*, in which the henpecked idler sleeps dreamlessly, timelessly, through the American War of Independence (and the unmourned decease of his termagant wife). Rather, the essential historical gap in Sleepy Hollow is one of comprehension, as if an insistent question mark had installed itself in the very soul of the little valley to trouble the sleep of its survivors and stalk its nightly byways in the figure of a monstrous, black Hessian, who embodies the gap both spatially in his very headlessness as well as temporally in his rushing belatedness. Something irreducibly enigmatic befell the Sleepy Hollow community in its survival of the war, something that eludes the hard facts of remembering and forgetting, but which expresses itself through the rhythms of these tales, firstly that of the unfortunate Hessian and then again that of Ichabod's romance and final ride. The tales of the survivors, which as this essay has shown are associated with the tale of the headless horseman (and precede the telling of that tale at the Van Tassels' fête), share an analogous status. They are essentially about an event, a death, that *didn't* happen, a musket ball that, by the most improbable happenstance, failed to arrive at its proper destination, a cannon explosion that, quite inexplicably, killed no one. Perhaps, one is tempted to speculate, the people of Sleepy Hollow repeat the tale of the headless horseman because in that figure, all at once, one is given the narrative comfort of an actual event (a head "carried away" by a cannonball), the visible embodiment of a gap (headlessness), an acknowledgment that the event *didn't really happen to them* per se, and a sort of explanation for why, in the aftermath of the war, the community continues to suffer the nightly effects of an event, a death, that didn't fully happen to them. The peculiar status of this historical event as a real *gap* that resists symbolization and narrativizing—and as something that nevertheless insists in the dreamy imagination of the community and struggles to find a certain expression in its speech—suggests why the tale of a community's war trauma had to be told in part through a ghostly Märchen proxy tale.

Yet the tale suggests, as we shall see, that they also tell the story because it is enjoyable to do so. Certainly, the tale is an enjoyable one to read as rendered in *The Sketch Book of Geoffrey Crayon, Gent.*, and for almost two hundred years readers have found themselves carried away by its fearful pleasures. But as critics, the theoretical dimensions of a pleasure that seems to situate itself in relation to trauma remains among our most pressing problems, since trauma would seem to locate itself as essentially beyond the domain of pleasure and incommensurable with it. In other words, having established the *historical trauma* that functions as the real kernel of the tale's persistent power, what is one to make of the fact that in the present case, the *tale* produces precisely *pleasure*?

For present purposes, let us follow Ichabod Crane, who is especially suggestive of the pleasures of the literary, since before he himself became the subject of the tale, Sleepy Hollow's man of letters was distinguished by the ferocity of his "appetite" for marvelous tales generally:

> His appetite for the marvelous, and his powers of digesting it, were equally extraordinary; and both had been increased by his residence in this spell bound region. No tale was too gross or monstrous for his capacious swallow. It was often his delight, after his school was dismissed of an afternoon, to stretch himself on the rich bed of clover . . . and there con over old Mather's direful tales, until the gathering dusk of evening made the printed page a mere mist before his eyes. Then, as he wended his way, by swamp and stream and awful woodland, to the farm house . . . every sound of nature, at that witching hour, fluttered his excited imagination. . . . (1063–64)

Irving will write two years later of the taste for the supernatural tale in terms of instinct,[14] but here already, in Ichabod's monstrous appetite (for tales as for food), we get a sense for something at work unreasonably in excess of mere need and beyond ordinary satisfactions. On one level, to say that the direful delights of such tales operate in excess of reason and beyond need seems like a banality, for these are surely hallmarks of the literary most broadly, but it is worth remarking that the particular pleasures of tale-telling in Sleepy Hollow (translatable to the printed word, as we see above) likewise exceed any ordinary, comparatively subdued, pleasures of literature. Ichabod's extreme voracity, like his figure ("the genius of famine descending upon the earth," 1061), suggests a link to death here and a driving hunger infinitely in excess of any possible object. Ichabod may spend his late afternoons reclining on a sensuous bed of clover, indulging his appetites with old Mather, leaving him only misty-eyed in the gathering dusk, but the effect is hardly one of the serenity of love fulfilled, nor even of the excitements of a typical bedtimely amour. Rather, we see that these very powerful excitements transform his nighttime world into a place of fluttering terrors.

This intimacy of pleasure and terror astonishes people far too little. To be carried away by a word, as Ichabod is by the Mather he so loves, to lose one's head, so to speak, amid the rhythms and charms of the dismal tales of history and legend, is plainly to give oneself over to a fearful death, if only one in imaginary anticipation. And yet this imaginary death, we find, is again and again contextualized amid familiar, homely comforts. The classic Sleepy Hollow venue would seem to be a cozy fireside hearth on a winter's evening:

> Another of his sources of fearful pleasures was, to pass long winter evenings with the old Dutch wives, as they sat spinning by the fire, with a row of apples roasting and sputtering along the hearth, and listen to their marvelous tales of ghosts and goblins, and haunted fields and haunted brooks, haunted bridges and haunted houses, and particularly of the headless horseman, or the galloping Hessian of the Hollow, as they sometimes called him. He would delight them equally by his anecdotes of witchcraft. . . . (1064)

Indeed, together with the haunting repetitions the critic might have expected from the traumatized community, with the sputtering, stuttering, breathless panting of the alliterations, we begin too to witness a certain poetic transformation, an essential degree of mollification in the manifestation of the strictly traumatic:

> But if there was a pleasure in all this, while snugly cuddling in the chimney corner of a chamber that was all of a ruddy glow from the crackling wood fire, and where, of course, no spectre dared to show its face, it was dearly purchased by the terrors of his subsequent walk homewards. What fearful shapes and shadows beset his path, amidst the dim and ghastly glare of a snowy night!—With what wistful look did he eye every trembling ray of light streaming across the waste fields from some distant window!—How often was he appalled by some shrub covered with snow, which like a sheeted spectre beset his very path!—How often did he shrink with curdling awe at the sound of his own steps . . . and dread to look over his shoulder, lest he should behold some uncouth being tramping close behind him!—and how often was he thrown into complete dismay by some rushing blast, howling among the trees, in the idea that it was the galloping Hessian on one of his nightly scourings.
>
> All these, however, were mere terrors of the night, phantasms of the mind, that walk in darkness. . . . (1065)

No doubt poor Ichabod suffers terrifying expectations on his night return through the snow. But we see here a shift in the status of the terror. This terror, unlike anything properly traumatic, enjoys an economic exchangeability with pleasure: a certain measure of pleasure in the tales enjoyed by the homely hearth is "purchased by" a certain measure of terror on Ichabod's subsequent walk homeward.

The shift in the position of the strictly traumatic—away from the pure and present directness of the nightmare image—is signaled too by the curious schema of the language here. If we had earlier described trauma as a sort of irreducibly insistent question mark installed in the soul of the valley (What's the difference between the surviving me and the exploded dead?), in the above paragraph we find something insistent and repetitive, and with the *form* of a question ("What fearful shapes and shadows . . . With what wistful look . . . How often was he appalled . . . How often did he shrink with curdling awe . . . how often was he thrown into complete dismay . . ."), but slightly *trans-formed* into something more exclamatory. It is as if the gap of trauma has been effectively *elided* by this rhetorical scheme, even while this scheme succeeds in *marking* that gap—by preserving both its repetitive insistence and as well as a trace of its question form—and in *transferring* some of its power into a different kind of excitement, a fearful, but *non*-traumatic, pleasure. We recognize this pleasure specifically as "the uncanny," something Freud described as that which is distinct from—but "reminds us of"—the traumatic repetitions beyond pleasure.[15] Curiously, Freud's German word here, "*mahnen*," isn't the usual word ("*erinnern*") meaning *to remind*. Mahnen does indeed mean to remind or to warn, but it also carries a suggestion of economic exchange, like a reminder of payment due. The uncanny legend, then, would in this sense issue a "reminder" to the listener or reader of the debt to be paid in words, in storytelling, and owed to a trauma originating in the War of Independence.

This transformation of the tale into the uncanny also makes possible a certain generalization that extends the range of that kernel of historical trauma into the unconscious of the broader social field, beyond any historical restriction to an actual witness of the original, traumatic event (or non-event) that we suppose first set the dream in motion. Irving suggests as much by describing the power of the tale as a sort of contagion communicated along unconscious lines:

> It is remarkable, that the visionary propensity I have mentioned is not confined to the native inhabitants of the valley, but is unconsciously imbibed by every one who resides there for a time. However wide awake they may have been before they entered that sleepy region, they are sure, in a little time, to inhale the witching influence of the air, and begin to grow imaginative—to dream dreams, and see apparitions. (1060)

So while the uncanny may always "remind us of" a trauma, the fact that it must do so unconsciously in "dreams and fancies" (1078), the fact that this reminiscence is one beyond the reach of conscious, critical appropriation, beyond the reach of daylight, one might say—all this likewise makes possible the fact of the tale's generalizable power, to the degree that we may expect to see this dreamy-nightmarish "contagion" carried even through the printed word (1078), as we saw in Ichabod's fascination with the histories of Mather, and as we dare propose in the case of Irving's still-loved tale.

The uncanny, reminiscent as it is of obscure trauma, suggests a class of tale with a specially unsettling power, as if invisibly woven into the expected excitement and familiar fright we bargained for, there were some troubling, enigmatic, *other* element, something that seems to address us very particularly from some other scene unavailable to our direct observation. The uncanny is not to be equated, therefore, with the thrills and satisfactions of the "merely" scary. The communicability of the odd horror, the ability of its fearful pleasures to survive through different tellings and retellings, the virulence of the tale—such aesthetic qualities, invisible and fleeting, are difficult to account for with any critical rigor, but we might propose, following Irving, that some quality of the telling, some contagion communicated at the level of the unconscious, is able to carry over some part of the weight of the original trauma, even if that originary event remains disguised or unrecognized by both the teller and the recipient.

"The Legend of Sleepy Hollow" testifies to this excessive significance of the uncanny in part by staging the tale as an essentially shared one. The communal provenance of the legend of Sleepy Hollow is made most explicit in the secondary event of Ichabod's disappearance, but the way this arises is suggestive too of the way the community claims or affirms its own identity as witness to a common trauma embodied in the spectral figure of the Hessian:

> The mysterious event caused much speculation at the Church on the following Sunday. Knots of gazers and gossips were collected in the church yard, at the bridge, and at the spot where the hat and pumpkin had been found. The stories of Brouwer, of Bones, and a whole budget of others, were called to mind; and when they had diligently considered them all, and compared them with the symptoms of the present case, they shook their heads, and came to the conclusion, that Ichabod had been carried off by the galloping Hessian. (1086)

The question of Ichabod's disappearance knots together these gazers and gossips in a community effort to situate this new mystery within the existing narrative field, to narrativize the symptoms of the present case under the authority of the galloping Hessian. Hence, the people of Sleepy Hollow seek to locate the event amid existing stories that the circumstances call to mind: the story of old Brouwer, for instance, a tale the reader will recollect from the Van Tassels', involving "a most heretical disbeliever" who met the horseman and was dunked in the brook with a clap of thunder for his lack of faith in the dominant spirit of Sleepy Hollow (1079). The events that Sunday are more than just social reinforcement of a central myth; they certify the continuing symbolic life of the headless Hessian, and we are not therefore surprised to find that the tale of the missing Ichabod, now bound together with the tale of the ghostly horseman, becomes "a favourite story often told about the neighborhood round the winter evening fire" (1087)—hearth fires where once the pedagogue snuggled so cozily.

Irving further signals the extraordinary virulence of the tale and broadens the field of its enigmatic inheritance by presenting the legend through fully four narrative frames:

[1819 Prospectus, 1120; 1819 Advertisement, 1121]
W.I. (1848 Preface, 742)
  Geoffrey Crayon, Gent. (*The Sketch Book of*, 731)
    Diedrich Knickerbocker ("Found among the Papers of the late," 1058)
      POSTSCRIPT story teller (1087)
        Old farmer; old country wives; authentic historians (1086)

The author of the Prospectus, Advertisement, and (later) the Preface, has an identity distinct from Geoffrey Crayon, the putative author of the collection, who indicates that "The Legend of Sleepy Hollow" was found among the papers of the "late" Diedrich Knickerbocker, who himself claims to have heard it repeated in Manhattan, from a storyteller who claims to have gotten it from an old farmer of Sleepy Hollow, where the tale appears to be in common currency among the old wives at least. In this lengthy chain of narration, "Sleepy Hollow" would appear to be, quite eminently, a tale to pass on, a tale that demands to be told by those who have heard it, and not just among the native inhabitants of the valley. Long after Irving has gone to sleep with his fathers beneath the green valleys of the Hudson, the fearful and bedtimely pleasures of this tale are still so vital that the event of Sleepy Hollow—regardless of the actual status of its historical referent, whether real or merely on the level of dream—might still be said to circulate through the American social body as the "possession of every American mind," to cite Van Wyck Brooks slightly askew.[16] We are indeed possessed. Possessed of a marvelous tale, certainly—but also possessed by the trace of a historical trauma captured and communicated and calling for further iteration in Irving's uncanny legend.

Postscript: The Moral of the Story and What It Goes to Prove

So, *The Sketch Book of Geoffrey Crayon, Gent.*, which opens with a denial of an American history, concludes with the strange and paradoxical history communicated—unconsciously—through the dreamy contagion of "The Legend of Sleepy Hollow." We remain, in the end, as much in the dark as ever about the specific nature of the trauma of this community in its survival of the war. Whatever it was, it remains an enigma that resists the daylight of critical consciousness and must be finally incomprehensible except as a forceful, empirical fact witnessed in the telling of the tale—perhaps, I propose, the affective force of some originary traumatic incomprehension. Similarly the question of the ending, *Brom Bones, Headless Horseman, What's the difference between the two?*, remains with us open and unanswered, though not without uncanny pleasures of its own.

The Postscript that immediately follows the tale proper seems to have anticipated the critical quandary engendered by such a compelling, yet irreducibly enigmatic tale. The scene is Manhattan, and a storyteller has just relayed the tale of Ichabod and the horseman of Sleepy Hollow. One cautious old gentleman, a familiar type in Irving's frames,[17] demands of the storyteller, "What was the moral of the story, and what it went to prove" (1087). For reasons untold, the cautious old gentleman has been unable to convert the unsettling and fearful pleasures of the tale into laughter, as the other burghers have succeeded in doing. It's as if he has sensed the open question of the tale, and identified it at the level of truth and ethics, but in demanding comprehension and satisfaction at the level of *information*, the cautious old gentleman displays his misapprehension of the *type* of question the tale has posed, as well as his blank immunity to the special power of the literary to communicate a truth beyond cognition, a communication all the more forceful for its essential deferral and indirection. "He was one of your wary men, who never laugh but upon good grounds—when they have reason and the law on their side" (1087). The cautious old gentleman has missed not only the pleasures of beauty and of a tale well told; he has also sought to deny another variety of truth following another law, one we have seen located at the level of affect: the unsettling and incomprehensible trauma preserved and communicated through the uncanny tale.

The tension between a literary communication and a developed theoretical understanding was in fact a long-standing interest of Irving's. Already in *A History of New York*, his Diedrich Knickerbocker was satirizing the perverse refusal of a fickle and wayward world to conform to the most ingenious truths of philosophy and theoretical understanding.[18] But in this Postscript, in the cautious old gentleman's direct and reasonable demand for the moral of the story and (as we shall see) in the curiously playful response of the storyteller who insists upon deference, Irving dramatized more starkly the gap between a literary communication and a developed theoretical understanding:

> The story teller, who was just putting a glass of wine to his lips, as a refreshment after his toils, paused for a moment, looked at his inquirer with an air of infinite deference, and lowering the glass slowly to the table, observed that the story was intended most logically to prove,
>
> "That there is no situation in life but has its advantages and pleasures, provided we will but take a joke as we find it:
>
> "That, therefore, he that runs races with goblin troopers, is likely to have rough riding of it:
>
> "Ergo, for a country schoolmaster to be refused the hand of a Dutch heiress, is a certain step to high preferment in the state."
>
> The cautious old gentleman knit his brows tenfold closer after this explanation, being sorely puzzled by the ratiocination of the syllogism; . . . [S]till he thought the story a little on the extravagant—there were one or two points on which he had his doubts.
>
> "Faith, sir," replied the story teller, "as to that matter, I don't believe one half of it myself." (1087–88)

In response to the demand, the storyteller might have responded directly, from *within* the field of the theoretical, either by saying, more or less reasonably, that literature proves nothing at all, or else by saying, for example, that the preceding tale most logically proves that certain tales may carry over some other meaning from outside of the rule of cognitive, conscious truth; the moral of the story concerns the ethical obligation to pay, in words and narrative, the debt owed to trauma originating in the War of Independence. But instead, he refuses the older gentleman's demand for direct communication and for a rationalization of the literary to the theoretical. The storyteller may give his reply in the syllogistic *form* of the purest theory, but he so playfully undermines this form's presupposition of simple cause and effect, that he finally reasserts the literary by insisting on the essentially extravagant, unsettling and indirect counterlogic working in the tale.

This conception of a truth outside of cognition expressed through the literary word would also seem to urge us to consider the possibility of an analogous ethics situated beyond understanding, an ethics located between the word and what we might call the aesthetic body—the body insofar as it is susceptible to the uncanny pleasures of the art of the well-told tale. Such a view remains latent in *The Sketch Book of Geoffrey Crayon, Gent.*,[19] but four years after the Sleepy Hollow Postscript, Irving's Crayon will make it more explicit in the medical language of his "To the Reader" in *Tales of a Traveller*:

> As I know this to be a story telling and story reading age, and that the world is fond of being taught by apologue, I have digested the instruction I would convey into a number of tales. They may not possess the power of amusement which tales told by many of my contemporaries possess; but then I value myself on the sound moral which each of them contains. This may not be apparent at first, but the reader will be sure to find it out in the end. I am for curing the world by gentle alteratives, not by violent doses; indeed the patient should never be conscious that he is taking a dose. . . .
>
> I am not, therefore, for those barefaced tales which carry their moral on the surface, staring one in the face; they are enough to deter the squeamish reader. On the contrary, I have often hid my moral from sight, and disguised it as much as possible by sweets and spices, so that while the simple reader is listening with open mouth to a ghost story or a love story, he may have a bolus of sound morality popped down his throat, and be never the wiser for the fraud. (384)

Irving's Crayon makes no pretensions to elaborate a theoretical account of truth or ethics. Of these things, he says, the reader of a literary tale should "never be conscious," and indeed he seems to take it as the task of the literary writer to proceed indirectly, by delivering these things to the body, mixed in unperceived with the sweeter pleasures of love and the spicier pleasures of ghostly legend. So, to extend our theoretical considerations of a literary ethics at the limit of theory, we shall turn elsewhere in the next chapter, to psychoanalysis, "the talking cure," with its crucial theoretical and practical interest in thinking about both ethics and the relation between the body and the word.

CHAPTER 2

Lacan and the Beyond of Language

From Art to Ethics

Irving's legend of love and death has given us a remarkable cluster of terms that seem all the more compelling for their collective resistance to the reason and cognition that we ordinarily associate with critical practice. The urgent sense that the pleasurable and paradoxical tale bears—in spite of itself, as it would seem—upon matters of truth and ethics, a fact intuited by the old gentleman of the Postscript who begs a rationalization of the moral of the story, brings us to an articulation of one of the fundamental questions of the present book. How, as a matter of critical practice and theoretical understanding, is one to think rigorously of that peculiar moral or ethical truth which lies by definition outside of the field of philosophical proof? Undeniably, a vast and important field of human values lies within the purview of reasoned, philosophical inquiry, and it is no surprise that ethics has traditionally been a category of philosophical inquiry. But Irving's legend has suggested that, in the event of literature, there may be a dimension of ethics that remains unexplained and inaccessible to this mode of thinking. If so, if in literature, ethics—or a certain, distinct part of ethics—can be seen to emerge from out of philosophy, how is one to conceive of the special relationship that literature bears to this other field of ethics?. Why, among all the arts, is literary art in particular "so near for us to the domain of ethics?"[1]

The discipline of psychoanalysis has been driven to theorize the human terrain of unreason out of the exigencies of its practice—that is, out of the fact that patients arrive with symptoms and sufferings that resist the suasion of reason, and out of the fact that patients are never reducible to their most reasonable selves. In tracing out, for its own practical necessities, the logic of the ways that bodies respond automatically to words and laws and dictates, and the ways that human subjectivity situates itself in relation to language, desire, and unreasonable, pathological enjoyments, psychoanalysis has developed a theory of human subjectivity that supplements the work of philosophy and the human sciences. By attending to the unique observations of psychoanalytic insight, we shall clarify the stakes and the dimensions of our key questions of a literature and an ethics outside the domain of reason. The present essay turns, therefore, to the psychoanalytic theorist whose work, after Freud's, has marked the most intense point of engagement between psychoanalysis and the human sciences, the Parisian analyst Jacques Lacan (1901–1981).

Lacan's seminar of 1959–1960, *The Ethics of Psychoanalysis*,[2] covers a characteristically broad and idiosyncratic range of material. The seminar opens with a consideration of pathological guilt feelings, proceeds to read Freud in relation to Aristotle (the *Ethics* and *Poetics*) and the Bible (St. Paul and the Mosaic texts), presents early formulations of Lacan's later essay on the ethics of Kant and Sade, ventures some preliminary formulations on courtly love and the formal innovations in art of the baroque period (anamorphosis), and, after an extended reading of Sophocles' *Antigone*, concludes by proposing an ethics of psychoanalysis situated beyond the ideologically bound ideals of normativity and beyond the anaesthetized moralism of a philosophy purified of desire. These seemingly disparate points of reference cohere along three related axes—psychoanalysis, ethics, and art—to articulate an ethics of desire, or, as several commentators have put it, an "ethics of the real."[3] Lacan sums up the project for his auditors at the midpoint of the seminar:

> All, I think, will have sensed that what I am showing to you this year may be situated between a Freudian *ethics* and a Freudian *aesthetics*. Freudian aesthetics is but involved insofar as it shows one of the phases of the function of the ethics. . . .
>
> Freudian aesthetics, in the broadest sense of the term—which is to say the analysis of the whole economy of signifiers—shows us this Thing inaccessible. (190f, 159e; my italics)

Lacan's interest in theorizing the experience of art, then, derives from what he believes a Freudian consideration of aesthetics can show us—namely, a Freudian ethics staged in terms of the inaccessible Thing and in terms of the human relation to the signifier.[4] The present essay will follow Lacan's effort to map out the intersection of ethics and aesthetics by tracing out how the seminar rethinks both categories, ethics and aesthetics, through the psychoanalytic understanding of the subject's relation to language and the signifier. In so doing, we will allow ourselves only the most elementary questions: What is this Thing Lacan speaks of? What is the experience of the beautiful? How do these terms bear upon other key terms such as the signifier and desire? And the present essay will follow Lacan in one further respect: as his seminar engages the work of art in order to open onto ethics, so we will engage the Lacanian aesthetics of the Thing in order to open onto the Lacanian ethics of desire.

The Work of Art, the Emptiness of the Signifier, the Representation of the Thing

If Lacan, the psychoanalyst, doesn't display the modesty of Freud when venturing into a field traditionally engaged by way of philosophy, one reason may be that Lacan believes his remarks on aesthetics remain essentially close to the experience of the analytic clinic and derive from that experience. Indeed, one might read the entire *Ethics* seminar as an exploration of the theoretical ramifications of a curious phenomenon observable in clinical practice:

> [Y]ou can pick it up by means of references to the aesthetic register that the subject will give you in his associations, in his broken, unknotted monologue, either in the form of quotations or of memories from schooldays. . . . [T]he more these references become strangely sporadic and incisive with relation to the text of the discourse, the more they are correlative of some thing that presents itself in this very moment, and that is always in the register of a destructive drive. At this moment when a thought is clearly about to appear in the subject, as in the narration of a dream for example, a thought one recognizes as aggressive towards the fundamental terms of his subjective constellation, the subject . . . will make some reference to a passage from the Bible,[5] to an author, either classic or otherwise, or else to some piece of music. (280f, 238–39e)

The analyst must ask why patients make recourse to the aesthetic register at this crucial moment in the analytic experience: What does the necessity of aesthetic reference reveal about this moment in the analytic encounter and what does it reveal generally about the relation of the subject to the destructive drive—in other words, to that most intimate and insistent problem of death? For Lacan, it is not (as it may be for the critic) that analytic theory can illuminate a philosophical question of aesthetics, but rather the reverse. Lacan's inquiry into the nature of aesthetics, then, serves to illuminate for his students something from the clinic. His claim above is that in the course of dream association, when the analysand closes in upon something related to the death drive and when the proximity to this Thing unties the thread of mastered speech and thought, the analysand is likely to make the presence of this enigmatic Thing felt indirectly by recourse to artistic reference and the "sphere of beauty." Between the aesthetic register and the unrepresentable of death, Lacan suggests, is a relationship intuitively felt and exploited by patients in the clinic, a rapport that begs consideration as a striking clinical fact reported by Lacan to his analytic trainees.

In the *Ethics* seminar, the single concept knotting together the clinical and the aesthetic, the aesthetic and the ethical, and the subject's relations to death, language, and desire, is what Lacan was then calling "the Thing" (*la Chose*) or, sometimes using the German, *das Ding*.[6] The preceding quotations have already suggested that the Thing is related to the enigmatic and unrepresentable of the death drive. We recall from the quotation above that the patient's associative approach to this Thing effects some sort of disruption both in the patient's discourse as well as in his or her "subjective constellation." We recall likewise Lacan's claim that, in an effort to invoke the presence of this Thing, the patient breaks from narrative discourse to make reference to some work of literature or music. Elsewhere in the *Ethics* seminar, Lacan describes the Thing in a variety of ways: as the beyond-of-the-signified, as absence and strangeness, as the Sovereign Good, as that which in the real suffers from the signifier.[7] Clearly, to speak of the Thing presents a palpable difficulty not only to patients in the clinic, but also to the theorist: the basic question in each case being, How is one to suggest the outlines of something that of itself is "fundamentally veiled" (142f, 118e), such that we are "unable to gain sufficient bearings" to orient our understanding of it (124f, 103e)? How, in other words, is one to represent the essentially unrepresentable? The answer Lacan proposes is that the Thing *is* representable, but only as something other than itself (143f, 118e). And art is the privileged mode of linking the Thing with signification.

Stealing his cue from Heidegger,[8] Lacan proposes that his auditors consider one of the most ancient of human arts. Imagine a simple vessel or vase, he says, crafted by the potter sinking his thumbs into the wet clay on the wheel. Right away the finished object presents itself to the eye as a human creation with a certain utility—namely, it is something to be filled. In this sense, the vessel or vase is also a signifier, both of *emptiness* and of the *fullness* that might be brought to it by the addition of some other object or substance, whatever it might be: water, rice, cut chrysanthemums and greens, whatever.

> I simply want us to grasp today the elementary distinction, in the vase, between its use as a utensil and its signifying function. If it is truly signifier, and if this is the first signifier crafted by human hands, it is but a signifier, in its essence as signifier, of nothing other than of all that which is signifier—put another way, of nothing particularly signified. . . .
>
> This nothing particular that it characterizes in its signifying function is indeed in its incarnated form that which characterizes the vase as such. It is indeed emptiness that it creates, introducing by that the same prospect of filling it. Emptiness and fullness are introduced by the vase into a world that of itself knows nothing of them. It is starting from this crafted signifier which is the vase, that emptiness and fullness as such entered into the world. . . .
>
> [I]f the vase be full, this is insofar as at first, in its essence, it is empty. (145f, 120e)

Lacan is underlining two important arguments here. The first regards the nature of language and the signifier in psychoanalytic theory. The second regards the privileged ability of art to highlight something introduced by the signifier into the field of the subject.

From the point of view of psychoanalysis, far more essentially than prompting a particular signified, the signifier acts upon the subject to introduce a real emptiness or gap—into the expectation of a natural and necessary relation between signifier and signified, into our denatured and split relationships with ourselves, and into the objects we turn to and the satisfactions we hope to find there. As he does so often, Lacan dramatizes the human condition revealed by psychoanalysis by casting it against a mythically supposed, lost natural world.[9] There, in a natural world, prior to the arrival of human meaning, Lacan would suggest that there can be no emptiness. Thus, one might say, a hollow in a rock or a tree cannot of itself be said to be empty. The hollow is simply shaped as it is at a given moment in time until a human expectation arrives to see what is *not* there and to name its essential emptiness in relation to what is not there. Thus, any signifier, but here quite visually the vase as signifier of emptiness, is able to reach beyond its utensil function (as a tool of communication) to *create* an emptiness that wasn't there prior to the possibility of representation. Indeed, Lacan argues here that, more than merely having the *potential* to represent something other than its proper signified, *all* signifiers, as part of their essence *as* signifiers in a flawed and incomplete field of human meaning, necessarily refer the subject to that essential emptiness or hole in human meaning. Hence, for the human subject, supplementary to any successful communication of a particular signified, the signifier also necessarily signifies an emptiness, a certain gap or nothing, that constitutes not another signified, but rather a "beyond-of-the-signified" that Lacan calls the Thing. The Thing, in this version of the argument, appears as a bit of the real that defies symbolization and that has been brought into existence by the subject's constitutive encounter with the signifier and the consequent alienation into language. We will see, however, that even though this real is excluded as such from the symbolic register, it nevertheless might be thought to drive the human relation to language and to shape and structure our relation to meaning—something again that the example of the vase was chosen to illustrate:

> Now if you consider the vase from the perspective I first proposed, as an object made to represent the existence of the emptiness at the center of the real that is called the Thing, this emptiness, such as presents itself in the representation, presents itself indeed as a *nihil*, as nothing. And this is why the potter, entirely like you to whom I am speaking, creates the vase around this emptiness with his hand, creates it, entirely like the mythical creator, *ex nihilo*, starting from the hole. (146f, 121e)

In Lacan's reading of Freud, all human creation, from language itself to the most sublime art, is essentially a creation *ex nihilo*, a creation driven and structured and rendered sensibly meaningful by that emptiness at the center of the real called the Thing.

We might clarify the outlines, at least, of the fundamentally veiled Thing, by distinguishing the Thing from the very emptiness that "invariably" serves to represent it (Lacan, *Seminar VII* 155f, 129e). If the vase, the cathedral, the perspectival painting, or the poetic word signifies emptiness, and if emptiness in turn represents the Thing, we cannot, merely on account of that, declare that the Thing is itself emptiness or nothing. Not only is the Thing not an object, it is not even nothing, properly speaking, since "nothing" is already within the field of meaning from which the Thing is excluded (78f, 63e). Hence, the subject's relation to this obscure Thing, like our theoretical understanding of it, is always complicated by the effort to relate from within the symbolic register to something excluded from it.

The ontological status of the Thing, then, is a peculiar one. Lacan tends to speak of the Thing topographically, for example speaking of "the place of the Thing," as if it were a place within the subject. But significantly, he is quick to deconstruct the claims of topology to locate the Thing within the subject it structures:

> Let's show in a simple soul, let's seat him in the front row, and ask him what Lacan means.
>
> The simple soul gets up, comes to the board, and explains: "Since the start of the year, Lacan has spoken to us of *das Ding* in the following terms: he puts it at the heart of a subjective world . . . defined by the fact that the signifier is, in man, already enthroned at the unconscious level. . . ."
>
> Already, by nothing more than writing it thus on the board, by putting at the center *das Ding* and all around it the subjective world of the unconscious organized in signifying relations, you see the difficulty of topographical representation. Because this *das Ding* is at the center precisely in the sense that it is excluded. That is to say, in reality it must be posed as exterior, as . . . something that is *entfremdet*, strange to me while being at the heart of this "me." . . . (87f, 71e)

Structurally speaking, the Thing is an excluded center: central in the sense of exerting a kind of gravitational field around which the speaking subject revolves and also central in its utterly intimate interiority to the subject to which it is, nevertheless, exterior—a paradoxical and uncanny quality Lacan describes with the neologism "extimacy" (167f, 139e).[10]

It is to this intimate and obscure structure of the subject that the experience of art refers us. Indeed, Lacan goes so far as to claim that *all* art, and not just the vase he used in his example earlier, "is characterized by a certain mode of organization around this emptiness" that represents the Thing (155f, 130e). One way of grasping the stakes of such a claim is to consider Lacan's remarks on the philosophical tradition that, since at least Plato's *Republic*, has regarded art in terms of mimesis:

> Of course, works of art imitate the objects they represent, but their end is not just to represent them. In giving the imitation of the object, they make of that object something else [*autre chose*]. Thus they but pretend to imitate. The object is

> established in a certain rapport with the Thing which all at once is made to encircle, to present, and to make absent.
>
> All the world knows this. At the moment when a painting turns once more upon itself, at the moment when Cézanne paints his apples, it is well evident that in painting those apples, he does something else entirely than imitating some apples—although his final manner of imitating them, which is most striking, would be mostly oriented towards a technique of presenting the object. But the more the object is presented as imitation, the more it opens up for us that dimension where the illusion is shattered, and aims at something else [*autre chose*]. Everyone knows that there is a mystery in the manner Cézanne painted the apples, for the relationship to the real as it is then renewed in art makes the object then appear in a manner which is lustrous, which constitutes a renewal of its dignity. . . . (169–70f, 141e)

The special quality of art derives from the fact that, in an everyday human world where signs are understood as transparent, as expressing an untroubled, flawless relationship between the signifier and the signified, art directs our interest to the essential *gap* between the signifier and the signified. One does not, in fact, look through Cézanne's canvas, as if the signifying paint were not there, as if one saw the signified apples themselves. Rather, supplementary to the success of the imitative illusion—and finally shattering that illusion—the work of art insists, paradoxically enough, upon the distance between the creation and the represented object itself. Art presents itself as essentially *created*, not as natural, and thus what it essentially *creates* is the sense of that emptiness that inhabits the gap between the representation and the supposed natural object. By placing pressure on that gap in signification, by making it the heart of the artistic event, the work of art aesthetically reveals the signifier *as such*. We are now in a better position to understand what Lacan meant when he remarked of art in the example of the vase that "it is but a signifier, in its essence as signifier, of nothing other than of all that which is signifier—put another way, of nothing particularly signified." When art presents the object it imitates, it also transforms the object by presenting together with it the very problem and phenomenon of signification—something that drives our interest insofar as the work of art is able to establish "a certain rapport," an aesthetic relation, between the artistic signifier and the subject's own relations with the Thing and the real of language. The possibility and existence of such a rapport explains why patients in the clinic are able to express their own encounter with the Thing by recourse to the aesthetic register of art. Art aims to present the object not mimetically in itself as an object, but rather in the artistic object's signifying function as a created signifier, something entailing a relation to the real loss necessitated by language.

The crucial event of art, then, does not in Lacan's view involve the contemplative admiration of an illusion—for example, of apples presented in their fullness through the masterful technique of the painter. Nor does art offer a mode of apprehension by which the subject encounters the truth of the object in its actual or ideal forms. While Lacan will indeed claim that art points to a beyond, it is important to note that this beyond is not of the order of objects and truth. When, in the event of art, Cézanne's apples point "beyond" themselves, the painted apples point beyond themselves as objects and beyond any particular signified to the emptiness that inhabits the signifier as such and that drives us as subjects of language. Thus, as Lacan describes it, the crucial event of art is the renewal of the subject's relationship with the Thing in the encounter with the artistically transformed object.

Indeed, we might locate here the "work" that the work of art does: it effects the transformation of the object into a signifier of the Thing, and thus re-articulates the subject with the real of language. In the ordinary course of events, culture "shies away from the sense of emptiness" that art creates (162f, 136e) and strives to master this emptiness by rendering it within the sign as a fullness. Once culture has successfully mastered the work of art, the vast cathedral renders palpable the fullness of God's presence, the perspectival painting gives the illusion of being full of space, Cézanne's painted apples make us see apples anew as apples, and even the emptiest vase is, as science well assures us it must be, full of air, dust, and pollen.[11] Directing itself against the reigning cultural-historical conventions that work to domesticate the real sense of the Thing and to "colonize" the field of the Thing with imaginary formations (119f, 99e), art works to elude our mastery and to unsettle us by demonstrating the mimetic illusion as a nontransparent signifier as such and thus to "make emerge something that would be precisely there where one has been thrown into a panic and lost one's head[12]—properly speaking, nowhere" (162f, 136e).

In this Lacanian aesthetics which conceptualizes art in terms of the subject's encounter with the Thing and the rediscovery of the real of the signifier, literary art in particular would appear to enjoy a special power. That is, since art essentially involves a manipulation of the *signifier* to put the subject into relationship with an object that represents the Thing (144f, 119e), literary art—which takes the signifier as its sole substance—would seem to offer the most elegant terms for exposing the artificial, illusory nature of mimesis, for the creation of the signifying emptiness, and hence for the representation of the Thing. Lacan puts it this way:

> [T]hat which we seek in the illusion is something in which the illusion as such transcends itself in some way, destroys itself, in demonstrating that it is but there as a signifier.
>
> It is this which so eminently gives back primacy to the domain of language, where we have, quite well and good, in every case to contend with the signifier. And it is this which restores to poetry its primacy in the order of the arts. (163f, [136e])[13]

The point to be underscored here involves not so much the relative place of literature among the arts[14]—whether or not, as Lacan seems to imply above, the essence of literary art is more evidently grounded in the signifier than are other arts—as the most basic fact that in literature we have an art form that performs its work exclusively through the medium of the signifier. In literature, in some mysterious way, these words, mere ink on a page, often representing stories understood to be entirely untrue, nevertheless, through their aesthetic association with the Thing, succeed in arousing our interest, in animating our bodies in excitement and fear and passion, and in pressing upon us with utter conviction a sense of urgency and meaningfulness far in excess of the signified object reasonably considered.

The Head of Beatrice: The Mystery of the Beautiful and the Limit of Death

Thus far, we have suggested the broad outlines of a Lacanian theory of aesthetics by describing the event of art as the subject's encounter with the Thing, or, to put it another way, by proposing that art places the subject into proximity with the real emptiness introduced by the signifier into the heart of subjective structure. We might illustrate these claims more concretely, however, and at the same time bring our key terms closer to those of Lacan's discussion of ethics, by working from a specific example of beauty, and seeing how art and beauty bring the subject into a relation with death and desire.

We shall turn to a painting that is scarcely remembered today and that of itself holds but little power to captivate those unacquainted with its history. Its principal remaining curiosity is that in the nineteenth century, before it became unmoored by art historians from its alleged story and fell from favor, it was widely renowned as among the most beautiful paintings in the world. It was thought then to be a portrait of young Beatrice Cenci, painted, on the eve of her beheading, by the Italian baroque master Guido Reni.[15] Such was the remarkable power of this famous portrait in its day that it inspired not only countless minor copyists, but even a five-act verse tragedy by Percy Shelley and a canny novella by Stendhal.[16] Among the Americans, Nathaniel Hawthorne wrote in his *Notebook* that it was "the most profoundly wrought picture in the world" (92–93) and Herman Melville not only alluded to it in a number of his later works,[17] but also owned a copy of the portrait himself. Today, the subject and attribution of the portrait hanging in the Palazzo Barberini are acknowledged as unknown, and the painting no longer enjoys any special reputation for beauty. Thus, in the present essay, when we turn to the painting, we really turn not to the painting itself, but to the reception of the painting by the Romantics. It will be Hawthorne's reading of the painting that interests us in particular, since not only is he very eloquent on the beauty of the portrait, but (as we shall see in a later chapter of this book) he is also engaged in an effort, like Lacan's, to think through problems at the intersection of ethics and aesthetics.

To those who know it, the tale of the beautiful Beatrice continues to exert a simple, mythic power in its atrocious crimes and uncanny reverberations. She was the daughter of Francesco Cenci, who lived in Rome toward the end of the sixteenth century, and who was both immensely wealthy and powerful, and also depraved and ruthlessly cruel.[18] His petty rivals he murdered, his peers he defied and intimidated, and the popes he paid enormous sums to look with indulgence upon his excess. His sons fled home upon reaching adulthood, and would have been abandoned to poverty, if not for the intercession of the pope. An older daughter escaped into marriage, again at the intercession of the pope to whom she had petitioned. Hence, it was the youngest daughter, Beatrice, who bore the weight of Francesco Cenci's passion. He held her captive within his palace, and there subjected her to the most appalling physical and sexual abuse—even, it would seem, flaunting this incest in front of Beatrice's stepmother, Lucrezia, and meeting any attempts at resistance with violence. The women together sent an appeal to the pope, but this, evidently, was intercepted and never received, and so they were left to consider more extreme measures to escape the atrocious torment heaped upon them. Thus, one night in September 1598, the mother and daughter succeeded in giving Francesco Cenci a large dose of opium and took the sleeping man to bed. There they looked on as two paid assassins seized a hammer and pounded one spike into the eye and then a second into the throat of old Francesco, killing him in his sleep. The women then removed the large nails and disposed of the body, improbably staging the father's bloody murder as an accident. For some months the death went without investigation, but suspicions remained and evidence accrued, until at length, Beatrice, Lucrezia, and two of the Cenci sons were arrested for the murder. And although all of Rome was aroused in compassionate defense of the abused family and the beautiful girl, nevertheless, confessions were extracted, and the pope was constrained to condemn the parricides to public execution. Almost exactly one year after the murder, then, and just days after her sixteenth birthday, Beatrice was led through the crowds, taken upon the scaffold, and beheaded before the eyes of all Rome.

The portrait that inspired Shelley, Stendhal, Melville, and Hawthorne is indeed a very beautiful one. The present essay cannot venture

Illustration 1. Portrait of a young woman, purportedly Beatrice Cenci, artist unknown. Galleria Nazionale d'Arte Antica, Palazzo Barberini, Roma

a full reading of the crucial role it plays in Hawthorne's last novel, *The Marble Faun* (1860), but we might exploit Hawthorne's description of the painting there to suggest something of the fascinating mystery it held for the nineteenth-century Romantics. "The picture," he writes,

> represented simply a female head; a very youthful, girlish, perfectly beautiful face, enveloped in a white drapery, from beneath which strayed a lock or two of what seemed a rich, though hidden luxuriance of auburn hair. The eyes were large and brown, and met those of the spectator, but evidently with a strange, ineffectual effort to escape. There was a little redness about the eyelids, very slightly indicated, so that you would question whether or no the girl had been weeping. The whole face was quiet; there was no distortion or disturbance of any single feature; nor was it easy to see why the expression was not cheerful, or why a single touch of the artist's pencil should not brighten it into joyousness. But, in fact, it was the very saddest picture ever painted or conceived; it involved an unfathomable depth of sorrow, the sense of which came to the observer by a sort of intuition. It was a sorrow that removed this beautiful girl out of the sphere of humanity, and set her in a far-off region, the remoteness of which—while yet her face is so close before us—makes us shiver as at a spectre. (905)

If the portrait of that "perfectly beautiful face" on the eve of beheading captured the imagination of the nineteenth century, Hawthorne shows us that it was not only because of the delicate lines and the sweet grace of the curves painted on the canvas, but also because of the viewer's shivering intuition of that terrible suffering, the violation of those primal taboos, and the spectral presence there of death anticipated.

Indeed, in Hawthorne's description of Beatrice's peculiar unapproachability, in the beautiful girl's removal from out of the spectator's sphere into "a far-off region, the remoteness of which—while yet her face is so close before us—makes us shiver as at a spectre," we get a more concrete sense for Lacan's own claim that beauty involves a relation with the absolute that is at once so very close and at the same time on the far side of a limit from where we stand, a line we are prohibited from crossing. Lacan describes the phenomenon of the beautiful in terms of a very specific relation to death. He speaks of the coincidence of beauty's radiance with a transgression of a limit, and says that

> It is there that a certain rapport is established for us to a beyond of the central field, but it is also that which prohibits

> us from seeing its true nature, that which dazzles us and separates us from its true function. The affectively moving side [*Le côté touchant*] of the beautiful makes all critical judgment vacillate, arrests analysis, and plunges the different forms in play into a certain confusion or, rather, an essential blindness.
>
> The effect of beauty is one of blindness. There happens something else beyond,[19] which cannot be seen. . . . When Antigone depicts herself as Niobe becoming petrified, with what is she identifying herself—if not with that inanimation where Freud taught us to recognize the form in which the death instinct is manifested? It is well indeed an illustration of the death instinct which is enacted here. (327f, 281e)

In the legendary portrait as the Romantics saw it, Beatrice sits—composed, still, sorrowful—and she casts a last look back over her shoulder to regard the viewer from the place of death she is already crossing into. The gaze, the soft appeal of her eyes, marks her closeness; her shoulder marks her distance and a limit beyond which the viewer may not penetrate. Ahead of her lies inscrutable darkness, yet the beautiful girl radiates in that last moment with a light as if divine. The spectator beholds not just a "perfectly beautiful face" in the fullness of its girlish beauty, but also the gaze of a beautiful young woman on the eve of execution, one against whom the law has pronounced its gravest, most absolute sentence. Hawthorne betrays this anticipation of Beatrice's death in his very first words: "The picture represented simply a female head." In *Pierre* (1852), Melville starts out almost the same way, writing of "that sweetest, most touching, but most awful of all feminine heads" (407). It is not literally true, of course: the girl in the portrait also has much of her upper torso visible—a torso still very much attached to her perfectly beautiful head. But in the viewer's imagination, Beatrice is always there, awaiting her own beheading, and so is frozen on the canvas in the inescapable presence of her own death.

The mystery of the beautiful signals a real limit. Partly this is a limit of critical comprehension, so that, even after his third visit to see the picture, a puzzled Hawthorne could write in his *Notebooks* that the alluring portrait of Beatrice, while "beyond measure touching," is also "quite indescribable, inconceivable, and unaccountable in its effect" (520–21). The stuttering inarticulacy in Hawthorne's remark is suggestive of the blindness effect that Lacan claims as essential to beauty, the fact that the encounter with beauty leaves us so moved and so dazzled by the radiance we perceive, that our critical judgment is blinded—prohibited from seeing the true, deathly nature of the attraction exerted by the beautiful, and separated from its true function.[20] In beauty, says Lacan, something takes place in a sort of "beyond" of perception and cognition, something that cannot be seen; and this unseen Thing is of the order of death.[21] If beauty, in our naïve consideration of it—the sparkling beauty of a winter's day or the beautiful form of a sleeping lover—if these events fail to call to consciousness the death that Lacan claims they indicate, and if even in the case of Beatrice's beautiful head Hawthorne marks the presence of death only latently in the language of his description, part of the explanation goes to the blindness effect.

More importantly, however, the deathly "beyond" both indicated and veiled by the radiance of beauty is simply not on the order of something that one might see if only one might part the veil. It is important to remember that, from a Lacanian perspective, despite appearances, beauty is not a native attribute of a thing or a person. It is not something that exists independently of the viewer or auditor. Rather, beauty is an effect produced and experienced in the intimacy of our subjective response to a given object or person. Hence, the death and the limit suggested by beauty also subsist at a more intimate level. When we recall Hawthorne's remark that the portrait arrests the viewer before a limit that works to remove the beautiful girl "out of the sphere of humanity, and set her in a far-off region, the remoteness of which—while yet her face is so close before us—makes us shiver as at a spectre," we note that Hawthorne doesn't shiver at the legendary portrait because it shows Beatrice as a ghost. He shivers because the sense of the girl's sorrow seems to haunt one from the inside, generating an uncanny specter within the nineteenth-century viewer. Lacan will claim to his analytic trainees that this intimation of death in the experience of beauty is not unique to the portrait so admired by Hawthorne, Melville, and others, and indeed that this suggestion of something related to the destructive drive in art is a generalizable phenomenon. "The true barrier," he tells them,

> that arrests the subject before the unnamable field of radical desire—as far as it is the field of absolute destruction, of destruction beyond putrefaction—is properly speaking the aesthetic phenomenon as far as it is identifiable with the experience of the beautiful, the beautiful in its shining radiance. . . . It arrests us, but it also indicates to us in which direction [*dans quel sens*] is found the field of destruction. (256f, 216–17e)

Within Lacan's psychoanalytic aesthetics, beauty is essentially an effect of a relation to a limit that he called "the limit of the second death" (302f, 260e). By "second death," Lacan means a death beyond the recuperative powers of nature, a death so radically alterior to the subject that it cannot be domesticated by the symbolic system and remains, therefore, quite traumatically, a Thing of the untamed real. Lacan, then, in speaking of the experience of beauty, isn't speaking of the death of one's corporeal body, the repulsive, unbeautiful death of rot and the grave. Rather, Lacan is speaking of death as an absolute void, a place where the subject has vanished from the order of being.

We can see that, though our terms have shifted, we haven't gone far from our earlier description of the artistic event as organized around the emptiness that represents the Thing of the real that defies symbolization. What *is* new is the recognition that the viewer's very sense of being is at stake in the artistic encounter with the Thing and the signifier as such:

> That which is beyond is . . . in part . . . the relationship with the second death, which is to say, with man insofar as language demands from him that he render an account of this fact that he *is not.* (345f, 298e)

In art, the subject comes into contact with the signifier in such a way that the artistic signifier "points to" the absence that is the beyond of the presence of the signifier. More to the point, however, in the event of art, the subject intuits that his or her place in the symbolic field (and in the very order of being discernible through the symbolic)[22] is not a secure one. The radical and deathly impulse of the real agitates against the fictions and misrecognitions that give that place consistency for the subject:

> [Q]uestion, . . . —how can man, that is to say a living being, accede to knowledge of this death instinct, his own relationship to death?
>
> Response—by the virtue of the signifier and under its most radical form. It is in the signifier and insofar as the subject articulates a signifying chain, that he touches upon the fact that he may be missed from the chain of that which he is.
>
> I had wanted to show you how the function of the signifier in the subject's access to his relation to death might be rendered more tangibly than by connotative reference. This

> is why I have tried to make you recognize it in these latest meetings under an aesthetic (that is to say sensible) form, that of the beautiful—the function of the beautiful being, precisely, to indicate to us the place of the relation of man to his own death, and to indicate it to us but in a dazzling radiance. (341–42f, 295e)

It is the special quality of art to bring the subject into proximity with the Thing, with a bit of the real death carried by the signifier. This element of the real is, on the one hand, utterly intimate to the subject—who is, after all, structured in and through the signifier—and, on the other hand, absolutely excluded from the symbolic and imaginary fields that give meaningfulness and consistency to the subject's own being and place in the world. Hence, out of that encounter with the signifying Thing, not only do we get the haunting quality of beauty that Hawthorne remarked upon in the spectral portrait of Beatrice's head, but we are also afflicted with a blank stupidity in trying to rationalize its "indescribable, inconceivable, and unaccountable" effect. We can now finally get a sense for why the aesthetic register emerges in the language of patients in the clinic, since in encountering the real of the Thing, they have likewise encountered the limit point of language and being.

Language, for Lacan, always carries with it an element exterior and incommensurable with itself. It promises on the one hand to structure and render meaningful our world and our place therein, and yet it succeeds only so far before, inevitably and necessarily, it fails us. Yet while language must fail *directly* to articulate anything outside of its own sphere, and can only ever hearken to yet more signifiers, paradoxically, as art demonstrates and as clinical experience confirms, language also retains a mysterious capacity to point beyond itself and thus to circumscribe, if only approximately, the place of its own failure.

Ethics: From the Vicissitudes of Being to the Passion of the Signifier

A moment's reflection will recall our attention to the fact that the preceding chapter, on Washington Irving's "Legend of Sleepy Hollow," arrived by close reading at much the same point we have now arrived at theoretically. There we described a tale motivated out of an overwhelming event in the Revolutionary War, confronted with some impossibility or failure in its own telling, and yet circulated nevertheless—circulated first among the locals and then down through a long chain of narrators, as if, by tongue and by pen, it bore some virulent and unconscious contagion of speech. The "impossibility" at the heart of the event and its tale, as we recall, testified to an insistent, traumatic confusion of identity between the living and the dead. From this question of death and the troubling *gap* it works to insert into the soul of the storytelling community, from the impossibility of placing the enigmatic Sleepy Hollow event properly into language, and from even the vibrant beauty of Irving's language, which nearly every early critic felt compelled to remark upon—from all of this, we now recognize not just an encounter with the headless horseman, but a true encounter with the Thing that lurks both between the lines and also beyond the emptiness carried on the shoulders of the horseman. We were struck, at the end of that chapter, with the force of what seemed to be an ethical imperative to speak and to tell the tale, to bear witness—if only indirectly—to an event whose precise nature must remain irreducibly enigmatic. We can now return to this question of ethics and restate it in the theoretical terms offered by our reading of Lacan: Given the subject's relation to the signifier as situated between being and death, given the real failure carried within the signifier, and given the indirect capacity (as in art) of the signifier to represent the Thing that drives the subject's relation to desire—how then are we to understand the psychological imperative to speak around that unspeakable event? Or, to put it somewhat differently, given the failure of language in an encounter with the real Thing that exceeds symbolization, and given our psychological need to circumscribe that place of failure with a chain of signifiers in a narrative, in what sense is this psychological necessity to speak the impossible word also an *ethical* one?

It is, in fact, the subject's relation to this place of real failure carried within the signifier that constitutes the core dynamic of the "ethics of desire" elaborated in Lacan's 1959–1960 Seminar. There, Lacan observes to his trainees that, in clinical practice, the pathological guilt feelings patients arrive with correlate not so much with having violated this or that law or social more, but rather with having "ceded on one's desire" (368f, 319e). That is, in their denials and repressions, guilty patients have betrayed not a particular object of desire; rather, they have betrayed the psychological and ethical imperative to give themselves over to experiences of desire more generally; they have refused to address themselves in lack to the hazards of the other person's desire. Psychoanalysis is an ethical practice, then, insofar as it aims to bring patients to a more sustained relation to the faculty of desire as such. Or, to put it in terms we've used in thinking about the work of art, since *desire*, in the Lacanian conception, is essentially bound up together with *language*,[23] human subjects must open themselves up to the desire that comes out of the absence or void inherent in language and the signifier.

The ethical relation of the subject to desire is a peculiar one, however. We recall the quotation, cited earlier, concerning the possibility that beauty may suspend the subject's approach to the field of the Thing:

> The true barrier that arrests the subject before the unnamable field of radical desire—as far as it is the field of absolute destruction, of destruction beyond putrefaction—is properly speaking the aesthetic phenomenon as far as it is identifiable with the experience of the beautiful, the beautiful in its shining radiance. . . . It arrests us, but it also indicates to us in which direction [*dans quel sens*] is found the field of destruction. (256f, 216–17e)

Here we see something of a paradox: desire involves an attraction to the Thing, and yet at the same time, requires that, under penalty of death—for what else is a symptom, if not the symbolic insistence of real death in the living flesh—the subject must not get too close to that Thing and is prohibited from seizing it for him- or herself. In this context, the Thing is both the ultimate object of desire, the object that would yield the fullest, most perfect pleasure or jouissance, and yet it is also something from which, despite its power of attraction, the subject must nevertheless shy away or maintain a certain distance, in order to avoid the destruction that its realization would bring.

In this recognition of the necessary barrier between the subject and the object, and in describing this ultimate object as a Thing of death, Lacan's ethics of desire shows itself opposed to any libertine ethics that would proclaim a universal law of the uninhibited pursuit of pleasure. On the contrary, from the very first day of the seminar, Lacan declared that libertine ethics had, historically and clinically speaking, proved itself a failure and that it had produced not a reduction, but rather an *increase* in the incidence of pathological symptoms (12f, 4e)—something that would mark it as "bad" in any ethics of psychoanalysis. One way to think about this tension (between the attraction to the object and the ethical barrier to it) is to make distinctions between desire and the object. In a certain sense, desire is motivated by the *lack* of the object; thus, to seize the object is to put an end to desire, since in such a case the subject would no longer contend with the absence of the object. But while Lacan is no libertine, nor is he an ascetic. It would be false to suppose that, in elaborating an ethics of desire, Lacan is thereby asserting that we must forgo each object of desire in order to maintain desire itself.

We might, then, make a further distinction in the nature of the object. There is, on the one hand, the ultimate object, the oedipal object that (one supposes) would yield unbounded pleasure or jouissance and would thus eliminate all desire from the subject. For Lacan, this ultimate object is not only barred to the subject (under the incest taboo), it is not even an object of *desire*, properly understood. Rather, this ultimate object implies an object of *jouissance*.[24] An object of *desire*, by contrast, is characterized by its being only *an* object of desire, by the subject's tendency to make a series of displacements in *the* object. In desire, in other words, the subject has elected to pursue not the object of ultimate jouissance, but rather has displaced, or "sublimated," that investment and that demand onto a series of other objects, each of which provides a certain compensatory satisfaction, while also sacrificing a certain amount of the pleasure that (one supposes) would have been afforded by achieving the ultimate object.[25]

Strikingly, it is the *signifier* that enables this capacity of desire to move from object to object and that governs the logic of desire's possible movements within the subject. Indeed, Lacan describes the movement of desire within the subject as a sort of metonymy:

> In the definition of sublimation as satisfaction without repression, whether implicitly or explicitly, there is . . . a recognition of this: that desire is nothing other than the metonymy of the discourse of demand. It is change as such. I insist here: the properly metonymic relation from one signifier to another that we call desire—this is not the new object nor the previous object: this is the change of object in itself. . . .
>
> In daring to formulate a satisfaction that isn't rewarded with a repression, the theme placed at the center, promoted in primacy, is—What is desire? . . . It is insofar as the demand is always at once both beyond and on the hither side of itself that, articulated with the signifier, it always demands another thing; that, in every satisfaction of need, it requires another thing; . . . that desire is formed as that which supports this metonymy, namely, as that which the demand wants to say beyond whatever it formulates. (340f, 293–94e)

Desire wants to say more. Out of an encounter with the limit of signification, more and more words are called for. If, in a portrait, the quiet, unsettling gaze of the beautiful Beatrice makes an appeal from beyond an unsurpassable limit, if as a viewer we find ourselves in the presence of something that vibrates within the fundamental terms of our subjective constellation, if, in short, we allow the work of art to call us forth as desiring beings, we are not surprised that we are called, quite precisely, to *speak*. Hence, the urgency and the passion of an aesthetic encounter carry, in the imperative to say more, a sort of ethics of criticism. Out of a painting come a tragedy, a short story, a novel, and more; out of these come criticism, operas, films, conversations, and folklore. The work of art, as we see in the portrait, ever urges us, like some great tragedy, to "go hence, to have more talk of these sad things." There seems always more to be said. The painting, together with the legend it carries, prompts the coming into being of the speaking subject as a subject of desire. In this sense, desire is at the same time "the metonymy of our being" (371f, 321e). As one speaks, as one enters into signification, there is a sort of parallel movement of the signifier, a parallel play of presence and absence between the signifiers of the text of one's discourse and the signifiers that give consistency to one's very being as a subject of language.

Lacan, then, makes two essential claims about ethics, each of them quite different from any ethics that would conceive of itself in terms of social constraint or conformity to a norm or ideal. The first of these essential claims has already been seen—namely, that guilt pertains to having "ceded on one's desire." Against an ethics that would trust one's conscience to properly identify sin, Lacan reminds us that the whisperings of the superego all too easily assume a cruel, predatory tone. In consequence, even good men, as they say, ever interpret themselves too meanly. Indeed, as Freud observes, the conscience of a saint may well be more meticulous, more insatiable, and more cruelly and paradoxically demanding than the voice heard by the common run of lawbreaker (Freud, *Unbehagen*, 485g, 126e). By contrast, clinical experience shows that, at the root of things, patients feel guilt where they have betrayed the ethical imperative to "metonymize" desire, so to speak, and have instead accommodated themselves to its repression. The second claim Lacan makes about ethics follows from this—namely that, from the perspective of psychoanalysis, "there is no other good than that which may serve to pay the price for access to desire" (370–71f, 321e). Desire requires a certain sacrifice of jouissance and a forsaking of the deadly pleasures of the Thing. The Thing will attract us and fascinate us—as it must—but the barrier between the subject and the Thing must remain intact, or else produce the symptoms that freeze us in the captures of death.

The present book has situated itself at the intersection of ethics and aesthetics and it has aimed, therefore, to consider two basic questions. First, how might we think of an ethical dimension to art? Second, how might we think of an aesthetic dimension to ethics? We can see that Lacan's seminar on *The Ethics of Psychoanalysis* and Irving's "Legend of Sleepy Hollow" have together already offered us a preliminary answer to the first question. In a Lacanian conception of ethics, art opens onto the ethical by maneuvering the subject's relationship with the Thing in the direction of the good—that is, in the direction of opening access to desire. In its opening maneuver, art renews our relationship with the Thing by insisting upon the real absence beyond the artistic signifier. Then, crucially, in the effect of beauty, art halts us before we get too close to the Thing—as if art first reawakened our desire, but then restrained us before we could lapse into the pure jouissance and the absolute destruction beyond the barrier. In the next chapter, on Brockden Brown's *Wieland*, we shall develop these themes further and we shall begin to address the question of how we might think about an aesthetic dimension to the ethical.

CHAPTER 3

Brown's *Wieland* and the Ethical Circumscription of Death

Literary Morality and the Romance of Family Murder

In an earlier period of critical history, it was sometimes remarked that, from its beginnings well into the nineteenth century, the thematics of American literature were principally concerned with morality. Indeed, with characteristic brashness and insight, D. H. Lawrence went so far as to declare that

> [s]urely it is especially true of American art, that it is all essentially moral. Hawthorne, Poe, Longfellow, Emerson, Melville: it is the moral issue which engages them. They all feel uneasy about the old morality. Sensuously, passionally, they all attack the old morality. But they know nothing better, mentally. Therefore they give tight mental allegiance to a morality which all their passion goes to destroy. (180)

However true or untrue this may be as a general claim, certainly it seems to describe America's first career novelist, Charles Brockden Brown (1771–1810). Brown's best-known novel, *Wieland, or The Transformation* (1798) opens with an Advertisement, one of those classic eighteenth-century prefaces that assure the reader that although the following work contains accounts both extraordinary and perverse, the writer's *purpose* is "neither selfish nor temporary, but aims at the illustration of some important branches of the moral constitution of man" (3). Of course Brown is hardly alone in announcing such an ambition, but we might pause here to appreciate the strangeness of such claims, especially as they express the power of this Gothic romance woven together from the triple strands of a contemporary newspaper account of a murder,[1] the biblical tale of Abraham and Isaac, and the wilds of Brown's own fevered imagination.

With few exceptions, eighteenth-century English language novels in the wake of Richardson's *Clarissa* openly engaged with morality principally in their supposed capacity as true exemplars for impressionable minds—for example, in displaying the virtues of honesty, chastity, and filial piety, together with the unhappy consequences of dishonesty, coquetry, and youthful passion.[2] When literary writers of the period imagined their own engagement with the religious sphere, they tended to proclaim their work both as promoting the glory of God and as inspiring the religiosity of the reader. More or less typical would be the words of the German writer, Christoph Martin Wieland,[3] who wrote in the Author's Preface to his *Trial of Abraham* (1754) that

> [t]he proper object of poesy, from the nature thereof, and its relation to the human heart, is the Deity, and man in the principal ends of his existence, consequently religion and virtue. The splendid scene of nature, with all its beauties, is exhibited to us, that from such displays we may know our infinitely adorable Creator, and . . . [that] we may form ourselves to acquire that harmony of dispositions and powers, which nature offers to our imitation, and which constitutes the excellence and happiness of the moral man. Therefore, when poesy is called an imitation of nature, this, in its best sense, means, that the poetical representations of sensible beauties and gay images should ever be heightened by intellectual and moral beauties; as in nature the beautiful and good are ever conjoined. (iii)

Christoph Martin Wieland is writing a poetic embellishment of the biblical tale of Abraham and Isaac, and—at least in the broad outlines of his poem—he remains faithful to the Genesis tale that is understood to be both eminently true and moral. It makes sense, then, that he can thus claim a high moral status to his own poem and can even assert the harmony of beauty, truth, and goodness within such a production.

Brockden Brown, however, makes a more radical departure, both from Richardson and from Christoph Martin Wieland, when he stages his own work in relation to the tale of Abraham and Isaac. Not only does Brown recast the characters to give them a late-enlightenment sensibility and restage the scene to suburban Philadelphia in the 1760s, but he also introduces critical questions that effectively undermine the element of divinity within the story. Brown's more direct source for the novel was the actual case, alluded to in his Advertisement, of J— Y—, who in Tomhanick village, New York, slew his wife and four children in December 1781. But again, Brown departs from the journalistic or historical account, by recasting and restaging the tale, by "romancing" matters of cause and motivation, and by inserting key characters.[4] One must ask the naïve questions here: Why are such changes necessary? Why make the departures from revealed or historical truth? If Brown "aims at the illustration of some important branches of the moral constitution of man," as he claims, why not write a biblical exegesis, a sermon, or a philosophical treatise? Or, since the tale also derives from the Tomhanick murders, why not present a journalistic account more faithful to the historical truth of those events? Why, in short, lie? Or, to recast the question again, what is it about literature that, despite its fictional status, allows for the emergence of some truth or moral insight unavailable to more straightforward accounts?

We might arrive at a preliminary formulation by considering Brown's essayistic writings. These suggest that he held two distinct views regarding the conjunction of literature and the field of ethics or morality. One of these views was akin to C. M. Wieland's ideal of offering, in literature, a harmonious and moral beauty to inspire the imitation of the reader—the claim, as Brown puts it in one essay, that literature ought to instruct and inspire us, "by the exhibition, in the principle character, of a model of right conduct" (102). However, it's not at all clear that Brown himself felt constrained to follow this exemplary dictum in his novels. Clara, for instance, the narrator and principle character of *Wieland*, may declare her heart "the shrine of all purity" (104), but in her hour of crisis, this otherwise admirable woman thirsts for the blood of a man guilty of perhaps little more than poor taste and ill-timed mischief—as she and the reader both know. And indeed a far more serious question mark hangs over the title character of Brown's *Arthur Mervyn*, who, depending on the faith one gives to his own account of things, is either an unlucky but well-intentioned innocent, or else a knave and an extravagant liar.

More interesting, and more consistent with Brown's own literary practice, are the claims he makes in his well-known essay, "Walstein's School of History. From the German of Krants of Gotha" (1799). Here, Brown directly speaks to the departures that a romancer will make from a systematic philosophical presentation or from strictly given historical facts. The abstract systems and theoretical reasonings of philosophy may indeed have their place within a narrow sphere, writes Brown, but the dryness of the material makes it too laborious to be correctly read by the greater number of people—and incorrectly read, it tends to impart error. Moreover, to this greater number,

> [m]ere reasoning is cold and unattractive. Injury rather than benefit proceeds from convictions that are transient and faint; their tendency is not to reform and enlighten, . . . but merely to pester the offender with dissatisfaction and regret. (35)

If we see here that the strictly philosophical is unattractive and liable to promote error, Brown argues further, in "The Difference Between History and Romance" (1800), that a strict adherence to known historical truth eviscerates precisely what we find most interesting in narrative: the (ultimately unknowable) human dimension of *motive* and the necessarily flawed and speculative declarations of a *cause* for a given effect:

> Curiosity is not satisfied with viewing facts in their disconnected state and natural order, but is prone to arrange them anew, and to deviate from present and sensible objects, into speculations on the past or future; it is eager to infer from the present state of things, their former or future condition.
>
> The observer or experimentalist, therefore, who carefully watches, and faithfully enumerates the appearances which occur, may claim the appellation of historian. He who adorns these appearances with cause and effect, and traces resemblances between the past, distant, and future, with the present, performs a different part. He is a dealer, not in certainties, but probabilities, and is therefore a romancer. (83)

Indeed, Brown goes so far as to claim that "the description of human actions is of moment merely as they are connected with motives and tendencies" (84). Because human interest directs itself to what *cannot* be certainly known, it is precisely *into* the unknown and the ultimately unknowable that literature must enter, if it is to succeed in engaging the interest and swaying the passions of the reader. Thus, for Brown, a literary dimension is requisite in lending to truth and morality a palpable sense of meaningfulness, even while this dimension introduces a subtle, irresolvable gap in the knowledge and truth of the text. Surprisingly, then, to illuminate the *understanding* requires that one also "charm curiosity, and sway the passions" (33). It requires *art*, in other words: a poetic manipulation of language and an imaginative departure into the realm of the merely probable.

Nevertheless, Brown's reader must still ask whether this is an adequate description of what Brown actually practices in his own novels. Certainly, in his best novels, Brown succeeds brilliantly in charming the curiosity and swaying the passions of the reader. But the complexity and ambiguity of a novel such as *Wieland* seem more to confound understanding than to illuminate it. Like the writers described by D. H. Lawrence, Brown seems to exhibit in his work an irreducible tension between a "mental," or intellectual, relation to morality and one derived from whatever motivates our passion. And so we ask again, if we take seriously Brown's moral ambitions as announced in his Advertisement, and if we concede the insufficiency of the *intellectual* moral lesson to account for the *passionate* ethical force of the tale, how then do we understand the intersection of literature and ethics in the case of *Wieland*? As the present essay describes an ethical force irreducible to understanding, one that emerges as the crucial and particular province of literature in the thinking of ethics, we shall see that this force is a matter of language at the limits of signification.

The Presence of the Divine Word and the Movement of the Signifier

Wieland is a gothic epistolary novel centered around the murder of a family. The principle action of the novel opens on a circle of four friends: the narrator, Clara; her brother, the future murderer Theodore Wieland; Wieland's wife, the gentle Catharine; and Catharine's brother, Henry Pleyel. This happy and enlightened society is plunged into chaos, false accusation, and murder, when to their number is added a fifth, Francis Carwin, a man of strange charm and vigorous intellect, whose unannounced powers of voice unhinge Clara's mystically inclined brother and precipitate his fall into insanity and murder. Exposed to the unexplained, seemingly supernatural ventriloquism of Carwin, Wieland begins to hear voices himself, and comes to believe he is under divine injunction to slaughter his wife and children in demonstration of his faith and obedience to God. After Wieland has accomplished this terrible charge, the agonized man again believes himself called by an incorporeal voice. This time it commands the destruction of his only surviving sister. Twice he fails to kill her, then one night Wieland escapes the bars of his asylum to make a third attempt. He finds Clara in her bedroom alone with Carwin, who has himself intruded on her and whom Clara is castigating for his responsibility in her brother's derangement and the deaths of her closest family. Carwin attempts to reason with Wieland by confessing his ventriloquist talents. However, Wieland is not to be stayed from the fulfillment of his divinely ordained mission. He seizes his sister and prepares her sacrifice, when, at the critical moment, Carwin intervenes with a timely deception. A voice, louder than human organs could produce, bursts from the ceiling, commanding Wieland to *hold!*:

> Man of errors! Cease to cherish thy delusion: not heaven or hell, but thy senses have misled thee to commit these acts. Shake off thy phrenzy, and ascend into rational and human. Be lunatic no longer. (214)

With his sublime fantasy of divine command shattered, and with the slaughter of his loved ones revealed as utterly insupportable, Wieland is crushed by the weight of his actions, fatally buries a penknife into his neck, and collapses in a pool of his own blood.

Although the structure of *Wieland's* plot derives more directly from the Tomhanick murders, a greater part of the novel's ethical force is really generated out of its mythological roots in another story of voices, sacrifice, and silence: the Genesis tale of Abraham and Isaac. In the biblical story, Abraham is called in his old age by the voice of God, and is commanded to take his son for a burnt offering on a mountain three days distant. At the mountain, Abraham builds an altar and prepares to slay his beloved son, but is stopped at the critical moment, when an angel calls from heaven, interrupts the sacrifice, and praises the God-fearing Abraham. In lieu of Isaac, then, Abraham offers up a ram, which he has found entangled in the bush nearby. Finally, the angel reports the Lord's promise to bless Abraham for hearkening to His voice and for obeying His command.

According to Søren Kierkegaard, whose *Fear and Trembling: Dialectical Lyric* (1843) is a poetic meditation on the Genesis tale, the general (or "universal") expression for Abraham's act is *murder* (30). That Abraham was stopped and Isaac survived, says Kierkegaard, is, from the ethical viewpoint of lawful human relations, immaterial to the brute fact that Abraham had made a decision to murder his son. And yet, paradoxically, the central fact of the tale, that act of decision, is remembered not as *murder*, but as the great, originary act of *faith*. Why? How is it possible to understand the celebration of the unethical Abraham? It is the weight of this paradox that motivates Kierkegaard's "dialectical lyric." Brown's novel poses the parallel question of the relation between Wieland and Abraham, and thereby gains some measure of its own weight—firstly by afflicting the reader with the Kierkegaardian paradox embodied in the "father of faith," and secondly by supplementing the power of Wieland's tale with this vital mythological engine. Wieland, Abraham—both hear voices they attribute to the divine, both make the decision to sacrifice to God family they are ethically bound to protect—but what does Brown's parallel go to show? That Wieland and Abraham are the same or that they are different? Are we to understand Wieland as we understand Abraham? These questions, inherent to Brown's text, together with the anxiety they aim to provoke at the nexus of universal reason and individual faith, suggest the dramatic stakes of Brown's novel. And they do something more, too: by insisting upon ethics while emphasizing the limits of both reason and faith, they hint toward an ethical dimension beyond the universal ethics that enlightened philosophy and reason have traditionally taken as their object.

Certainly, Wieland himself conceives of his ordeal in Abrahamic terms. Even apart from Clara's interpretation along these lines, we know this from Wieland's own testimony. Wieland had been quickly seized after the murder of Catharine and their four children, but before he can escape to seek his sister's sacrifice, he is placed on trial, where he gives an account of the slaughter and of the events that led up to it. Clara, who has been recovering from the shock of discovering her sister's mangled body and who remains ignorant of the murderer's identity (she had assumed it to be Carwin), takes up a roll of papers left by her uncle, and, full of fear and trembling all her own, reads her brother's words from a transcription of his courtroom testimony:

> It is needless to say that God is the object of my supreme passion. I have cherished, in his presence, a single and upright heart. I have thirsted for the knowledge of his will. I have burnt with ardor to approve my faith and my obedience.
>
> My days have been spent in searching for the revelation of that will; but my days have been mournful, because my search failed. I solicited direction: I turned on every side where glimmerings of light could be discovered. I have not been wholly uninformed; but my knowledge has always stopped short of certainty. Dissatisfaction has insinuated itself into all my thoughts. My purposes have been pure; my wishes indefatigable; but not till lately were these purposes thoroughly accomplished, and these wishes fully gratified.
>
> I thank thee, my father, for thy bounty; that thou didst not ask a less sacrifice than this; that thou placedst me in a condition to testify my submission to thy will! What have I withheld which it was thy pleasure to exact? Now may I, with dauntless and erect eye, claim my reward, since I have given thee the treasure of my soul. (153)

When Wieland conceives of himself in Abrahamic terms—called by God, willing to offer in bloody sacrifice the "treasure of his soul," yielding the utmost expression of faith and obedience—he is thinking about Abraham very much along the lines that convention has laid down since at least the time of Christoph Martin Wieland's *The Trial of Abraham* in 1753. As we shall see, these are precisely the conventions that the texts of Brown and the later Kierkegaard are asking their readers to revise.

Kierkegaard may wish to claim, in his Preface and in his subtitle, that the status of *Fear and Trembling: Dialectical Lyric* is more poetic than philosophical, but his "lyric" is indeed also a "dialectical" one, or a philosophical one, that allows him an essayistic space unavailable to Brown's novel or to Clara's dramatic situation, and he punctures the conventional thinking of Abraham succinctly and forcefully:

> We glorify Abraham, but how? We recite the whole story in clichés: "The great thing was that he loved God in such a way that he was willing to offer him the best." This is very true, but "the best" is a vague term. . . . What is omitted from Abraham's story is anxiety, because to money I have no ethical obligation, but to the son the father has the highest and holiest. We forget it and yet want to talk about Abraham. So we talk and in the process of talking interchange the two terms, Isaac and the best, and everything goes fine. But just suppose that someone listening is a man who suffers from sleeplessness—then the most terrifying, the most profound, tragic, and comic misunderstanding is very close at hand. He goes home, he wants to do just as Abraham did, for the son, after all, is the best. (28)

Kierkegaard could very nearly be writing about Brown's Wieland here.[5] Wieland too seems to have understood—or rather misunderstood—the nature of Abraham's sacrifice as a sort of economic exchange, in which his family translates without loss into "the treasure of his soul" and its sacrifice in turn purchases the reward from God that Wieland now feels he may rightfully claim.

But Jacques Derrida reminds us, in his reading of *Fear and Trembling*, of three essential qualities in Abraham's sacrifice[6]—qualities we see missing in the case of Wieland. Where Abraham consents to the sacrifice in all humility, in the spirit of a true gift and without expectation of any return from God, Wieland's trial testimony reveals him to be oriented toward the reward he may now claim "with dauntless and erect eye." Where Abraham bears in silence his singular responsibility to the divine command, Wieland cannot bear his silence, and shares first his burden with his victim and then his glory with the courtroom. And where Abraham's faith in God is never to be equated with certain knowledge, Wieland's quest for knowledge of God's will is revealed to be motivated precisely by an absence of faith, by an enlightened demand for *certainty* in place of *faith*. Indeed, as we recall from his quotation above, the fulfillment of Wieland's supreme passion comes when knowledge no longer stops short of certainty and the dissatisfaction that had hitherto insinuated itself into his every thought is evacuated from his soul in the pure and perfect gratification of his wish for certainty. We see that whereas Abraham lives supported within a world of faith, faithless Wieland can only long impotently for such an exalted existence, because his enlightened devotion to reason has cast him irretrievably from any such world of faith. The impossibility of Wieland's return to the shelter of faith, with its promise of almost mythical wholeness, contributes a sort of postlapsarian pathos to Wieland's madness and to his aching desire for the palpable presence of God.

As Wieland's testimony describes his thoughts prior to hearing the divine command, one can observe a series of economic equivalencies that determine his sacrifice in terms of pleasure and pain:

> The series of my thoughts is easily traced. At first every vein beat with raptures known only to the man whose parental and conjugal love is without limits, and the cup of whose desires . . . overflows with gratification. . . . The transition was not new from sensations of joy to a consciousness of gratitude. The author of my being was likewise the dispenser of every gift with which that being was embellished. The service to which such a benefactor like this was entitled, could not be circumscribed. . . .
>
> For a time, my contemplations soared above the earth and its inhabitants. I stretched forth my hands; I lifted my eyes, and exclaimed, O! that I might be admitted to thy presence; that mine were the supreme delight of knowing thy will, and of performing it! The blissful privilege of direct communication with thee, and of listening to the audible enunciation of thy pleasure!
>
> What task would I not undertake, what privation would I not cheerfully endure, to testify my love of thee? Alas! thou hidest thyself from my view: glimpses only of thy excellence

> and beauty are afforded me. Would that a momentary emanation from thy glory would visit me! that some unambiguous token of thy presence would salute my senses! (154)

Wieland takes the blessing of his family as a debt to God that he owes and wishes to discharge. For the pleasure and gratification of his beloved family life, there would seem, by this logic, but one equivalent price he might pay: the pain and torment of its sacrifice. Thus, inside the anguished breast of Wieland, we might suppose there to be an exact compensatory pleasure of believing he has paid his debt to the author of his being, and that, alone of all humanity, he no longer stands in a relation of loss and obligation to God. Indeed, Wieland's vanity urges him to the belief that, touched by the divine ray, he has surpassed humanity and approached the divine.

But Brown's text reminds us that loss and obligation are essential to human subjectivity, and there can be no once-and-for-all sacrifice, unless it be our own death, to discharge this primordial debt. As we recall from the preceding chapter, and as Wieland's testimony reveals, because we exist within a language that always to some degree escapes our control, we can escape neither the loss and ambiguity of that language nor the passion that it drives. One might fantasize of the "bliss" of a communication that would be absolutely direct in its fullness and presence, but such would be a language ascribable only to God, and unavailable to a mere man. When Wieland describes Catharine's murder, his very language shows just how thin his fantasized transcendence of the human really is:

> Till her breath was stopped she shrieked for help—for mercy. When she could speak no longer, her gestures, her looks appealed to my compassion. My accursed hand was irresolute and tremulous. I meant for thy death to be sudden, thy struggles brief. Alas! my heart was infirm; my resolves mutable. Thrice I slackened my grasp, and life kept its hold, though in the midst of pangs. Her eye-balls started from their sockets. Grimness and distortion took the place of all that used to bewitch me into transport, and subdue me into reverence.
>
> I was commissioned to kill thee, but not to torment thee with the foresight of thy death; not to multiply thy fears, and prolong thy agonies. Haggard, and pale, and lifeless, at length thou ceasedst to contend with thy destiny.
>
> This was a moment of triumph. Thus had I successfully subdued the stubbornness of human passions. (159)

Wieland's "moment of triumph," as he terms it, is an unstable one, however. In the courtroom testimony he gives above, we can see that, though he feels he remains God's chosen agent, his language betrays a persistent humanity, both in his passion and in the decomposition of his language. The power and the pathos of the scene, after all, lie partly in the way he shifts his address without notice, from the listeners in the courtroom, to the dead wife he loved: "Haggard, and pale, and lifeless, at length thou ceasedst to contend with thy destiny." Something about the testimony he gives and the witness he bears to his wife's passing carries him into the presence of death, or the presence of the past, and he is momentarily overthrown. Wieland's apostrophic language here, perhaps like human language generally, seems necessarily to aim itself at a very particular missing element, but this must be an element—like death or the past—whose nature is to remain essentially, finally, unreachable.

Wieland's instability continues in the moments following the murder: from triumph to despair to regained calm to renewed strife. He regains balance, however, by a sort of double-movement that seems, on the one hand, to return him to the presence of God's word, and simultaneously to accommodate itself to the propulsive deferral at the heart of human language and subjectivity:

> I will not dwell upon my lapse into desperate and outrageous sorrow. The breath of heaven that sustained me was withdrawn, and I had sunk into *mere man*. I leaped from the floor: I dashed my head against the wall: I uttered screams of horror: I panted after torment and pain. . . .
>
> I thank my God that this degeneracy was transient, that he deigned once more to raise me aloft. I thought upon what I had done as a sacrifice to duty, and *was calm*. . . .
>
> From these thoughts I was recalled by a ray that was shot into the room. A voice spake like that which I had before heard—"Thou hast done well; but all is not done—the sacrifice is incomplete—thy children must be offered—they must perish with their mother!—" (160)

In representing and figuring his experience, Wieland's punchy, asyndetic clauses carry one along by substituting a colon for a period ("I leaped from the floor: I dashed my head against the wall: I uttered screams of horror: I panted after torment and pain . . .") and suggest thereby that the *mere man* he lapsed into was one more characterized by the movement of language and no longer sheltered under the presence of the divine. Strikingly, however, Wieland takes that ineluctable linguistic movement from the isocolon and seeks to recuperate it into the incompleteness of the divinely ordained task: there is yet more to accomplish. Thus, he acknowledges the exigencies of language *and* he maintains his status as the chosen instrument of God, but in doing so, he expresses the monstrous insatiability and obscene ferocity of the "divine" voice. Or, to put it differently, he remains a divine murderer, but can do this only by denying the alterity (and thus subverting the divinity) of the divine.

So, where Brown's text exploits its comparison with the tale of Abraham and Isaac to provoke an appreciation for an ethical dimension beyond universal ethics, it also exploits its contrast—not to undermine the biblical tale, but rather to underline a genuine distinction between the divine word and the all too human signifier that motivates Wieland, betrays his "mere" humanity, and impassionates this text through and through.

The Unforsaken Image

Clara's narrative gives us an even more evocative picture of how an understanding of the human relation to the signifier might help to "illustrate some important branches of the moral constitution of man." At the heart of the matter lies a crucial distinction between the power of the word and the power of the violent image. Theories of art going back to Aristotle have suggested that a superior catharsis of pity and fear is produced not by the direct image of violence (however sensational for the spectator) but rather via the mediation of the reported word. As Aristotle puts it in his *Poetics*, "Now, what is fearful and pitiable can result from spectacle, but also from the actual structure of events, which is the higher priority and the aim of the superior poet. For the plot should be so structured that, even without seeing it performed, the person who hears the events that occur experiences horror and pity at what comes about" (1453b). There seems to be something relatively intractable about the image of violence, something, as we shall see, that inhibits the more productive effects that can follow from the human voice and the word of the superior poet.

Let us now recall Carwin's intervention in the bedroom and try to highlight a few of its essential structures. At this point in the novel, Clara has returned to her deserted home to retrieve a journal before departing with her uncle to convalesce in France, far removed from the murderous passion of her imprisoned brother. By chance, she is found there first by Carwin, who confesses his ventriloquism and his role in some of the deceptions and voices, and then by Wieland, who has escaped his confinement, driven to fulfill his divine mission in the sacrifice of his beloved sister. It is indeed a moment of terror and pity,[7] as Clara faces her brother there. Ever more desperate to escape the death that seems so certain, she has tried to redirect Wieland's violence onto Carwin, by exposing Carwin's ventriloquism and by speciously proclaiming his ruinous intent (this, despite the fact that Carwin explicitly denied direct responsibility for the voices prompting the murders). Wieland, however, has no ears for Clara's argument and dismisses Carwin, leaving only brother and sister, face to face, alone in the bedroom. After the reasonable explanation of Wieland's voices has been offered and refused, and just as Wieland and Clara grasp each other, trembling with fear and panting with dread, each having made the decision to use deadly force against the other, the ventriloquist speaks and a voice, as if from heaven, echoes through the chamber:

> *Hold*! . . . Man of errors! Cease to cherish thy delusion: not heaven or hell, but thy senses have misled thee to commit these acts. Shake off thy phrenzy, and ascend into rational and human. Be lunatic no longer. (214)

As readers with a certain presence of mind unavailable to poor Clara or her brother in this moment of terrible passion, we must be struck by the rhetorical strangeness of this scene. It is a command, *not* a voice of reason that gets through to our serial murderer. The only voice Wieland will hear, and listen to, essentially commands him not to listen to voices. That is, only by believing in this voice can he understand that voices ought not to be believed. And this is the paradoxical structure that grounds his condition for insight. This voice is still further complicated by the fact that it is a ruse, a trick, a false impersonation. This time we know for certain it's not God Himself who issues the command and speaks the truth: it's the all too human Carwin speaking *as if* in the voice of God. Is this not troubling? *Why*, we must ask, can truth only be heard through false impersonation? And this voice of Carwin's that yields its insight through the paradox of its own structure, how are we to understand *it*? What *is* the truth that Wieland hears; what is his insight and how can we share it? As if to add to our anxiety, Wieland, though showing signs of great psychic animation, falls silent between the intervention of the voice and his suicide shortly thereafter.[8] What Brown is getting at, I propose, has something to do with literature itself, or with the specific way that literature can speak a truth to us in ways distinct from the truths of scientific, philosophical, or (one might suppose) divine discourse.

There are several reasons for us to consider the problem of Carwin's intervention in terms of a *literary* relation to ethics. For one, the very first word of the voice—*hold!*—is a self-conscious literary eruption from *Macbeth.*[9] In the course of his confession to Clara—this is some time before Wieland has entered her bedroom to find them together—Carwin describes an earlier instance of his ventriloquism. He says,

> The mode in which heaven is said by the poet to interfere for the prevention of crimes . . . never failed to occur to me at seasons like this. . . . [F]or this end I uttered the powerful monosyllable, "hold! hold!" (189)

A footnote by the author identifies "the poet" as Shakespeare and Brown scholarship has identified the source play as *Macbeth.* And certain parallels in the action of *Wieland* and *Macbeth* are clear: in each we have a man who hears supernatural voices, who murders his kin, and who then fatally self-destructs. And both works also concern themselves with powers and the limits of language, with voices that predicate a horrific deed, as well as horrific deeds that defy the circumscription of language.[10] So Carwin's intervention is, in its conception and its execution, a poetic one, *as he knows,* and as the author makes certain the reader knows with the inclusion of an authorial footnote (one of only four in the novel). So it is the voice of the poet that Wieland finally hears. To refine a question posed previously: Is there perhaps some way in which poetry, or the literary, allows for a truth one would otherwise refuse to hear—or prove unable to comprehend?

Let's return to the bedroom, where all the ethical and literary questions of the novel come to bear. With the moment of Carwin's Shakespearean intervention, the scene in the bedroom has still not yet reached its climax. Clara writes her own interpretation of the events that follow the voice:

> My brother opened his lips to speak. His tone was terrific and faint. He muttered an appeal to heaven. It was difficult to comprehend the theme of his inquiries. They implied doubt as to the nature of the impulse that hitherto had guided him, and questioned whether he had acted in consequence of insane perceptions.
>
> To these interrogatories the voice, which now seemed to hover at his shoulder, loudly answered in the affirmative. Then uninterrupted silence ensued.

> Fallen from his lofty and heroic station; now finally restored to the perception of truth; weighted to earth by the recollection of his own deeds; consoled no longer by a consciousness of rectitude, for the loss of offspring and wife—a loss for which he was indebted to his own misguided hand; Wieland was transformed at once into the *man of sorrows*![11] (214)

Onto the silence, the muttering, and the inquiries she admits are difficult to comprehend, the ever-intellectual Clara projects an image of her brother as a fallen "man of sorrows," fortune's fool, a classic tragic hero. She elides over the gaping chasm of paradox and uncertainty that Carwin's intervention has opened, in order to produce a narrative that can support a stable ethical system. As Clara wants to read the scene here, there is a Supreme Good, and Wieland at last knows the truth that the rest of us have known all along: *thou shalt not kill.* Her brother's disordered speech and then conspicuous silences testifies, in her interpretation, to his terrible insight, and for the moment it appears that death has been forestalled. All this would be comprehensible to Clara and to the reader.

But Clara's attempt to rationalize an ethical schema that would account for these events holds only for a moment, and then, at first slowly, and then faster than thought itself, Clara's narrative begins to collapse:

> His lips moved, but no sound escaped him. . . .
>
> For a time his movements seemed destitute of purpose. . . .
>
> [Then] A beam appeared to be darted into his mind . . . and now he eagerly gazed about him. . . . His eye now lighted upon [the penknife], he seized it with the quickness of thought. I shrieked aloud, but it was too late. He plunged it to the hilt in his neck; and his life instantly escaped with the stream that gushed from the wound. He was stretched at my feet; and my hands were sprinkled with his blood as he fell.
>
> Such was thy last deed, my brother! For a spectacle like this was it my fate to be reserved! Thy eyes were closed—thy face ghastly with death—thy arms, and the spot where thou liedest, floated in thy life's blood! These images have not, for a moment, forsaken me. Till I am breathless and cold, they must continue to hover in my sight. (214–15)

The trauma of her brother's death and her survival is registered not just in Clara's belated shriek, but also in her very language and her mode of address. Customarily a model of self-possession and enlightened intelligence, and sharing Brown's characteristic tic of posing deliberative questions, Clara herself is shattered and her tone here shifts abruptly from the rationally speculative to the spectacularly imagistic. The blood on her hands, the face of the suicide, the images that have not, in her curious and plaintive phrasing, "forsaken" her. What we witness in this most crucial moment of the entire novel is the collapse of language in its universal capacity to symbolize experience. It is the graphic image, *not* the word, that communicates the lasting impact here. When at last Wieland opens his throat, it is *not* to speak, but to bring silent death back into the room with Clara's pen-knife. "These images," writes Clara, "have not, for a moment, forsaken me." Captured by the images of her dead brother, Clara ceases to address the world and the universal reader, and, in an eerie repetition of her brother's apostrophic turn to Catharine during his trial testimony, she instead addresses Wieland in particular: "Such was thy last deed, my brother." She moves from a conventional past tense to one with an emphatic present sense to it: "now he eagerly gazed about him. . . . His eye now lighted upon [the penknife] . . ." Time itself seems disrupted.

Together with the trauma of unexpected death and survival comes too a radical shift in Clara's ethical vision—predictably, from the universal to the particular. After the suicide, Carwin re-enters the room proper to make further avowals of his innocence. But, writes Clara:

> I did not listen—I answered him not—I ceased to upbraid or accuse. His guilt was a point to which I was indifferent. Ruffian or devil, black as hell, or bright as angels, thenceforth he was nothing to me. I was incapable of sparing a look or a thought from the ruin that was spread at my feet. (215–16)

And so Clara's silence is joined to that of her brother. What, then, is the reader left with? There are words, of course, but these seem only to register the failure of words when faced with the overwhelming image of death. This novel of voices has metamorphosed into a novel of silences. Instead of catharsis, the reader faces images of death, "obscure and disjointed like the parts of a dream" (162). Instead of being given the content of Wieland's insight, the reader is seemingly ignored by the narrator, and must contend with the anxiety and the rapturous horror of those unforgettable images given in Clara's account. Fenimore Cooper was one such reader and his words, in his *Notions of the Americans*, offer a strange echo of Clara's own lament: "I remember to have read . . . *Wieland*, when a boy, and . . . amid a thousand similar pictures which have succeeded, the images it has left still remain distinct and prominent in my recollection" (Brooks, 25n).[12] It is a remarkable and unsettling testimony to the power of Brown's novel—and indeed to the power of the literary word generally—that something of the shattered experience inside the fictional world of the text is able, through the force of the traumatic image, to carry over into world of the reader.

It was surely to exploit this power of the literary word that Kierkegaard chose to write *Fear and Trembling* in the very particular way that he did. He described this mode as "dialectical lyric," a near oxymoron that suggests a sort of biloquism in itself, at once literary and philosophical. At one point he will say, perhaps in modesty, that he is "not a poet" (90), and in the end it is clear that Kierkegaard's sympathies are not fully literary, but clearly too he wishes to make a break from systematic philosophizing and from the universal strivings of the Hegelian tradition. "The present author is by no means a philosopher," he twice repeats emphatically.

> He is *poetice et eleganter* [in a poetic and refined way][13] a supplementary clerk who neither writes the system nor gives *promises* of a system. . . . He writes because to him it is a luxury that is all the more pleasant and apparent the fewer there are who buy and read what he writes. He easily envisions his fate in an age that has crossed out passion in order to serve science. (7)

For Kierkegaard, the poetic dimension of his dialectical lyric bears upon passion: in the first instance upon his love for Abraham, but also upon the necessity of marshalling one's art in order to afflict the reader with a similar passion for the shattering paradox of Abraham's celebrated decision to murder his beloved son. For Kierkegaard, the dialectical dimension will describe the necessity of thinking and working through that paradox, but it is the literary dimension that seizes readers and engages their passion and anxiety. It is art that lays the groundwork for a philosophical thinking through of ethics.

Half a century before Kierkegaard, Brockden Brown must have intuited some similar insight, for when Clara—and Brown—sharpen the quill to write the present narrative, not only is that pen marked by death, but the narrative itself is pocked by ethical paradoxes and impossibilities that will not forsake the reader and that demand a sort of working through on the part of the reader, both despite and because of the collapse, in this moment of trauma, of the universal capacity of language to represent experience. The point for Brown, as for Kierkegaard, is not that such paradoxes and gaps signal a final collapse of ethics (nor, for that matter, some colossal failure of reason and ordinary language), but rather that ethics, taken seriously, involves a passionate engagement with something beyond the reach of philosophical science narrowly conceived. Brown's literary fiction aims to accomplish just such an engagement. It may enrapture its readers with the charm of literature, but it does so only to then force upon them the weight of those troubling questions and paradoxes that inhabit the limit of human ethical experience.

Writing out of Death

Clara's own exercise in writing—the two letters that compose the whole of the novel—may be considered in this same light. She, too, in the act of writing, is aiming at something beyond reason and beyond the referential power of language—something, as we shall see, that bears upon ethics in the most fundamental way. We've already come to understand the work as having lapsed into silences. This lapse manifests itself in the decomposition of Clara's language in the bedroom scene and in the unforgettable images at the conclusion of her narrative—violent, captivating images which to some degree have disabled her capacity to address others in speech and which must hover before her sight until, as she fully expects, she lies "breathless and cold." And yet, as with Kierkegaard's narrator, Johannes de Silentio, it's not a pure silence she gives in this account. She, too, writes, and addresses her words to another person. Indeed, she writes and writes and writes. Clara may well understand the witnessing of her brother's death as an encounter with the limit of language, but when we consider the broader narrative framework of Clara's story, we find that this very encounter with the limit of language is the kernel that motivates a letter more than two hundred pages in length.

It is surely one of the most strikingly strange formal features of this full-length novel that it should be composed of only two letters—the first consisting of the opening twenty-six chapters, the second of the closing twenty-seventh chapter. It is tempting to dismiss the artifice as a careless flaw in *Wieland*'s hasty composition or else as a vestigial trace of the Richardsonian tradition Brown's novel has inherited. But, as his final two sentimental novels attest, Brown was perfectly capable of composing epistolary novels with letters of ordinary length. As we consider Clara's massive letter in light of the very particular circumstances of its composition, we can see that its very length testifies to the profound problem of language the novel poses.

Let us approach this problem by considering the doubled time line of the novel's first letter. The primary time line is the one we have been considering up to this point. It begins with the tale of Clara's paternal ancestry and her father's youthful readings about the Cathars; it concludes with her brother's suicide and Clara locking herself in at the scene of the havoc. There is, however, another, secondary time line unfolding in tandem with this first one. It begins in the days immediately following Wieland's suicide, but then doubles back, as Clara composes her letter to an unnamed friend, recalling, recounting, and reliving the events of the first time line, expecting to die at the conclusion of her task:

> A few words more and I lay aside the pen for ever. Yet why should I not relinquish it now? All that I have said is preparatory to this scene, and my fingers, tremulous and cold as my heart, refuse any further exertion. This must not be. Let my last energies support me in the finishing of this task. Then will I lay down my head in the lap of death. Hushed will be all my murmurs in the sleep of the grave.
>
> Every sentiment has perished in my bosom. Even friendship is extinct. Your love for me has prompted me to this task; but I would not have complied if it had not been a luxury thus to feast upon my woes. I have justly calculated upon my remnant of strength. When I lay down the pen the taper of my life will expire: my existence will terminate with my tale. (205)

Thus, each time line within this first letter ends with a death—the one with Wieland's suicide and the other with Clara's own prospective death. We shall return shortly to the second letter, dated three years afterward, in which Clara has passed through the death she so confidently predicted and has survived to write again. The important point for now is that, from the perspective of the first letter, Clara's act of writing spans between the two deaths, her brother's and her own, each in its way both the origin and the aim of the writing.[14] The parallel arrangement of the two deaths suggests not only the way Clara has been seized by the traumatic image of Wieland's death and has embraced it as her own, but also (as we shall see) something of the way her survival is linked to her act of writing and bearing witness.

Clara's romance of death, hinted above in imagining the sweetly erotic swoon of the grave, is a tribute to Brown's ingenious and compelling perversion of the sentimental novel; but in its own terms, it also begs the question of why Clara wavers in her devotion when she is finally about to win the object of her love. That such a strongly sympathetic character as Clara—all at once so passionate, so smart, and so clueless—fails in love with the two eligible men of her circle has contributed an undercurrent of pathos up to this point. Forcefully seduced by the power of Carwin's passionately modulated voice, but pinning her expectations for romantic happiness on a proposal from Pleyel, she has played the two against each other, only to find herself dangerously mistaken in Carwin and bitterly forsaken by Pleyel. When the climactic scene in the bedroom arrives, it comes quickly after Pleyel has finally departed to join his former lover. And here, after a dark and desperate struggle with her beloved brother, she is, beyond all expectation, ravished by the images of his death, and these she clings to like a lover. These alone remain faithful to her, refusing to forsake her when all others have disappointed or departed. It is death she loves, ardently desiring it, enamored beyond hope, and luxuriating in her melancholy passion.

Yet Clara does survive. As the moment of the two deaths comes into convergence, as Clara writes of her brother's entrance into her bedroom that fatal night—and as at the same time she approaches the termination of her tale and the expiration of her mortal existence—she feels again its original terror: "Even now, when this scene exists only in memory, when life and all its functions have sunk into torpor, my pulse throbs, and my hairs uprise: my brows are knit, as then; and I gaze around me in distraction" (209). It is as if, in this moment of writing and memory, her very body is torn between past and present, life and death, and she hesitates between the two:

> Here let me desist. Why should I rescue this event from oblivion? Why should I paint this detestable conflict? Why not terminate at once this series of horrors?—hurry to the verge of the precipice, and cast myself for ever beyond remembrance and beyond hope? . . .
>
> Yes, I will rise above the sphere of mortal passions: I will spurn at the cowardly remorse that bids me seek impunity in silence, or comfort in forgetfulness. My nerves shall be new strung to the task. Have I not resolved? I will die. The gulph before me is inevitable and near. I will die, but then only when my tale is at an end. (211–12)

It is an exceptionally rich passage quoted here, but we might first ask the basic question: why *does* Clara outlive her tale? Why, when she is so smitten by the seductions of death, does she defer its final embrace?

The language of her resolve suggests that writing, and literature in particular, has something to do with her survival. Her questions above express an urgency and seriousness the reader must acknowledge: Why write? Why rescue these horrific events from oblivion? Why indeed paint this detestable scene? Why not hasten to forget, in the dreamless sleep of death, the nightmare images of this world? If she has earlier found it a luxury to feast upon her woes, if she earlier anticipated the quietly erotic pleasure of laying down her head in the lap of death, it would seem that the nature of her effort has changed now as she approaches the heart of her task—writing out those traumatic images that have not, for a moment, forsaken her. Now, she must string her nerves *against* this passion for death. Now, she must refuse the soft seductions of silence and forgetfulness. For, now, she *must*, psychologically and ethically, write this letter and tell this tale. The ethical status of her writing is unmistakable. She wishes to forget. She longs for the peace of the grave. She is confident of her fate. But rather than hastening toward the (seemingly) inevitable, and rather than allowing herself relief from exhaustion and the insistent images of death, she concedes her obligation to write, defers the fulfillment of her romance with death, and consents to live.

We might discern an ethic of life at the heart of this obligation to circumscribe the problem of death with language. We have already seen that, for Clara's first letter, writing and living are bound inseparably together. While she writes, she lives; while she lives, she writes. In a literal sense, writing is what sustains her against the dreamy, beckoning call of death. Someone once proposed, hearkening to Scheherazade and other literary examples, that "writing so as not to die . . . or perhaps even speaking so as not to die, is a task undoubtedly as old as the word."[15] Certainly, this is true of Clara. Given her expectation that death awaits her at the conclusion of her letter, is it any wonder that her letter stretches on and on through twenty-six chapters and more than two hundred pages? Her writing in that first letter represents time against death, and that act, more than the literal content of her words, testifies to Clara's desire to write *through* this trauma and, in the writing of the trauma, to live on.

Strikingly, Brown's language also implies a movement from the ethical nature of writing within the fictional world, where it is seen in Clara's obligation to write out her traumatic survival in the bedroom, outward to the ethical potential of the literary word more generally. One recalls Clara's words as she deliberates between writing and dying in the lengthy quotation above: "The gulph before me is inevitable and near," she writes. "I will die, but then only when my tale is at an end." The image of the gulph is in fact an echo of a dream she reports early in the novel, before the murders, from when she is napping one summer evening in a recess under a secluded trellis, and is there awakened by a mysterious voice, the status of which is confused between dream and reality:

> I at length imagined myself walking, in the evening twilight, to my brother's habitation. A pit, methought, had been dug in the path I had taken, of which I was not aware. As I carelessly pursued my walk, I thought I saw my brother, standing at some distance before me, beckoning and calling me to make haste. He stood on the opposite edge of the gulph. I mended my pace, and one step more would have plunged me into this abyss, had not some one from behind caught suddenly my arm, and exclaimed, in a voice of eagerness and terror, "Hold! hold!" (58)

The dream, of course, foreshadows Clara's attraction to death and the iconic role of her beloved brother in summoning her there—and perhaps also suggests that these things lurked unsuspected within Clara's breast even before the murders and the climactic suicide. More remarkably, however, the "hold! hold!" of Carwin's Shakespearean intervention makes its first appearance in the story, and here, as it will later in the bedroom with Wieland, the poetic word restrains the subject in a career toward death, seizing her and stopping her on the verge of the abyss. Thus, much later, as Clara writes and wavers between death and life, past and present, it is literature, through the dreamy image of the fatal "gulph" and its associated poetic intervention, that lends the power to defer death, allowing Clara to write through this trauma and survive to write another day.

Without doubt, literature intersects with ethics in many ways. Its capacity to exemplify and inculcate moral values is only the most obvious and has been well appreciated since the eighteenth century and before. However, Brown's claim that literature finds its distinctive voice and its abiding interest in the ultimately unknowable suggests that the most properly *literary* dimension of ethics must likewise engage with the unknown—with the ultimately unknowable of cause, loss, and death, as we see in the instance of *Wieland*. This is, as Kierkegaard's dialectical lyric on Abraham's incomprehensible sacrifice also argues, an ethics beyond universal ethics, an ethics beyond that available to a systematic philosophy of reason. Thus, literature itself seems an impossible venture: it must somehow write about the thing it cannot know, it must somehow speak about the thing it cannot say, it must somehow circumscribe within the literary word the radical alterity of death. And yet, Brown seems to suggest, the engagement of literature with its own impossibility is precisely what yields its fascination and power over the passion and interest of the reader. Thus, the ethics that literature speaks to—an ethics of life as we have described it—involves not a repression of death, but rather a very specific engagement with death that nevertheless succeeds in circumscribing that death and capturing its trauma in the power of the word.

CHAPTER 4

Heideggerian Ethics

The Voice of Art and the Call to Being

Literature is commonly held to be a moral or ethical force in the life of a given culture and in the formation of its citizens. One needn't look to those wonderful eighteenth-century prefaces protesting the wholesome values to be learned from the sufferings of romantic heroines and scoundrels; the belief that literature has a powerful influence on the moral and political values of readers remains the basic assumption on both sides of the continuing culture wars. But if the most common way of thinking about the intersection of literature and ethics has involved the capacity of literature to create, reinforce, or challenge moral and political values, there have also been, in recent decades, efforts in disciplines other than literary studies—for example, in psychoanalysis and philosophy—to reconsider the nature of ethics itself. Hence, the psychoanalysis of Jacques Lacan and Luce Irigaray and the continental philosophy of Emmanuel Levinas, Jean-François Lyotard, and Jacques Derrida, have proposed dimensions of ethics outside of, and perhaps more fundamental than, the specific moral and political values embraced or rejected by individuals in their particular historical moments. For the literary scholar, it stands out as a remarkable fact that, in thinking about this sphere of ethics beyond, or on the hither side of moral codes, these philosophers and psychoanalysts often turn to the resources of literature and art. Thus, the work of Derrida and Lyotard has turned as much to art and literature as to the question of foundational ethics. Lacan and Irigaray, moreover, develop their ethics in readings of Sophocles' *Antigone*, and even Levinas opens his early masterwork on ethics, *Totality and Infinity*, by citing the French poet, Arthur Rimbaud.[1]

One begins to wonder whether the ethical dimension of literature has truly been exhausted by the problem of moral values or whether there is in fact still more to be said regarding the intersection of literature and ethics. Most of these thinkers don't generally have an interest in theorizing the work of literature as such, but their very recourse to literature in order to bring something ethical into view does point to their shared interest in language. Indeed, each of them will claim, with their varying points of emphasis and differing developments, that a fundamental *ethical* dimension is implied in the human relation to *language* itself. It is a striking assertion, if at first somewhat mysterious. Modern philosophers have long claimed that language is the basic ground for the possibilities of human thought as well as the sole material substance of the literary text. Now, more recently, it has been proposed that language lends its structures also to the ethical event.

This turn toward language and literature in the effort to think through problems in foundational ethics begs our interest in the present essay—and not only for the very basic questions of how, exactly, one might think of ethics outside of moral codes and what, exactly, language might have to do with such an ethics. Perhaps even more importantly for the literary scholar, lies a question at the very heart of literature itself: How is one to understand the relation of literature to language such that literature is able to bring into focus the ethical dimension inherent to language? To address these questions, the present essay turns in its inquiry to the later work of Martin Heidegger (1889–1976), the German thinker whose profound influence is a common thread among all the psychoanalysts and philosophers named above. Heidegger is not usually considered a philosopher of ethics—his abiding concern was really for the nature of being[2] and human existence. But he came to be deeply interested in thinking about the work of art and, as this essay will argue, he found a dimension we might call ethical there at the heart of art and poetry—an ethics he conceived in terms of a call of language that summons being into the open and that puts the responsible listener into proximity with mystery, truth, and the uncanny limits of mortal existence itself.

Language, Poetry, and the Unconcealment of Being

In an everyday consideration of the matter, language is held to be a kind of tool for communication. Such a conception seems to describe adequately enough the human relation to language as one goes about one's daily and professional business. One has, for example, points one wishes to communicate to students, messages to leave for colleagues, and requests to submit to one's chair. So, one picks up a pen to write, or opens one's mouth to speak:

> What does it mean to speak? The current view declares: speaking is the activation of the organs for sounding and hearing. Speaking is the audible expression and communication of human feelings. These feelings are accompanied by thoughts. . . .
>
> From the first and before all else, speaking is expression. (*Unterwegs* 14g, 190e)

Language is thus ordinarily thought of as the first, most fundamental technology, an instrument of sight or of sound that carries thought and feeling from the mind of one member of a language community to the mind of another in the same community. In this respect, human language differs not essentially from the language of machines and computers: it encodes and decodes a signified concept or message and carries it from one port to another.

But while it is undeniably correct to say that language can serve expression, Heidegger will insist that expression and signification nevertheless "do not genuinely reach into the realm of the primordial, essential determination of language" (*Vorträge* 204g, Logos 64e).[3] Language does something else, something more. It does not exhaust itself in signifying:

> [Language] serves as a means of discussion and agreement, in general for achieving understanding. But language is neither merely nor primarily the aural and written expression of what needs to be communicated. The conveying of overt and covert meanings is not what language, in the first instance, does. Rather, it brings beings as beings [*das Seiende als ein Seiendes*], for the first time, into the open. (*Holzwege* 61g, 45–46e)

Language, for Heidegger, is intertwined in the most intimate way with the problem of how a world comes to be present. When Heidegger proposes, as he does above, that language brings things into presence, that it somehow summons them to be what they are, he's making a double claim about the capacity for language to open up being: one claim regards things in general and the second regards human beings in particular. We shall return to the second claim in discussing Heideggerian ethics in later sections of the present essay.

The first claim, that language brings what *is* into the open, is initially a rather mysterious one. Heidegger is not, after all, proposing that there was nothing in existence before the first humans spoke. Rather, from within the human horizon—which for Heidegger matters much more than any objective stance—prior to any event of language, entities remain somehow veiled and withdrawn:

> Where no language is present, as in the being of stone, plant, and animal, there is also no openness of being, and consequently also no openness of that which is not a being [*des Nichtseienden*] or of the empty. (*Holzwege* 61g, 46e)

When language brings things into being, it calls them forth, to emerge into presence, open and unconcealed, amid beings, as beings themselves. It is not a matter of brute existence; it's a matter of openness, of whether a thing appears as itself in its proper relations to its world, "face-to-face"[4] with the other things nearby. Moreover, being *requires* this sort of event of language in order to come into its own as presence and to be sustained as being in the world. Without language, or with only everyday language (as distinct from poetic language), what remains obscured and muted is not only the absent and what ought properly to remain concealed, but also that which ought to come into unconcealment, into the open.

Language that proves still capable of summoning being into its own is what Heidegger calls "poetry." "The purely spoken," as he succinctly puts it, "is the poem" (*Unterwegs* 16g, 192e). Thus, poetry for Heidegger is not strictly verse—"pure" prose, as he says, can be just as poetic (and hence as rare) as poetry itself (*Unterwegs* 31g, 205e). For that matter, poetry in this sense need not even take its form in the spoken or written word, since for Heidegger, "*All art*, as the letting happen of the advent of the truth of beings, is, *in essence, poetry*" (*Holzwege* 59g, 44e). If Heidegger does indeed sometimes seem to give priority to verse among the arts, devoting many essays and several seminars to the poetry of Friedrich Hölderlin, for example, and declaring that "the linguistic work, poetry in the narrower sense, has a privileged position among the arts as a whole" (*Holzwege* 61g, 45e), he nevertheless holds that all works of art are directed toward the same experience of truth, and his writing shows little interest, generally speaking, in developing theoretical distinctions between the arts. Poetry in the wider sense might then be as truly painted on a canvas or piled stone upon stone on a hilltop over Athens.

Thus, so far as Heidegger is concerned, the crucial distinction to be made with poetry is not between verse and the other arts, but rather between poetic language and everyday language:

> Mortal speech is a calling that . . . bids thing and world to come. The purely bidden in mortal speech is what is spoken

> in the poem. Poetry proper is never merely a higher mode (*melos*) of everyday language. It is rather the reverse: everyday language is a forgotten and therefore used-up poem, from which there hardly resounds a call any longer. (*Unterwegs* 30–31g, 205e).

Heidegger's claim here is reminiscent of Emerson's from "The Poet" (1844), that

> though the origin of most of our words is forgotten, each word was at first a stroke of genius, and obtained currency, because for the moment it symbolized the world to the first speaker and to the hearer. The etymologist finds the deadest word to have once been a brilliant picture. Language is fossil poetry. . . . [L]anguage is made up of images or tropes, which now, in their secondary use, have long since ceased to remind us of their poetic origin. (Emerson 457)

In each case, both for Emerson and for Heidegger, the poetic word—language in all its original brilliance and power—calls forth the world (and the whole of what is) in a way that everyday language, fossilized and long since dead, can no longer do.[5] Moreover, both for Emerson and for Heidegger, what is ultimately at stake in the poetic force of each original word is not an isolated signified or referent, but rather the *world* that the poetic word summons into the open. From this perspective, the task of poetry, like the task of criticism, is to revive and to restore the human relation to language and thus to bring the careful reader to an experience of the unconcealedness of what is: to the world and the whole of Da-sein. This unconcealment of world and being that emerges in the poetically (or artistically) pure encounter with language is one way Heidegger conceives of truth. To distinguish this notion of truth as *unconcealment* from the common conception of truth as referring to the *correctness* of a proposition, he sometimes borrows the word *aletheia* from the pre-Socratic philosophers. As Heidegger will argue, alethetic truth lies at the heart of any event of great art.

Heidegger's van Gogh: The Shoes That Stared, the Painting That Spoke

Without doubt, Heidegger's writing about art finds its greatest force in his readings of specific works of art. The best known of these derives from a series of three lectures, which he gave in 1935–36 and which he then revised periodically over the ensuing years, until he published it as the essay, "The Origin of the Work of Art" (1950). In this essay, Heidegger asks what it is that "works" about a work of art—or, to put it somewhat differently, what kind of "work" it is that the artwork performs on one who listens or reads attentively. The answer Heidegger will propose, as we have already seen, is that great works of art[6] constitute an event of truth, the disclosure of a particular being in its being. But it will be instructive to follow Heidegger through on this one reading, both to gain a more concrete sense of how the event of art bears upon being and to understand how this being revealed by art bears upon a Heideggerian ethics. The work in question is the "well-known painting" by Vincent van Gogh,[7] of two old shoes set against a plain backdrop.[8]

Heidegger turns to van Gogh's painting of the shoes, he says, in search of the "equipmental quality of equipment" [*das Zeughafte des Zeuges*]. Earlier in the essay, Heidegger has proposed that the key to understanding the *work of art* was to distinguish it from its *mere thingliness.* After all, as he reminds his reader, works of art can surely be regarded as mere things under certain circumstances—by dealers and investors,

Illustration 2. Vincent van Gogh, *Shoes* [F255]. Van Gogh Museum, Amsterdam (Vincent van Gogh Foundation)

for example, or by the charwoman at the museum. But since works of art also seem to be something more or something other than "mere things," one must wonder what it is about art that sets it apart from its own mere thingliness. In order to open up the distinction between the work and the thing, then, Heidegger proposes to examine closely a common piece of equipment, a pair of shoes, since equipment enjoys certain qualities both of mere things (which can be use-objects) and also of works of art (which are produced by the human hand):

> We choose as an example an ordinary piece of equipment: a pair of peasant shoes. For their description, we need not exhibit an actual example of this sort of useful article. Everyone knows them.[9] But since it is a matter here of direct description, it may be good to facilitate their visual realization [*die Veranschaulichung zu erleichtern*]. To this end, a pictorial representation [*eine bildliche Darstellung*] suffices. We choose a well-known painting by van Gogh, who painted such shoes several times. But is there much to be seen here? Everyone knows what shoes are like. (*Holzwege* 18g, 13e)

One notices right away the peculiar back-and-forth movement evident in Heidegger's series of "buts": there's no need to exhibit actual shoes, *but* the author will make them visually present anyway, *but* such visualization really won't reveal anything new or unexpected about the form and matter of shoes, *but* we choose this example notwithstanding. Reading this paragraph, one half expects Heidegger to drop the van Gogh example before he even presents it, as if it were a mistake, as if the writer had not assiduously revised this essay over many years. Or else, one is tempted to discount the instability that emerges from this back and forth movement, by noting that to propose and then rebut is one of Heidegger's characteristic modes of presenting an argument—in fact, much of the earlier part of the essay has followed this structure by consecutively proposing, but then rebutting, three philosophical notions of the thing. However, Heidegger hasn't yet begun to make an argument out of his van Gogh example. Indeed, the expected argument (about equipmentality) has evidently gotten hung up on the problem of its own example. And a problematic example it surely is, for what kind of unmediated, "direct" description [*unmittelbare Beschreibung*] proceeds not from a really existing pair of shoes, but rather from daubs of color on a two-dimensional canvas—for that matter, representing shoes that may well exist only in the imagination of the painter? But Heidegger is also here following a long tradition in philosophical writing that turns to art so that art might serve as an example to clarify a philosophical point. We shall see very shortly that if at first Heidegger seems to be following this tradition, he does so only to turn it on its head.

Before the interruption by a very different sort of voice, the next paragraphs continue their critical questioning of the usefulness of van Gogh's painting as an example. Heidegger appears to argue against it himself, by noting, reasonably enough, that, since *equipment* is essentially *useful*, if one wishes to open up the essential equipmentality of shoes, one ought to examine the shoes *in use*, rather than, as van Gogh's painting has them, standing alone against a plain backdrop:

> So long as we only imagine [*vergegenwärtigen*] a pair of shoes in general, or just see [*ansehen*] in the picture the mere empty, unused shoes standing there, we will never learn [*erfahren*] what the equipmental being of equipment in truth is. From van Gogh's painting we cannot even tell where these shoes are standing. Surrounding this pair of peasant shoes is nothing to which and within which they could belong; only an undefined space. Not even clods of earth from the fields or from the country path stick to them, which could at least point toward their use. A pair of peasant shoes and nothing more. And yet. (*Holzwege* 18–19g, 14e)

Until the final two words of the paragraph, Heidegger seems on the verge of aborting his use of van Gogh's painting as an example or tool of argumentation. Simply looking at this painting of shoes will produce nothing, yield no significant experience of truth. But the precise nature of the failure remains ambiguous at this point: is it a limitation of this particular picture or a limitation of simply looking? That is, will the experience of truth fail to arrive because the painting was poorly selected as an example in this case? Or even—one must wonder, since the author himself selected the example he now appears to disavow—is Heidegger suggesting some broader incommensurability or resistance between the general strivings of philosophy and the particularities of a given work of art? But perhaps the limitation does not lie in this direction; perhaps the problem is that the experience of the truth of being (presumably in this case equipmental being) does not unfold in the visual register: "But is there much to be *seen* here?" he asked before. And above: "So long as we . . . just *see* in the picture the mere, empty, unused shoes standing there, we will never learn what the equipmental being of equipment in truth is." As the passage proceeds, truth does, finally, issue from van

Gogh's canvas, and yet when it does, it happens more as a voice, and not as a simple vision.

The voice that speaks to interrupt Heidegger's argument against his own example has an ambiguous status of its own, but it suggests, forcefully and compactly, Heidegger's contention that at the heart of any work of art lies a poetic experience of truth. Just as he seems on the verge of abandoning van Gogh, he is caught, as if in wonder and surprise, and says, simply, "And yet":

> From the dark opening of the well-worn insides of the shoes the toil of the worker's tread stares forth [*starrt*]. In the crudely solid heaviness of the shoes accumulates the tenacity of the slow trudge through the far-stretching and ever-uniform furrows of the field over which a raw wind stands [*steht*]. On the leather lies the dampness and richness of the soil. Under the soles slides the loneliness of the field-path as evening falls. In the shoes vibrates the silent call of the earth, its silent gift of the ripening grain and its unexplained self-refusal in the desolate fallows of the wintry field. This equipment is pervaded by uncomplaining worry as to the certainty of bread, wordless joy of having once more withstood want, trembling before the impending birth, and shivering at the surrounding menace of death. This equipment belongs to the *earth* and it is sheltered in the *world* of the peasant woman. (*Holzwege* 19g, 14e)

It is a richly lyrical passage, and one might suspect Heidegger of seeking to render van Gogh's painting directly in poetic form, except that the painting is, on the level of representation, of two simple shoes and little else, whereas Heidegger's lyricism expends itself upon a mortal peasant life, the mysteries of the earth, and the world of harvests and lonely evenings on the field-path. The closest the renowned phenomenologist would seem to get to the shoes themselves is not the leather and soles, but rather the dampness that lies *on* the leather and the loneliness that slides *under* the soles. Thus, what happens in Heidegger's reading is more complex than any ekphrastic translation of the painting's visual imagery into corresponding linguistic signs. Rather, what happens in Heidegger's text is an event we might consider an effect of pure language.

This experience of language generated by the painting is made possible in the first instance by a curious displacement of the observing subject. Consider the complexity of the gaze Heidegger describes. From one side of the canvas, Heidegger and his reader had "simply looked" at the painting, evaluating its usefulness in explicating a philosophical point. But attention came to be gathered upon the nothingness and the undefined space surrounding the shoes, and then all of a sudden, with Heidegger's "And yet," there is a radical shift. With this sudden break, all critical use of the artwork is interrupted and the philosopher overthrown, first by a gaze and then by the voice that speaks: "From the dark opening of the well-worn insides of the shoes the toil of the worker's tread stares forth." The complex and curious gaze, or "staring forth" of the painting,[10] together with the transformation of the authoritative philosophical voice into a more lyrical, more poetic voice, suggests the kind of event that Heidegger conceives as an experience of language. As he puts it elsewhere in writing of the experience of language:

> To undergo an experience [*eine Erfahrung machen*] with something . . . means that this something befalls us, strikes us, comes over us, overwhelms and transforms us. When we talk of "undergoing" an experience, we mean specifically that the experience is not of our own making; to undergo here means that we endure it, suffer it, receive it as it strikes us and submit to it. (*Unterwegs* 159g, 57e)

Thus, the unexpected and uncanny *stare* that gazes from the dark opening of the empty shoe places the autonomy of the subject in question, interrupts habitual patterns of thought, and makes it impossible to maintain a utilitarian relation to the painting (as if it were a mere tool to illustrate a point). Instead, the work of art comes into its own—it comes into being as itself—as the viewer submits to being carried away on a path that radiates out into the world from the painted shoes themselves and that opens up metonymically from their toilsome tread: from the dark opening of the shoes, to the presumed peasant woman who wore them, to the windswept fields and lonely paths she trod, to the seasons of the earth and the vicissitudes of mortal life and death in this world.

Thus, what we see in Heidegger's reading is not simply a painting translated into linguistic terms; instead, the painting operates linguistically to open up the world lying dormant in the image itself. In the interruptive encounter with the gaze of the painting, the viewer is compelled to forsake totalizing grasp on the work of art: no longer is the being of the painting (or the being of the shoes) subordinate to the use the viewer might wish to assign. And—even more than this—in the metonymy of the word, where the painting comes poetically into its own and where a world is opened up, the human observer encounters not just him- or herself—but him- or herself as a being face-to-face with other beings in the world: with the peasant woman and her shoes, of course, but also with the whole of her world: the wintry fields and the approach of night, the anxious uncertainties of bread, the labors of life, and the menaces of death.

And, remarkably, we have, by the way, learned something of equipmentality after all—namely, that use-value operates negatively on the being of a thing. In other words, the more thoroughly something becomes subsumed under the human category of use—and thereby becomes "usual"—the more difficult it is for its being to come into the open as anything other than a mere object for human use (*Holzwege* 20g, 15e). It is difficult to focus on a commonplace pair of shoes, for example, since what we tend to see are not the things in themselves, but rather their quotidian usefulness (or potential usefulness) for us. One might consider in an analogous vein the surprising turn given by the painting, when it asserted itself as a work over and against the effort to exploit it as a tool to serve an argumentative point. One might say that Heidegger's lyricism demonstrates how the being of the work of art emerges into unconcealment as its philosophical use-value recedes.

Altogether, then, the experience of aletheia in the painting aims toward bringing the observer into a truer, more authentic relationship with his or her own mortal being as one of limitation and not mastery:

> Truth happens in the van Gogh painting. That does not mean that something present is correctly portrayed; it means, rather, that . . . that which is as a whole [*das Seiende im Ganzen*], world and earth in their counterplay, comes into unconcealment.
>
> In the work truth is at work—thus not only something that is true. The picture which shows the peasant shoes, the poem that says the Roman fountain,[11] manifest not only what these isolated beings as such are—if they manifest anything: they let happen unconcealment as such [*Unverborgenheit als solche*] with regard to beings as a whole. The more simply and essentially the shoe-equipment is absorbed in its essence, . . . the more immediately and engagingly do all beings become, along with it, more in being [*wird mit ihnen alles Seiende seiender*]. (*Holzwege* 43g, 54e)

Remarkably, if indeed, as Heidegger suggests above, the observer attains to truth and becomes "more in being" through van Gogh's painting, this happens not through the reflective words of the philosopher, nor the descriptive words of the phenomenologist, but rather through the poetic speaking of the painting itself. The van Gogh painting "spoke," as Heidegger puts it in a trope every bit as unsettling as the stare of the shoes (*Holzwege* 21g, 15e). What this speaking *calls for*, and what is *obligated* on behalf of our existence, then, is either a special kind of thinking distinct from traditional modes of metaphysics, or else a special kind of attentiveness to the poetry of art and the song of being.

The Call of Language and the Obligation to Bear Witness to One's Existence

Almost from the very beginning, Heidegger seems to have intuited that the experience of truth opened up by art, poetry, and language is partly ethical in nature. Indeed, his remarks in "Hölderlin and the Essence of Poetry" (1936), a reading of five verses by Friedrich Hölderlin, are already quite suggestive in this respect. In this essay, Heidegger gives a preliminary outline of how "the primary language [*die Ursprache*] is poetry as the foundation of being" (*Erläuterungen* 43g, 61e)—the almost Emersonian claim we have already seen developed in the 1950s publications on language and poetry. More to the point, however, here Heidegger also locates the foundation of being human at the nexus of language and responsibility. The responsibility at the heart of human being, he says, is a matter of giving testimony to one's mortal existence in the world, a matter of bearing witness to one's own belonging among beings as a whole:

> Who is man? He is the one who must bear witness [*zeugen muß*] to what he is. To bear witness can signify to testify [*Bekunden*], but it also means to be answerable for what one has testified in one's testimony. Man is *he* who he *is* precisely in the attestation of his existence [*der Bezeugung des eigenen Daseins*]. This attestation does not mean a subsequent [*nachträglichen*] and additional expression of man's being; rather, it forms a part of man's existence. (*Erläuterungen* 36g, 54e)

The general context of the quote is familiar. We have already seen that in order to become "more in being," one must struggle to experience oneself as standing *in* the world, face to face with other beings in the world, rather than (as our everyday mode of apprehending would have it) merely *before* the world and other beings, objectifying them in acts of cognitive representation and thus seeing these things not as they are in themselves, but rather as objects of use or potential use. But the language above of bearing witness binds the human problem of *being* together with *law and obligation* on the one hand, and with a whole new problem of *language* on the other hand. We have already seen that when van Gogh's painting "speaks" and thereby opens up the world, it implies the necessity of *listening* and thus of attending and responding to the work of language in the work of art. The essay here, however, in speaking of "bearing witness," suggests that it is further incumbent upon the thinker or the reader of art to respond and to *speak* themselves.

Moreover, it is only a special kind of speaking that will bring us to the fullness of our human essence. In his later essays Heidegger will occasionally describe this special speaking in terms of singing. To understand this, we might think of Heidegger's fondness for the phrase, borrowed from the German Romantic poet Novalis, "language speaks" (*Unterwegs* 12g, 188e). One of the things Heidegger means by citing this dictum is that language—and we saw this in the poetic voice of van Gogh's painting—calls to us, summoning us to being. But our task, as human beings striving for a greater degree of being, is not only to listen but also to respond, harmonizing with the speaking of language, joining and amplifying its voice.[12] This indeed is the only kind of speaking that bears on what is essential:

> [I]t is language that speaks. Man first speaks when, and only when, he responds to language by listening to its appeal. Among all the appeals that we human beings, on our part, may help to be voiced, language is the highest and everywhere the first [*der höchste und der überall erste*]. Language beckons us, at first and then again at the end, toward a thing's nature. But that is not to say, ever, that in any word-meaning picked up at will language supplies us, straight away and definitively, with the transparent nature of the matter as if it were an object ready for use. But the responding in which man authentically listens to the appeal of language is that which speaks in the element of poetry. (*Vorträge* 184g, 214e)

So, in our speaking, in bearing witness to our own being and singing to the call of being issuing from language itself, we "say again the Saying [*Sage*] we have heard" (*Unterwegs* 255g, 124e). We can understand, then, the most basic sense for why Heidegger describes language as the "house of being [*das Haus des Seins*]" (Brief 313g, 217e), for it is by going through this house of language, by listening attentively and then joining our own voice in speaking our testimony, that we might arrive at being.

But if this language of being that we speak does not operate strictly in terms of word-meanings that "supply us, straight away and definitively, with the transparent nature of the matter," how then are we to think of this essential task of speaking? The "saying again" of ethical speaking is indeed not a matter of making representations or of repeating particular words and word-meanings. Rather, ethical speaking amplifies and restages the original poetic event or experience of language. At its best, as in the reading of van Gogh's painting, Heidegger's own critical practice gives a brilliant example of such a maneuver. While Heidegger shows himself to be deeply read in the work of his favorite poets, his own critical practice displays no devotion to the scholarship of literary history and quite explicitly announces its departure on a different path from that taken by the psychoanalytical, sociological, biographical, or historical readings dominating that era. The virtues of his readings lie elsewhere. Heidegger thought of his own critical elucidations as dialogues of thinking and poetry that aimed to preserve "what has been purely composed into a poem [and to bring it to] stand forth a little clearer" (*Erläuterungen* 8g, 22e). We might think of his reading of van Gogh's painting in this sense. The poetic interruption certainly comes from Heidegger's own pen, but we can see too that through this lyrical moment Heidegger aims to reenact for the reader, only through words rather than with paint, the experience of being that is called forth by van Gogh's work. We can also see that, by bringing his reader face to face with the work of art and thus preserving the possibility for undergoing an experience with pure language in that work of art, Heidegger aims ultimately at allowing his reader to live again within language and to be in the world. Thus, we might propose that ethical speaking, in the sense of a Heideggerian ethics, involves an attentiveness to the world of mortal human life such as is opened up in the experience of art. At the same time, this ethical speaking also involves entering into a kind of lyrical speech that harmonizes one's own voice with the speaking of pure language: something that opens onto the whole of being both for oneself and potentially also for one's reader or viewer or auditor.

It may be somewhat surprising that, even while aiming at what he conceived as the most foundational calling of human existence, Heidegger was always reluctant to cast his work as constituting an "ethics" per se. The reason for this, as he tells it in his "Letter on Humanism" (1946), appears to have been a discomfort stemming from the tradition that that word (and other words like it: "logic" and "physics") has inherited from philosophical tradition since the school of Plato. Heidegger's correspondent, Jean Beaufret,[13] had asked him to clarify the relation between a possible ethics and the fundamental ontology Heidegger had described in *Being and Time*. Rather than do so, Heidegger takes his letter as an occasion to repudiate as a miscalculation his earlier claim to have written a fundamental ontology:

> [I]n order to make the attempt at thinking recognizable and at the same time understandable for existing philosophy, it could at first be expressed only within the horizon of that existing philosophy and its use of current terms.
>
> In the meantime I have learned to see that these very terms were bound to lead immediately and inevitably into error. For the terms and the conceptual language corresponding to them were not rethought by readers from the matter particularly to be thought; rather, the matter was conceived according to the established terminology and in its customary meaning. The thinking that inquires into the truth of Being and so defines man's essential abode [*den Wesenaufenthalt*] from Being and toward Being is neither ethics nor ontology. Thus the question about the relation of each to the other no longer has any basis in this sphere. (Brief 357–58g, 259e)

Heidegger believes the experience of the truth of being that is opened up and called for by language is indeed foundational, but for that very reason it is prior to the disciplinary distinctions that metaphysical tradition has imposed on this sphere. What is essential is that we enter being through language. When Heidegger finally consents to Beaufret's question concerning ethics, he does so only by redefining terms—or, as Heidegger would have it, by returning them to etymological possibilities dormant since the pre-Socratic philosopher Heraclitus:

> If the name "ethics," in keeping with the basic meaning of the word *ēthos* [ἦθοζ], should now say that "ethics" ponders the abode of man [*den Aufenthalt des Menschen bedenkt*], then that thinking which thinks the truth of Being as the primordial element of man, as one who ek-sists, is in itself the original ethics. (Brief 356g, 258e)

Thus, ethics, in its original sense and as Heidegger wishes to redefine it against the metaphysical tradition, pertains to "the abode of man," that is, to being and the world of human existence. We are not surprised, then, given his theory of the work of art and this new understanding of ethics, that Heidegger will conclude that, as great works of art, the tragedies of Sophocles preserve the *ēthos* "more primordially" than do Aristotle's lectures on ethics (Brief 354g, 256e).

The present essay opened by remarking upon the twentieth-century effort to rethink the nature of ethics in terms of the human relation to language. For Heidegger, as we have seen, the ethical imperative inherent to language lies at the very heart of our humanity. Since we are most essentially beings who speak, to undergo an experience with language is therefore to "touch the innermost nexus of our existence" (*Unterwegs* 159g, 57e). Thus, in cultivating a humanity that is truly human—neither inhuman nor inhumane—we must enter into a relation with language that brings us into our proper nature and opens us onto what most concerns our being. This, for Heidegger, is the single law foundational to all others: "[M]ore essential than instituting rules," he says, "is that man find the way to his abode in the truth of Being" (Brief 361g, 262e).

Not at Home: Heidegger and the Ethical Uncanny

Heidegger's key claim—that art and ethics bear essentially upon how human beings come to a proper relation to being itself—requires some further thinking here, for how, more specifically, are we to understand what would it mean for human beings to arrive at their proper nature or to be opened onto what most concerns their being? For that matter, if being is truly "the primordial element of man," then in what sense must man "find the way" to this site? Such questions are fundamental if, as Heidegger proposes, "the original ethics," more originary than everyday moral codes, lies in thinking this truth of being as the primordial element of man. Let us begin our questioning by first considering one aspect of the poetics of Heidegger's own late writing.

Arguably, the central trope of all Heidegger's late writing on poetry, ethics, and being involves the home and its companion words: house, abode, dwelling, hearth. Language, we recall, is the "house" of being. Ethics, as we also recall, ponders the "abode" of man. Elsewhere we might read that "dwelling" is the basic character of being (*Vorträge* 155g, 158e). And, referring to the pre-Socratic thinker Philolaos, Heidegger declares that being is the "hearth" wherein all beings are "at home" as beings (*Hölderlins* 140g, 112–13e). Altogether, these metaphors suggest a site where human beings might, at least potentially, find their own proper place within the sphere of being. In order to clarify the situation of human beings in relation to this abode of man that lies at the heart of Heideggerian ethics, we turn now not only to one of those tragedies of Sophocles, in which Heidegger says he finds the *ēthos* so primordially preserved, but also to consideration of a longstanding aesthetic category, the uncanny—in German, *das Unheimliche*: if one takes the German root literally, the "unhomely."

Contemporary critical conceptions of the uncanny in art and literature look primarily to Sigmund Freud's well-known essay of that title ("The Uncanny," 1919), in which the psychoanalyst proposed that uncanny aesthetic effects in literature are produced when the content of the narrative resonates with the repressed childhood traumas of the reader's own subjectivization. It is less widely known that, in his seminars of 1925, 1935, and 1942, Heidegger himself turned and returned to the uncanny, reflecting in his elaboration his own philosophical care for how human beings might come to a more authentic relation to their own existence. For both thinkers, Freud and Heidegger, the unsettlement and angst produced by the uncanny point to an obscure, ontogenetic problem, a primordial absence, lack, or lostness at the heart of human being that, in the ordinary, everyday course of things, is covered over by the ego's protective mechanisms or crowded out by the idle preoccupations of quotidian life. Still, as we will see, Heidegger's philosophical account of the uncanny is quite distinct from Freud's psychoanalytic account of the uncanny Oedipal dramas unsettling human beings.[14] Literary theorists may in fact find Heidegger's account of the uncanny nearly as thought-provoking as Freud's. Not only, like Freud, does Heidegger stage his later discussions as extended readings of a literary work, in this instance Sophocles' *Antigone*, but Heidegger also has a more refined and respectful relation to what we might call the "literariness" of the literary. Freud is a superb reader, of course, but his main effort as a literary essayist seems to be to map out literary characters onto a strongly posed, finely developed psycho-theoretical framework. Heidegger, by contrast, strikes a more responsive relation to the literary object and elaborates a theory of the uncanny using a very different—and in some respects even more basic—set of terms.

For Heidegger, the uncanny is not primarily a matter of affect, or aesthetics, or anything on the order of mere circumstance. Uncanniness may indeed be signaled by an aesthetic affect such as dread or angst,[15] but, for Heidegger, "uncanny" is really one way of describing the "fundamental kind of essence belonging to human beings" (*Hölderlins* 89g, 72–73e); indeed, it is itself "the basic trait of the human essence, into which every other trait must always be drawn" (*Einführung* 116g, 161e). So, the crucial feature of the uncanny, then, is not that we *feel* unsettled or that we enjoy an *impression* of weirdness, but rather that we *are*, in our essence, *unsettled*—that is, unseated from the site where we might properly claim our own being, so that we *are*, in our essence, *weird* or wayward, forever journeying toward our own proper destiny within being, but without ever quite arriving there. As we think through this "law" of being unhomely (*Hölderlins* 155g, 125e), and as we consider the specifically Greek "pathos" of this uncanny unhomeliness, we will come to a better understanding of Heidegger's claim that ethics ponders the home, or the abode, of man. Let us then venture a few observations concerning the being of human beings and consider why Heidegger thinks the matter of human being requires some care.

Heidegger's thinking proceeds from the claim that the essence of human being is that human beings never quite have access to their own essence. Hence, in a way that echoes Romantic thought[16] and prefigures Lacan's subject of the real, Heidegger proposes an essential absence at the heart of human being, such that we never quite come into our own, never quite are who we are. Something at the level of being always remains in (mere) potentiality. As Heidegger puts it, with a palpable ethical force,

> Whatever is their own is that to which human beings belong and must belong if they are to fulfill whatever is destined to them, and whatever is fitting, as their specific way of being. . . . All this is true only on the presupposition that initially human beings are not and indeed never "of themselves," or through any self-making, in that which is their own. In that case, however, to dwell in what is one's own [*Im Eigenen zu wohnen*] is what comes last and is seldom successful and always remains what is most difficult. (*Hölderlins* 23–24g, 21e)

A little later in that same seminar from 1942, Heidegger develops his thinking on "dwell[ing] in what is one's own" into his key trope of being (or rather *not* being) *at home*:

> This *coming to be* at home [*Dieses Heimisch*werden] in one's own in itself entails that human beings are initially, and for a long time, and sometimes forever, not at home [*nicht heimisch*]. And this in turn entails that human beings fail to recognize, that they deny, and perhaps even have to deny and flee what belongs to the home [*das Heimische*]. Coming to be at home is thus a passage through the foreign [*das Fremde*]. (*Hölderlins* 60g, 49e)

Hence, the simplest face of Heidegger's *Unheimliche*, the unhomely or uncanny, is this not-at-homeness implicit in the existential task of coming to be at home in one's own. Part of it consists of a claim about who we are: we are those who are not authentically at home in ourselves; we are those who are in some way lost, stranded amidst the foreign. Part consists of a kind of ethical claim about our difficult—perhaps impossible—task as human beings: we ought to strive for whatever is our own and we ought to seek our home there.

We might pause to ask the question, though: If uncanniness or unhomeliness is a condition of not being at home, what would homeliness itself look like? How are we to think this thing which we must fail to be, and yet must come to be? One way to conceptualize becoming homely is to conceive of human being as the nexus of a certain set of relations. Heidegger makes little pretense here to speak for anything other than Western humankind, but of it he says:

> [I]n the concept of the essence of Western humankind we also necessarily, and therefore always, think those essential relations within which this humankind stands: the relation to world, the relation to earth, the relation to the gods and to alternative gods and false gods. These relations are not, however, simply added on to "human beings" in addition to "their" being human; rather, to be human is in itself to be the unity of this configuration. The becoming homely [*Das Heimischwerden*] of human beings thus in itself comprises this full essence of being human. (*Hölderlins* 51–52g, 43e)

So, as Heidegger would have it, becoming homely is a matter of coming to assume one's proper place in relation to the world and the things in it, in relation to the earth and the mysteries it conceals, and in relation to the gods and what they give or withhold to sustain us as mortal human beings facing privation and always, ultimately, death.[17] No doubt, from a physical, psychological, or biological perspective, human beings are always, inevitably, in relation to these things. But Heidegger very self-consciously resists the scientific impulse that, in his view, regards human beings as though they were mere objects. So, the question of human being here posed by Heidegger is not whether one has matter enough to count as an existent, or whether one has DNA sequences tagging one as human. Rather, more humanistically, it is a question of whether or not one can stand before things as they are in themselves. To put it in terms used earlier in this essay, it is a question of whether things emerge into presence, open and unconcealed, or else, to the contrary, remain as they are with all of us, almost all of the time: muted and obscured.

A certain structural paradox is already visible in Heidegger's discussion of homeliness and unhomeliness to complicate how we might think of the uncanny. Namely, if human beings are, in their essence, unhomely, might there not be a sense in which human beings are at home precisely in their unhomeliness? So far, we have considered the human being as one who is unhomely yet who is simultaneously becoming homely. As we put it before, human being is a coming to be at home in one's own. Put that way, it sounds like a matter of logical inference: we are becoming homely only because we are not already homely—that is, only because we are unhomely. Or it sounds like a temporal matter of present and future: initially (and presently) we are unhomely; perhaps later (or in the end) we will have become homely. But our structural paradox begs us to consider unhomeliness and homeliness as more intimately bound together into the same uncanny knot. At one point in the 1942 seminar, Heidegger distinguishes a human being in his or her proper fullness from a mere adventurer. The adventurer, he says, is merely not homely in a rather pedestrian sense. The δεινοτατον [*deinotaton*], by contrast, the name given in the choral ode of *Antigone* to man as the most uncanny being,

> is the most uncanny being in a specific manner of being homely, namely, that which, within its own essence, finds no entry to this essence, remains excluded from it and without any way out that could allow it to enter the center of its own essence. The one who is properly unhomely [*Der eigentlich Unheimische*] relates back precisely to the homely, and to this alone, yet does so in the manner of not attaining it. The adventurer, by contrast, finds the homely precisely in what is constantly and merely not-homely, in the foreign taken in itself. To put it more precisely: For the heart that seeks adventure, this distinction between the homely and the unhomely is altogether lost. . . .
>
> The unhomely one is deprived [*entbehrt*] of the homely; deprivation is the way in which the unhomely one possesses the homely, or to put it more precisely, the way in which whatever is homely possesses the unhomely one. What becomes manifest in these relations is the essence of uncanniness itself, namely, presencing in the manner of an absencing, and in such a way that whatever presences and absences here is itself simultaneously the open realm of all presencing and absencing. (*Hölderlins* 91–92g, 74–75e)

So, to answer the question: Yes, the properly unhomely one is indeed at home in his or her unhomeliness, but not in a manner that adventurously effaces the distinction between homeliness and unhomeliness. Rather, in coming to be *at home* in one's own *un*homeliness, one comes to dwell in the presence of an absence, bearing in relation to one's own essence a kind of existential deprivation, assuming this absence, sustained as absence, as one's own.[18] This presence of absence is at once the essence of the uncanny, as well as the uncanny structure of our own essence as human beings. It is also, suggests Heidegger, at the poetic core of Sophocles' *Antigone*.

Heidegger's 1942 seminar is ostensibly dedicated to a meditation on Hölderlin's hymn, "Der Ister," but, in fact, the German philosopher spends an almost equal amount of time in that seminar with *Antigone*, the Greek tragedy Hölderlin had been translating as he was also composing his river hymns, between 1800 and 1806.[19] As he had also done earlier, in his 1935 seminar, *Introduction to Metaphysics*, Heidegger spends some time in 1942 with the first choral ode of the tragedy, in which the chorus famously sings that there is nothing more uncanny (δεινον)[20] than man, that man ventures forth everywhere, mastering much, yet everywhere coming to nothing. Having reprised this interest in the ode as a poetic thinking of the uncanny essence of human being, Heidegger then goes further and elaborates his reading of *Antigone* beyond the choral ode to the fascinating and uncanny drama of Antigone herself. The present essay cannot offer a full reading of Sophocles' play, but we might follow Heidegger's own reading a short way in order to clarify what it might mean to take up a "proper" relation to uncanny being.

So far as Heidegger is concerned, *Antigone* has tripped up commentators because the core of Antigone's drama is more basic—and also more explicitly stated—than one tends to assume. In the play, Antigone first solicits and then bitterly refuses help from her sister, Ismene, in tending to the remains of their brother, the rebel Polyneices, whose proper burial has been prohibited and declared a capital crime by Creon, the new regent of Thebes. Inevitably, Antigone is caught and—loudly, unrepentantly, publicly—she claims her deed before the angry new regent. But though she is betrothed to his son and excites the sympathy of the chorus, Creon sentences her to be entombed alive, and she is taken away, ecstatically bewailing her early marriage with Death. Later, shaken by doubt and finally swayed by the chorus, Creon yields funeral rights to Polyneices and remits Antigone's sentence. He is too late: Antigone has already killed herself, and his son, and then his wife, follow soon thereafter. But while Creon presents the play's concentration of hamartia, peripeteia, and anagnorisis, it is passionate, doomed Antigone who is universally recognized as the center of the play. Understandably, then, one puzzles on her comportment, motives, and actions as a way of getting to the heart of the famous tragedy. For Heidegger, though, one must attend closely to what Antigone actually says of her motives, however strangely put, without too swiftly assigning a meaning that renders her comprehensible by psychologizing or idealizing her stance. In Heidegger's reading, *Antigone* is not, ultimately, about Antigone's personality or about the Greek cult of death or about the importance of blood-relatedness in that culture. *Antigone* is rather, like Greek tragedy more generally, the presentation of a specific kind of παθειν [*pathein*], or suffering, a suffering pertaining to the truth of being as a whole (*Hölderlins* 128g, 103e), a truth of being we have already identified as uncanny.

Let us look at how Heidegger supports this claim. First, as Heidegger notes, Antigone explicitly declares that she is acting in fidelity to neither the law of the gods nor the law of man. Here, in (an English translation of) Heidegger's idiosyncratic German translation of the Greek, is what she says to justify herself in her confrontation with Creon:

> It was no Zeus that bade me this.
> Nor was it Dike, at home amongst the gods below,
> who ordained this law for humans.
> And your command [Creon] seemed not so powerful to me,
> that it could ever override by human wit
> the immutable, unwritten edict divine
> [*den ungeschriebenen wankellosen Götter-Spruch*].
> Not just now, nor since yesterday, but ever steadfast
> this prevails. And no one knows from whence it once
> appeared.[21] (*Hölderlins* 145g, 116e)

So, in Antigone's own account of herself, she is indeed behaving lawfully, responding to an "immutable, unwritten edict divine," that issues not from Zeus on high, nor Dike (Justice) below, nor, certainly, from Creon at Thebes. Yet what kind of law can this be? Such a sovereign edict, legitimated by no known or specifically named authority, but prevailing "immutable" and "ever steadfast," must indeed excite our critical interest. Earlier in the play, in the introductory dialogue between Antigone and her sister Ismene, Antigone describes it as a "supreme necessity" and also offers a more specific sense for how she understands the content of this law. Here is how Heidegger renders the exchange, as Ismene tries to dissuade Antigone from an act certain to inflame the wrath of Creon:

> Ismene: You have a fiery heart, though turned toward the cold (dead).
>
> Antigone: Yet I know from whence I am greeted, there falls to me supreme necessity [*am höchsten zugefallen mir die Not*]. . . .
>
> Ismene: Yet to commence in pursuit of that remains unfitting, against which nothing can avail.
>
> Antigone: If you say this, in hatred you stand, arising from me,
>
> and the hatred of he who is dead will come to meet you, as is fitting.
>
> Yet leave this to me, and to that within me that counsels the dangerous and difficult:
>
> to take up into my own essence the uncanny that here and now appears [παθειν το δεινον τουτο].[22] (*Hölderlins* 123g, 98–99e)

So, beyond Zeus, beyond Dike, a "supreme necessity" reigns, she says, one that counsels the dangerous and difficult—namely, παθειν το δεινον τουτο: "to take up into [her] own essence the uncanny that here and now appears." For Heidegger, this line is decisive: it at once pronounces Antigone's act as an assumption of uncanny being, declares it to be of supreme necessity, and at the same time connects her to the choral ode's description of man as the uncanniest being.

Heidegger celebrates Antigone for exactly this reason. He sees in her one who is in herself "the supreme uncanny" (*Hölderlins* 129g, 104e), "utterly unhomely" (129g, 103e), and avowedly belonging "to the realm of δεινον" (136g, 109e). But, in addition to her explicit naming of this law of the uncanny, what especially attracts Heidegger's interest in these lines is the fact that Antigone describes her own, proper, ethical relation to the δεινον as one of παθειν [*pathein*], a word with the same root as "pathos," meaning to suffer or to bear:

> παθειν does not mean the mere "passivity" of accepting and tolerating but rather taking upon oneself . . . making it through to the end, that is, properly experiencing. This παθειν—experiencing the δεινον—this enduring and suffering, is the fundamental trait of that doing and action called

> το δραμα [to drama], which constitutes the "dramatic," the "action" in Greek tragedy. Yet this very παθειν is also the proper relation to the δεινον. . . .
>
> In the Greek tragedy the "heroes" and "heroines," if we may use these terms at all, are neither "silent sufferers" nor "martyrs" in the Christian sense. . . . "The tragic" is not to be measured, as modern human beings think, according to the passion of which we can have a psychological "lived experience" . . . but rather according to the truth of being as a whole and in keeping with the simplicity in which it appears. This is why in the Greek tragedy virtually nothing occurs. . . . The uncanny [in which Antigone knows she has been ultimately counseled] is nothing other than this: the fact that she takes as her all-determinative point of departure [*alles bestimmenden Ausgang*] that against which nothing can avail, because it is that appearing that is destined for her and of which no one knows whence it has arisen. (*Hölderlins* 128g, 103e)

Given his general ideas about art, as we have considered them earlier in the present essay, we cannot be too much surprised by Heidegger's suggestion that the tragic art of the Greeks is essentially concerned with the assumption of being we now recognize as uncanny. Nor, by extension, can we be surprised that, in Heidegger's view, the central drama of this play, the "supreme action" of Antigone's own suffering, and indeed the fundamental ethical charge of human existence as such, is centered upon this same task of at once being unhomely and becoming homely, that is, of properly taking upon oneself the immutable, impossible law of unhomely human being. But what, in the end, does Antigone take upon herself? Precisely this: a kind of being unhomely that, "properly," shows itself as "a not yet awakened, not yet decided, not yet assumed potential for being homely and becoming homely" (*Hölderlins* 144g, 115e). So, she endures the not-yetness and (mere) potentiality present at the heart of uncanny being. She persists and takes, as her "all-determinative point of departure" and as her destiny, a law whose origin she cannot name, but which functions as a kind of existential call of conscience[23] summoning her toward a more authentic relation to her own being (and her own lack of being). In short, she suffers and takes her own place in the uncanny gap between being and becoming, unhomely and homely.

Though the uncanny has always taken a certain indefiniteness as one of its peculiar characteristics,[24] nevertheless, one searches among the unhomely, uncanny particulars of Antigone's life for a way to make Heidegger's claim more concrete. Perhaps one recalls the fateful wanderings of the Labdacids and their tribulations on the road. Perhaps one recalls Antigone's own actual homelessness accompanying her blind father, Oedipus, through his final exile. Perhaps one recalls the uncertain position of Oedipus's daughters (and Polyneices' sisters) in the house of the new regent of Thebes. But, in Heidegger's reading at least, Antigone's act is not, ultimately, determined by her long years of vagabondage and actual homelessness, or indeed by anything on the level of mere circumstance. When Antigone heeds that voice that counsels her "to take up into [her] own essence the uncanny that here and now appears," when she holds to that "immutable, unwritten edict divine," she suffers an *intrinsic* unhomeliness, as Heidegger takes some pains to point out (*Hölderlins* 129g, 104e). True, it is not some arbitrary impossibility Antigone has embraced. True, its drama pertains, in the first instance, to her blood-relation, Polyneices, and, in the second instance, to the law of the dead. But, according to Heidegger, through taking up these causes, Antigone is really thereby taking upon herself "the fundamental law of the living" (*Hölderlins* 126g, 101e)—namely that law of the unhomely, which is simultaneously, uncannily, the law of the homely. So, the interest of the play in matters of blood and death is not accidental or frivolous, but, seen in the context of the choral ode and of Antigone's declarations to Ismene and Creon, these actual matters appear more truly as indices of the work's more essential concern for human being—and, ultimately, for being itself. Thus, the heart of the matter—the heart of the tragedy and the heart of the uncanny itself—is not actual blood and death per se, but rather what determines our relation to death and to blood and, even, to actuality as such—namely, "the relation of human beings to being itself" (*Hölderlins* 147g, 118e).

From one perspective, Heidegger's 1942 seminar on Sophocles' *Antigone* has demonstrated much the same thing as his essay on van Gogh's painting: that the work of art and the poetic word open upon being itself and bring human being (and the world) into unconcealment. Thus, through Heidegger's intense meditation on δεινον, as the word appears specifically in the context of the play's choral ode and the heroine's account of her "supreme necessity," our attentiveness is awakened to human being as, in its uncanny essence, being unhomely in becoming homely. But the seminar reading of *Antigone* also suggests another, different way of considering what ethics might mean from a Heideggerian perspective. The essays published in the 1950s, as we saw, proceed from two basic claims: that human beings are essentially beings who speak and that pure, poetic language, such as we see it in great works of art, has the capacity to bring things into presence and unconcealment—that is, into their proper relations with what is as a whole. Correspondingly, in our first formulation, Heideggerian ethics involves a specifically *poetic* kind of speaking and bearing witness: a listening and attending to the speaking of the world and poetically harmonizing one's own voice with this speaking of the world in order to bring things into the open and thereby attain to a greater degree of being, becoming "more in being." By contrast, the seminars on *Antigone*, though they are themselves readings of poetic works, proceed not from any central, explicit claim about language and poetry generally, but rather from the claim that human being is essentially unsettled, that is, not at home in itself. Correspondingly, in our later formulation, Heideggerian ethics locates the ethical in the uncanny, in suffering and bearing the unhomely deprivation and essential absence intrinsic to human being. Certainly, in both accounts, Heideggerian ethics is about human beings coming to a proper relation to being itself. However, the way Heidegger describes the path to that home within being has shifted from, in our earlier account, adopting a certain "poetic" relation to language and the testimony of being, to, in our later account, coming to be at home with unhomeliness.

But whether this primordial ethics involves a bearing witness *to* being or a bearing *of* being in its uncanny presence and absence, in Heidegger's account of things, literature and art are shown to be intimately intertwined with our most fundamental obligation as human beings called to assume a more authentic existence and a higher degree of being. This is true equally of works that, like *Antigone*, take obligation and ethics as key thematic elements, and of works that, like van Gogh's shoes, make no explicit thematic demand upon our moral and ethical consideration. As we have seen, these different works of art lead Heidegger (with his reader) onto different paths in the thinking of being. Van Gogh's painting, in Heidegger's own very poetic reading of it, takes one from the dark opening of the shoes themselves and then radiates out to the world as a whole: the earth and the soil, the desolate fields trod by the peasant woman, the wintry evening, the wants and vicissitudes of a mortal life. Heidegger's reading of *Antigone* is less lyrical, more critical, and perhaps more conceptually dense than his reading of van Gogh's painting. For Heidegger, one might suppose, Sophocles' uncanny tragedy is dramatic enough, its alethetic force proved and powerful still, after almost two and a half thousand years, that his reader will readily register its power as truth simply through Heidegger's intense working and reworking of Sophocles' dramatic language. More to the point, it is also, as we have seen, irresistibly explicit in putting a name to the ethical import of Antigone's heroic action and its own aesthetic effect:

παθειν το δεινον τουτο, the supreme necessity to take up into one's own essence the uncanny that here and now appears. But these different ways of thinking the truth of being through art are not so different, really, and we might better think of them as complementary considerations of the same problem of a Heideggerian ethics. That is, if the poetic word brings things into being, calling them forth to emerge into presence, and if poetic testimony bears witness to one's own belonging among beings as a whole, then the question naturally arises: What then? How then is one to comport oneself as a human being in the world, among beings as a whole? One might do anything at all—even, adventurously, refuse all foreignness, efface otherness, and fail to take up the unhomeliness proper to human being. Heidegger's Antigone, by contrast, is celebrated because she sustains an essential relation to what we might call the paradox of the ethical uncanny: that one must become homely precisely in one's unhomeliness; one must dwell in the uncanny, open realm of all presencing and absencing.

In the next chapter, we will turn to the work of a philosopher deeply indebted to the work of Martin Heidegger and absolutely committed to thinking foundational ethics as structured through an encounter with otherness. We will turn to the work of Emmanuel Levinas.

CHAPTER 5

Levinas

Art and the Transcendence of Solitude

The work of Emmanuel Levinas (1906–1995) was an indispensable touchstone for the post-Heideggerian French constellation that also included Maurice Blanchot, Jean-François Lyotard, Jacques Derrida, and Luce Irigaray, and it remains the most eminent contribution to thinking ethics provided by the contemporary and late-twentieth-century continental tradition. It must be said, however, that this philosopher of *ethics* is not usually considered a thinker of *art.* Certainly it is possible to bring Levinas into discussions of art by reading narratives as illustrating or dramatizing his description of ethics—that is, as exhibiting an encounter with the other in which one gives oneself over, in respect, to the alterity of the other, surpassing one's own egoistic solipsism and one's tendency to domination. In fact, in his rare ventures into literary reading, Levinas himself occasionally read literature in just this way: reading Shakespeare's *Macbeth* and Maurice Blanchot's "Madness of the Day," for example, as allegories of the desperate difficulty in escaping from the solitude of being and of the subject's longing for a transcendence of being in movement toward the other. But however illuminating such critical exercises may be of Levinas's philosophy or of the ethical relations prevailing among characters, they really can't be said to think Levinas's work together with the problem of art as such. Nonetheless, we will see that, scattered in stray comments and in several short essays over a long career, Levinas's work suggests the outlines of a more general theory of art, one shaped in fascinating ways around the contours of his far better-known ethics. Indeed, in his devotion to elaborating an ethics of the other and in the unusual phenomenological or, even, "pre-phenomenological" terms of that ethics, Levinas recasts Heideggerian and Blanchotian ideas on art and literature to offer a more complex and innovative understanding of the ethics of art, insofar as it bears upon the fundamental structures of human subjectivity.

The claim that Levinas's thinking about art proceeds from a basically Heideggerian stance perhaps deserves a brief comment before we proceed further. Among readers of the continental tradition, Levinas's strained relation to the philosophy of Martin Heidegger is well known.[1] In 1981, looking back over his long career, Levinas described his own work as an effort to do philosophy otherwise than Heidegger, but, at the same time, Levinas also maintained that a philosopher in the twentieth century could not escape Heidegger's thought, especially as represented by *Being and Time* (1927), but also the later Heidegger, since this thought is a "great event" of our century (*Éthique* 33f, 42e) and *Being and Time* one of the most beautiful and most admirable texts in the entire history of philosophy (*Éthique* 27f, 37e). It will not be the business of the present essay to sustain an explicit comparison between Heideggerian and Levinasian theories of art and ethics. Yet, as we consider Levinas's writing about art, we will see implicitly both his profound debt to Heidegger, together with a profound effort to surpass what Levinas saw as limitations in the possibilities of a Heideggerian ethics. Hence, we will see that, like Heidegger, Levinas made a self-conscious break with what he called the "contemporary dogma of knowledge through art" (Réalité 125f, 2e)—that is, with prevailing pedagogical and critical claims that novel reading, for example, is a useful way to learn valuable moral lessons or facts about the world (Réalité, 123f, 1e). Likewise, and again explicitly, Levinas ridicules the notion that what is important about art ultimately proceeds from authorial intent or meaning (*Noms* 135f, 92e). Finally, against the Sartrean insistence on the engagement of art with history, Levinas shares Blanchot's view that "the poster, newspaper article and scientific treatise serve history far better than does the poem" (*Sur* 12f, 129e). Altogether, then, the entire field of representation—including the appearance within art of ideology and real-world sociohistorical forces—is left aside as inessential to the real question of art, which is better understood, with Levinas as with Heidegger, as an event that befalls the subject in his or her very being. At the same time, as we will also see, Levinas is able establish his own distinctive understanding of this event and its relation to being: namely, against the claim of a Heideggerian existentialist ethics that art has the potential to open upon a greater degree of being, Levinas will ultimately consider art's ethical potential precisely as a surpassing of being. Hence, we will also see that Levinas will offer a rather different description of art's ethicity from anything one would read in the Heideggerian oeuvre. The present essay, then, will try to capture that specific contribution of Levinas to thinking the foundational ethics of art and literature.

The interest of the present essay is not a historical one and will not follow Levinas through his early waverings on the ethicity of the work of art.[2] Rather, our interest will be to outline Levinas's vision of the ethical potential of art from the perspective of his most mature thinking on the topic—especially as this is represented by his late masterwork, *Otherwise than Being or Beyond Essence* (1974) and his essays on Paul Celan and Maurice Blanchot in the 1960s and 1970s. What we will find in these later writings is that Levinas develops his ideas on art and ethics around three terms: language, time, and sensibility. Art, when it succeeds as an ethico-aesthetic event, makes an intervention, through language, time, and sensibility, into the very subjectivity of the subject, casting the ego out of its habitual solipsism and powers of objectivity and cognition, surpassing one's ordinary relation to being, and moving the subject into ethical proximity with alterity and the other.

Art and the Grammar of Being

It has already been remarked that Levinas takes the work of Heidegger as his point of departure in thinking about art. Part of this lies in his bracketing off of a vast range of potential critical concerns—sociology, psychology, science, history, biography, authorial intent—as lying outside the key event of art. But Levinas's debt on this point is also far more precise: Levinas is persuaded that art *works*, at least in part, to call into the open the very being of being. That is, for Levinas, as for Heidegger, art makes something at the most fundamental level of being "resonate" or "vibrate"—a musical trope perhaps reverberant with something of Levinas's son, Michaël Lévinas, a composer in the French spectralist movement whose work was just beginning to attract attention in the early- and mid-1970s. Thus, in *Otherwise than Being*, Levinas describes a piece by the "proto-spectral" composer Iannis Xenakis in terms of its "resonance of essence"—that is, in its renewal or recommencement of being:

> In the inexhaustible diversity of works, that is to say, in the *essential renewal* of art [*le* renouvellement essentiel *de l'art*], colors, forms, sounds, words, buildings—already on the verge of being identified as entities, already disclosing their nature and their qualities in substantives bearing adjectives—recommence *being*. . . . [In] the touch of color and pencil, the secrecy of words, the sonority of sounds—all these modal notions—there is a resonance of essence. The research of

> modern art, or, perhaps more exactly, art in the stage of search, a stage never overcome, seems in all its aesthetics to look for and understand this resonance or production of *essence* in the guise of works of art. As if the differences of pitch, register and timber, color and forms, words and rhythms, were but temporalization, sonority and key. . . . Music, in Xenakis' "Nomos Alpha for Cello Solo" for example, bends the quality of the notes emitted into adverbs. Every quiddity becomes a modality, the strings and wood turn into sonority. What is taking place? Is a soul complaining or exulting in the depth of the sounds that break up . . . ? What misleading anthropomorphism or animism! The cello *is* a cello in the sonority that vibrates in its strings and its wood, even if it is already reverting into notes, into identities that settle into their natural places in gamuts from the acute to the grave, according to the different pitches. The *essence* of the cello, a modality of *essence*, is thus temporalized in the work. (*Autrement* 70–71f, 40–41e)

Like Heidegger, Levinas sees art as working against an everyday regard for phenomena in which objects may be seized by hand or by thought or by sign, but in which being itself remains veiled. By contrast, for the attentive subject, art reawakens the very verbality[3] of being, shifting it *from* substantive slumber (*a* being) *to* an event in the process of happening, a vibrating *resonance* of essence (be*ing*). To take Levinas's example above, in its essence as a work of art, Xenakis' "Nomos Alpha" calls us to attend not to a *noun*—to a given sound-image or to a given composition or to a given cello taken as an objective entity with various qualities attached—but rather to a *verb*—to the cello *as it emerges in its essence*, actively enacting its very cello-ness as its particular mode of being.

Xenakis' "Nomos Alpha" is a dense, difficult work for solo cello that develops not through evolving variations on a melody (in fact the fifteen-minute piece has almost no conventional melody whatsoever), but rather through an evolving series of eight "sound complexes," sequenced and resequenced in ways determined partly by chance and partly by Xenakis' recourse to mathematical group theory. There is, in fact, a rigorous organizational structure at work,[4] but this fact is grasped only obscurely by the lay listener, as by an intuition of order not immediately perceptible, calling upon his or her utmost attentiveness. Given this obscurely intuited sense of order, the listener can neither dismiss the piece (as if it were a merely random series of dissonant drones, whistling glissandi,

Illustration 3. Iannis Xenakis, first page from the score of *Nomos Alpha*. Boosey & Hawkes Music Publishers Limited, 1967.

and peculiar spiccato and col legno effects), nor fully grasp its ordering principles. Consequently, the listener is cast into the "stage of search," alluded to by Levinas. Furthermore, because the organizational principle unfolds on a much larger scale than conventional melody and because of the novel terms of its exposition, the minuteness of the listener's attentiveness tends not toward disclosure of the compositional entity and its implicit logic, but rather toward an engaged immersion in the unfolding of sound itself in the specific sonority of the cello. That is, the listener's grasp of the piece is deferred; the everyday comprehension of musical entities and identities is postponed; and yet the work exerts an undeniable power to engage the listener in a search for intelligibility. The pleasure of the piece is not so much that it delivers on this promise of intelligibility, but rather that the sense-making quest it inspires opens instead upon something unsought and surprising: the strong sense of being caught up, listener and performer alike,[5] in the active unfolding of an event of art, wherein the manifold textures and sonorities of the cello succeed each other in ever-surprising, ever-engrossing juxtapositions. This is music as an event, an unfolding of be*ing*, not music as an object or *a* being.

Through art, then, being and essence come forth not as concepts, but as a singular event in time, new in their every evental instance. This moment, however, in which art is an event of being that befalls the subject, is transitory: everydayness reasserts its privileges and the subject lapses back into objective existence—say, identifying the composition, seeking to comprehend its novel arrangement of notes within the prevailing musical language of the West, grasping its peculiar relation to musical tradition and contemporary art music, perhaps psychologizing the event to imagine that the composition expresses a mood or state of mind shared between the composer and his audience. This essay will return later to the ethical implications Levinas sees in the *temporal* nature of art considered as an event. For now, though, let us note simply four things: (1) the bracketing off of history (broadly considered), (2) the work of art defined as an event and not as an object, (3) Levinas's description of art as simultaneously also an event of language, a transformation in the grammar of being from noun to verb, and (4) the claim that the event of art reaches us at the most fundamental level of our existence to militate against an everyday attitude that, in the ordinary course of things, holds us within its captures.

One of the most compelling features of Levinas's philosophy generally is surely his description of this everyday disposition. For Levinas, the problem is not quite (as it is for Heidegger) that everydayness veils our relation to being generally and to our own existing in particular—and thus must be overcome in the name of an existential ethics. Rather, for Levinas, the problem with everydayness is that it traps us within the solitary sovereignty of our selves—enjoying, to be sure, a certain kind of power (of cognition, conception, perhaps volition and action), but also utterly isolating us from any ethical relation to anything or anyone beyond ourselves. Levinasian ethics, including any possible ethics of art, is from this perspective entirely a matter of transcending the bounds of solitary everyday existence, forsaking ego and power, and opening ourselves to an ethical encounter with alterity.

But how profound is this tendency of the ego [*le moi*] to draw everything into a universe that is eminently its own! Like other thinkers in the phenomenological tradition, Levinas conceives of the ego as the irreducible given fact at the center of all cognition. Consequently, when knowledge and reason grasp the world of objects and grasp the other, they claim the world and claim the other inexorably for the ego *as one's own*. And, insofar as knowledge and reason grasp and claim the other, Levinas would argue, they emerge as unethical. As he writes in *Time and the Other* (1948):

> In thus going back to the ontological root of solitude we hope to glimpse wherein this solitude can be exceeded. Let us say at once what this exceeding will not be. It will not be a knowledge [*une connaissance*], because through knowledge, whether one wants it or not, the object is absorbed by the subject and duality disappears. It will not be an ecstasis, because in ecstasis the subject is absorbed in the object and recovers itself in its unity. All these relationships result in the disappearance of the other. (*Temps* 19f, 41e)

For Levinas, then, there can be no other, no authentic encounter with exteriority or alterity, within the solitude of the ego's "own" universe. For any properly *ethical* event, wherein the subject encounters and respects the alterity of the other, solitude must be escaped and surpassed. Yet one must wonder what the relation of subject and other would look like, for what can it mean for the subject to encounter the other without grasping the other? Somehow, this must be a "relation of non-relation," where there can be no possibility or power of grasping, such that the subject is no longer "able to be able," so to speak, and is unseated (*Temps* 62f, 74e). Consequently, an ethical event must not only transpire outside of the realm of knowledge, since "knowledge [*la connaissance*] never encounters anything truly other in the world" (*Temps* 53f, 68e), it must be outside reason itself:

> By encompassing everything within its universality, reason finds itself once again in solitude. Solipsism is neither an aberration nor a sophism; it is the very structure of reason. This is so not just because of the "subjective" character of the sensations that it combines, but because of the universality of knowledge [*connaissance*]—that is to say, the unlimitedness of light and the impossibility for anything to be on the outside. Thus reason never finds any other reason to speak. The intentionality of consciousness permits one to distinguish the ego from things, but it does not make solipsism disappear: its element—light—renders us master of the exterior world but is incapable of discovering a peer for us there. The objectivity of rational knowledge [*savoir rationnel*] removes nothing of the solitary character of reason. (*Temps* 48f, 65e)

According to Levinas, then, my consciousness and my powers of reason can never present any object or objects—a painting of two shoes, the sparkling blue and yellow eyes (not green!) of my lover, a composition for solo cello, a philosophical proposition, the wretched of the earth—except insofar as these are objects *for me.* In terms of knowledge or of my consciousness, the object is only ever the object *as* present to my consciousness; it can never be its own pair of shoes, its own composition, its own proposition apart from what I can or will make of it. Another person, likewise, is only ever present to my cognition as subordinate to my knowledge of that person and to my conceptualization and contextualization of that person—however beautiful and brilliant or however abject—in terms of my universe and my symbolic matrix. In the everyday course of things, I am the point of reference by which I comprehend another person. By contrast, says Levinas, "The best way of encountering the Other is not even to notice the color of her eyes!" (*Éthique* 79f, 85e). Knowledge and perception and reason itself are surely indispensable for philosophy and critical thought, romantic love and humanitarian sympathy, but they lie outside of the ethical encounter considered at the heart of Levinas's philosophy.

According to Levinas, then, in our everyday mode of existence, we are trapped within a world of what he calls entities and identities. We are surrounded by objects, which we can revolve as objects of our reflection, which we can grasp with our powers of perception and conception and reason, and upon which we may attempt to exercise our powers of agency and volition. Such powers are made possible by a certain everyday relation to language, in which language "doubles up" the world of actual entities, denominating and identifying every object and relation with a name, to the extent that even verbs, in this everyday sense, are regarded as a kind of noun denominating an action, so that *to read*, for example, denotes the "thing" that one does with one's eyes and one's thought in relation to a book. This is the solitary world of the ego and its powers within perception, cognition, and everyday language. This is the also the very world overthrown in the event of art. Art, Levinas claims, works to make the verbality of being resonate, and the consequence is that the everyday, ego-centered, objective grasp of one's world is cast aside and one is unseated from one's place as a thing among things and instead thrown into an event in time.

We have already touched upon Levinas's description of art as an event that befalls the subject as a transformation in the grammar of being: that, through art, being is wrested from the everyday captures of denomination, nouns, identity, and representation, and is instead restored as an event to its essential verbality. We might get a more concrete sense for how this appears in an actual encounter with art by recalling again Xenakis' solo cello, or by considering another passage from *Otherwise than Being*. Through art, he writes,

> *essence* and temporality begin to resound with poetry or song. And the search for new forms, from which all art lives, keeps awake everywhere the verbs that are on the verge of lapsing [*retomber*] into substantives. In painting, red reddens and green greens, forms are produced as contours and vacate with their vacuity as forms [*vaquent de leur vacuité de formes*]. In music, sounds resound; in poems, vocables, material of the said, are no longer effaced [*ne s'effacent plus*] before what they evoke, but sing with their evocative powers and their diverse ways to evoke, from their etymologies; in Paul Valéry's *Eupalinos*, architecture makes buildings sing. Poetry is productive of song, or resonance and sonority, which are the verbalness of verbs or *essence*. (*Autrement* 70f, 40e)

When the red reddens and the green greens, when the sound resounds and the vocables sing, something befalls the subject which is not quite perception, if we take perception to imply the identification of an image within one's cognitive and symbolic apparatus. Hence, the reddening red in the event of a painting does not refer one to the *idea* of a particular color within the color spectrum. As an event of art, and before lapsing into a topic for introspection and thought, the reddening red simply strikes us, verbally and adverbially. It strikes us redly, so to speak, strikes us to register a particular sensuous impression but without yet entering into cognition. Thus, when the reddening red strikes us with the particular mode in which red *is*, it nonetheless does so without, at this level, making a differential or conceptual contrast between various modes of being—without, say, contrasting it with the greening in which green *is* in its essence.

One way of thinking about Levinas's claims here is as a way of accounting for a common experience of art: the way art casts the subject out of the memorial time of objects and entities, into some more immediate time of being. Certainly, one can refuse to give oneself over to the time of art. Certainly, too, one can adopt a critical relation to art, refusing it as event and taking it instead as an object of analysis. But when one gives oneself over to the work of art, one is cast out of time, unseated from one's habitual command of the world and its phenomena, and one is instead, according to Levinas, thrown into a sense of the very flow of time itself in the verbality of being. The reddening of the red and the singing of the architecture or the poem are strictly unplottable on our internal clocks and calendars because one has been overthrown in the event of art. Indeed, in a Levinasian perspective, to think about an event as a plottable "place" in time represents an inappropriate spacialization and reduction of temporality to an entity—in short, a failure to recognize the very temporality of time and the verbality of be*ing*. The lost time of the subject in the cinema or the concert hall, the temporal confusion of the reader "awakening" from a novel, the disparate experiences of time among museum-goers: such phenomena testify to the fact that the time of art involves a vanishing of the powers of the sovereign ego and a shift out of our usual command of time and into some other temporal mode. Hence, for Levinas, art and literature, taken as event, lead to "the unthinkable" of being (*Sur* 18–19f, 134e), because they cast the subject into an alternate temporality, beyond cognition and thought, and out of the solipsism and command of agency, ego, entities, and identities.

The reader of Levinas must ask, given Levinas's larger project insisting upon the primacy of ethics, how one is to consider the ethical status of this restoration, through art, of the verbal sense to being. Levinas thinks of the ethical as the "otherwise than being," as the title of his major work would have it. Is this it? Is the verbality of being, such as we see called forth in the event of art, to be considered as "otherwise than being" in the precise ethical sense Levinas has in mind? After some vacillation earlier in his career on the question of the ethics of art,[6] after reflecting on the possibilities of literature suggested by Paul Celan and Maurice Blanchot, by the early 1970s Levinas finally concedes the possibility that literature can indeed be "an unheard of modality of the *otherwise than being*" (*Noms* 66f, 46e). But what exactly is this "otherwise than being"? How does Levinas see here an opening for the ethical? And is there some way to think more concretely of the work of art in terms of this "otherwise than being"?

Levinas can give no easy answers to such questions. He does, however, give a hint when he proposes that questioning itself suggests something of the otherwise than being. We read earlier of "the research [*recherche*] of modern art," and "art in the stage of search [*recherche*], a stage never overcome." For Levinas, the otherwise than being is a modality akin to searching, to questing, to questioning, to desiring, to anticipating. All of these involve an errancy, a certain subjective departure from one's ego in which one's habitual grasping is suspended or deferred, and in which one has not yet arrived at something concrete that one can claim or incorporate as one's own. This is why "the poem goes toward the other" in a movement that proceeds "from place to the non-place, from here to utopia" (*Noms* 61–62f, 41–42e) as well as why, more generally in Levinas's ethics, at stake is not an arrival at alterity (a contradiction in terms), but rather an ethical movement toward mere "proximity" with the other. If, as Drucilla Cornell writes, there is a "thereness" to the (otherwise than) being of the other (Cornell 179), there can in any case never be a demonstrable "hereness" to the being of the other. This *movement toward* the ethical is accomplished in art through two essential features long recognized as constituting the heart of the event of art—language and sensibility—as well as through a third feature unique to Levinas's description of the event of art: the flow of temporality itself.

Aesthetics, Vulnerability, and Proximity to the Other

Emmanuel Levinas seems not to share the uneasiness, common among critics and philosophers of art, at binding together in the single word *aesthetics* the distinct problems of sensibility (suggested by the Greek root *aisthesthai*) and art (as the word has come to signify since the eighteenth century). Thus, in an early essay devoted to the problem of art more generally, he declares of art that "the aesthetic element is, in conformity with its etymology, sensation" (Réalité 130f, 5e). Consequently, when Levinas writes about art, the problem of sensation is not far away. In fact, we have already seen that, if art bears ultimately not upon the field of representation, as the common view would have it, but is rather an event of the verbality of being, this event is registered by the subject as a modality of being particular to a given work of art: the way, in a performance of Xenakis' piece for cello, the subject is cast into a vibrant resonance of being—and not being in some abstract or ideal sense, but rather the singular being of *this* cello resounding right now in its very "celloness." In other words, through the sensuous encounter with the resounding cello, the verbality of being acquires its particular cast and the work of art transpires as a singular event in the temporal flow. We might say that, for Levinas, sensibility yields the indispensable adverbial mode of the verbality of being in a given event of art. More than this, we will see that Levinas understands sensation as involving a passivity, immediacy, and vulnerability that open *ethically* upon responsibility and proximity to the other. Before we consider the ethicity of sensation in Levinas's theory of art, however, we might first gain a more precise sense for sensibility itself by considering the distinction Levinas draws between, on the one hand, sensation, sensibility, and the sensible and, on the other hand, perception and experience.

As Levinas uses the terms, the distinction between perception and sensation involves the way perception is psychologically bound up in the synthetic apparatus of cognition and representation. To perceive, for Levinas, is to seize an object, to grasp it, to know it, to have it available (at least in some degree) to conscious thought. Perception is moreover aligned with Husserl's philosophy of intentionality: perception is always perception *of* an object and is therefore always in relation to that object of perception. Perception, one might say, is the ego's representation of qualities belonging to a preexisting object.

Sensation, "the aesthetic element," is absolutely distinct from perception. For Levinas, "sensation that one may seize by introspection is already a perception. . . . [N]othing psychological would correspond to the simplicity of the physiological definition of sensation" (*Totalité* 203–204f, 187e). Sensation is more immediate and more fundamental than perception. It is also more passive: sensation is something that befalls the subject before agency can assert itself. An encounter with the statue of Laocoon in the Vatican Museum, to take an example from Levinas's "Reality and its Shadow" (1948), is first a matter of sensation—of enjoyment and pain—before it becomes a matter of perceiving the phenomenal qualities of the object and recognizing its name or story. Sensation has an *affective* content (of pain and enjoyment) that is the beginning and end of it. If, in some way, it may signify by indicating proximity of the other, it nonetheless cannot signify as a *representation* that opens onto the symbolic field. Consequently, sensation is not to be considered as if it were some variety of "inferior theoretical knowledge" (144f, 136e). Rather, sensation is "essentially naïve" (143f, 135e), and issues of clarity of thought or rational insufficiency do not touch it. Nor does it aim at an object—it's not sensation *of* an object. Or, rather, when it begins to be, it ceases any longer to be sensation, and has instead *converted* or been "anaesthetized" into perception and knowledge (*Autrement* 104f, 64e). Sensation, one might say, is the brute affectivity of being, an event without object that befalls the subject in his or her sensate corporeality.

When Levinas claims that sensation is the true domain of art, he argues that art, as art, is able to enact a "disincarnation" of the representational world into the sensible artistic image. Let us consider the fuller context of our earlier quotation from "Reality and its Shadow":

> If art consists in substituting an image for being,[7] the aesthetic element is, in conformity with its etymology, sensation. The whole of our world, with its givens and rudiments and intellectual elaborations, can touch us musically, become image. That is why classical art attached to objects—all those paintings, all those statues representing *something*, all those poems which recognize syntax and punctuation—conforms no less to the true essence of art than the modern works which lay claim to pure music, pure painting, pure poetry, under the pretext that they drive objects out of the world of sounds, colors and words . . . under the pretext that they break up representation. The represented object, by the simple fact of becoming image, is converted into a non-object. . . . The disincarnation of reality by the image is not equivalent to a simple diminution in degree. (Réalité 130–31f, 5e)

The radical conversion of representation into a naïve image that can "touch us musically," the disincarnation of the perceived object into sensible affect—it is as if the dialectical forward-movement of perception and cognitive thought "looped back" on itself, in the encounter with the statue of Laocoon or Xenakis' "Nomos Alpha," and fell back onto the hither side of such processes in aesthetic sensation. If one follows Levinas to take art and literature seriously as aesthetic events in this sense, there can be no question of any subordination to the universe of representation and knowledge, object and veridical truth. The "true essence" of art, regardless of either classical representationalism or the utmost modern degree of abstraction, poses itself as sensation, anterior and outside of that universe. Art conspires against the world of objects and their representation; indeed, art effaces this world in the work of aesthetic conversion. This is why Levinas, like Martin Heidegger and Alain Badiou, speaks properly of the *work* of art, or the *event* of art, rather than the mere artistic *object*, phenomenally considered. For Levinas, art can surely be dominated by perception (as if it were an object), but what is specifically the work of art is what cannot be reduced to that object.

Levinas is able to claim an ethical status for art and the aesthetic because of his conception of an ethical subjectivity that is grounded not in reason, cognition, and free will, but in the sensate corporeality of human being. As flesh and blood beings, we enjoy living, we enjoy our physiological satisfactions, and, indeed, we enjoy enjoyment itself. But because we are embodied beings, finite and mortal, our enjoyments equally imply a vulnerability to loss, to pain, to suffering, wounding, and trauma. When Levinas writes that sensibility is the very "subjectivity of the subject" and that the ethical "resounds" in sensibility (*Autrement* 31f, 15e), he is describing an ethical subject who gives him- or herself over, in radical passivity and exposedness, to an encounter with alterity that requires forsaking the ego. He is describing a sensate ethical subject who, in thus touching upon alterity and submitting before the face of the other, risks the possibility of pain and loss. It is no wonder, then, that Simon Critchley, in his essay on Levinas and trauma, concludes that "the bond with the other is affective" (Critchley 239). If one is to encounter anything outside of oneself, as Levinasian ethics calls upon the subject to do, then one must bear the loss of ego and self-identity, must bear the patience of passivity, and must suffer vulnerability itself. This is why Levinas writes, with an ear for the near homophony of "to offer oneself" (*s'offrir*) and "to suffer" (*souffrir*), that

> The subjectivity of subjection of the self is the suffering of suffering—the ultimate offering of oneself [*l'ultime s'offrir*], or suffering in the offering of oneself. Subjectivity is vulnerability. Subjectivity is sensibility. (*Autrement* 92f, 54e)

Why are ethical subjectivity and aesthetic sensibility coupled for Levinas? Because sensibility's terms—enjoyment and vulnerability—signify also as ethical terms of proximity, signifying one's proximity to alterity and the other. Where the ego would be complacent in itself and would posit itself for itself, the vulnerability immediately inherent to sensibility opens upon the possibility of the subject's being instead "for the other," and not just for itself, and thereby touches the subjectivity of the subject. This is why Levinas can declare that the immediacy of sensibility is "the for-the-other of one's own materiality, the immediacy—or the proximity—of the other" (*Autrement* 120f, 74e).

So, by offering oneself up to the aesthetic work of art and, in the passivity and vulnerability of sensibility, allowing the work to have its way, one thereby enters upon the Levinasian ethical: an interruption of the complacency and self-identity of the ego and an ethical opening to alterity and the other.

Saying the Word and Seeking the Other in the Poem

It has already been remarked that *language*, together with *sensibility* and *time*, is one of the three key terms through which Levinas's mature philosophy considers the ethicity of art. Yet we have also seen that Levinas locates the essence of art beyond all representation—that he describes the very event of art as sloughing off this representational dimension in some aesthetic event of pure sensation. We have also seen that, for Levinas, ethical subjectivity is located outside one's powers of cognition and beyond one's usual domestication of alterity as a mere object of thought and reflection. It cannot be altogether surprising, then, that, for Levinas, the ethical essence even of language itself is located elsewhere than in its representational power, as dazzling as this can be in the hands of a true artist. In contrast to Heidegger, who also locates the ethics of language beyond representation, but who locates it in its capacity to open upon being, Levinas locates his ethics of language precisely in the way, beyond representation, it "opens up a passage" to the other (*Noms* 12f, 6e). This ethical language beyond representation is what Levinas calls "the saying."

That is, in his later thinking about language as a feature of ethics, Levinas distinguishes sharply between two dimensions of language: the saying [*le Dire*] and the said [*le Dit*].[8] The *said* refers to that part of language that designates within the field of essences and entities, phenomena and truth, cognition and knowledge, representation and thematizability. But prior to "the linguistic systems and the semantic glimmerings," more originary than thought and the thematization of being, there is, says Levinas, a *saying* that resonates as the ethical signification of language and thus "weaves an intrigue of responsibility" (*Autrement* 17f, 5–6e). Levinas describes the saying as an exposure to the other.

> The ethical sense of such an exposure to the Other, which the intention of making signs—and even signification itself—supposes, is now visible. The intrigue of proximity [of one to the other] and of communication is not a modality of cognition. The unlocking of communication, irreducible to the circulation of information which supposes it, is accomplished in the Saying. It [the ethical sense] is not held in the contents inscribed in the Said and transmitted to interpretation and

> decoding done by the other. It is in the risky uncovering of self, in sincerity, in the rupture of interiority and the abandon of all shelter, in exposure to traumatism, in vulnerability. (*Autrement* 82f, 48e)

In Levinas's view, the most manifest, most material aspects of language—the words that are said and the meaning or thought communicated by this said—are in fact predicated on some more originary moment: a "saying" that constitutes an unlocking and a venturing forth, a forsaking of the shelter of inwardness, an exposing of oneself to the risk of wounding and pain, and an approach to the other:

> The Saying, where the subject speaking it is exposed to the other, is not reduced to the objectification of the theme stated. Who then came to wound the subject so that he should expose his thoughts or expose himself in his Saying?! He is subject to being affected [*l'affection*] by the other, which through its very irreversibility, does not molt into a universal thought. The subject affected by the other cannot think that the being affected [*l'affection*] is reciprocal. (*Autrement* 133–34f, 84e)

Opening one's mouth to speak or picking up the pen to write—before one even has any thing to say—is, Levinas suggests, a moment of giving oneself over to the other who befalls the subject and with whom one cannot share any reciprocal relation as equals participating together in a dialogue. This event of saying, of relation to the other, is "pre-original" in the sense that it is bound to a temporality irrecuperable and unrepresentable (in memory, in history) to any said, to any form or content that presupposes it. The ethics of the saying, then, is located in turning away from oneself, in venturing beyond one's solipsistic universe, in exposing oneself to proximity with the other and suffering the risk of suffering. It cannot be wholly contained in the said or stated *theme* of the utterance, however self-effacing or self-revealing; nor is it equivalent to any conscious *intention* of self-abnegation or self-disclosure or reaching out; nor is it a communication in fellowship among equals.

Thus stated, it would seem that the ethical dimension of language—from an irrecuperable "pre-original" temporality, beyond representation, unavailable to universal thought—is always already lost. But this is not altogether the case, as Levinas sees it, for the saying and the said are necessarily bound together—even if the saying is ordinarily absorbed and slumbers forgotten within its said. Consequently, however obscured, there remains a trace of the saying inscribed in every element of the said. This is why, in *Otherwise than Being*, Levinas is able to affirm that, indeed, "language permits one to say, be it in betrayal, this *outside of being*, this *ex-ception* to being, as if the other of being were an event of being" (*Autrement* 18f, 6e). In a Levinasian perspective, then, the ethical question of language and signification thus regards how one might awaken something of this saying slumbering in the said while effectively minimizing its betrayal:

> The *otherwise than being*—which, from the start, has been sought here and which, since its translation before us [into the recognizable idiom of entities and identities] is found betrayed in the said dominating the saying which states it—poses a methodological problem here. It consists of wondering whether the pre-original of the Saying (whether the anarchical, the non-original, as we designate it) can be brought to betray itself in showing itself in a theme (if an an-archeology is possible)—and whether this betrayal can be reduced; whether it is possible at the same time to know and to free the *known* of the marks that thematization imprints upon it in subordinating it to ontology. (*Autrement* 19f, 7e)

In fact, we have already seen this question posed several times before in a different aspect: How is one to have a relation with the other that does not imperialize the essential alterity of the other? How is one to bring the otherwise than being into the language of being without altogether losing its otherness? Levinas spends an entire career exploring these central questions of his philosophy of ethics. As we have already begun to suspect, literature—and art more generally—is one way Levinas imagines the complex impossible-possibility of the appearance of alterity, the saying, and the otherwise than being.

Levinas's engagement with the writings of Maurice Blanchot and Paul Celan marks a shift in his thinking about the relationship between literature and language that only deepens as language (as *saying*) becomes a central feature of his ethical philosophy. If, previously, he had considered the question of literature and language primarily through a Heideggerian lens and with a certain guardedness, hereafter, from the mid-1950s and especially by the 1970s, Levinas's thinking grew more complex and more consistently open to the possibility that literature could indeed open upon the ethical. In particular, as his philosophy of ethics becomes more significantly devoted to the ethics of language—of the saying and the said—and as his thinking about literature comes increasingly under the influence of Blanchot and Celan,[9] Levinas begins to endorse a theory of literature as a language event that offers an especially "scintillating" or vibrant sense of the saying (*Sur* 39f, 147e).

From this perspective, perhaps the most essential, most salient phenomenal fact of poetry and literature is a kind of strangeness at the heart of the event of art. One might locate this strangeness perhaps in the "disproportion between the writing and the work" that defines for Levinas the essence of the literary—the disproportion, that is, between the sense of significance asserted by the event of literature, on the one hand, and the poem's mere textual meaning, on the other hand (*Noms* 135f, 92e). Perhaps, more precisely, the strangeness resonates in what Levinas refers to as the "musicality" of the language of the poem: the obscure sense that, supplementary to its textual meaning, there is some signifying element that signifies beyond the order of meaning to indicate proximity to the other (*Sur* 57f, 157e). This very strangeness, this "irreducible exoticism" of poetry and literature, "invokes a saying [*en appelle au dire*]," as Levinas puts it (*Sur* 56f, 157e). And if, as he claims further, echoing Celan, "the poem leaves the real its alterity" and "yields to the other some portion of [its proper alterior] truth" (*Noms* 63f, 44e), it does so not at the level of reference, but at the level of language itself: "The mode of revelation of what remains *other*, despite its revelation, is not the thought, but the language of the poem" (*Sur* 14f, 130e). This dimension of language is, of course, the saying. Thus, if the poem, to a degree far greater than most everyday language, succeeds in preserving some element of alterity and allowing it some less-betrayed appearance, this is because poetry, in its strangeness and disproportion, in its exoticism and its musicality, allows the saying to be registered, despite the power and the brilliance of its said.

When Levinas describes such a revelation of the saying in poetic language, he returns to the tropes of movement and searching we have already seen him use in describing the "otherwise than being." We cannot be surprised that the saying would never appear as a reified, identifiable phenomenon, but would register only as a fleeting, scintillating sense of strangeness. In writing of Paul Celan, though, Levinas goes further. After claiming that the poem's essential work is situated in its language, a "language of proximity for proximity's sake," a language that constitutes a kind of "for the other" (*Noms* 60f, 41e), Levinas proposes that

> [t]hings will appear, certainly—the said of this poetic saying—but in the movement that carries them toward the other, as figures of this movement. "All things, all beings, as they make their way toward the other, will be figures, for

> the poem, of that other." (*Noms* 63f, 43e; Levinas's quotation is from Paul Celan)

Without minimizing the capacity of poetry and literature to make things appear and to bring beings into presence, Levinas nonetheless shifts the frame of this traditional insight from its prevailing Heideggerian perspective to a more distinctively Levinasian one. He does this by endorsing, reiterating, and reclaiming for himself Paul Celan's view that the *appearing*, perhaps the most celebrated characteristic of poetry, is itself an effect of a movement toward the other—that, in some sense, when the poem does its work of presenting beings, it simultaneously also bundles that work together with a saying that constitutes a movement toward the other and that this movement itself figures the other within the poetic event. Consequently, the poem registers itself upon the ethico-aesthetic subject as an arrangement of figures of alterity. The exoticism and strange musicality of art thus find their cause in the dissonance between the *ethical figures* of the poem which are registered aesthetically and the *textual figures* of the poem which are registered critically and which function as a proxy for the ethical figures they secretly carry below the level of conscious perception.

Strikingly, at the same time, this quotation from Levinas's essay on Paul Celan also enlarges our understanding of the locus of poetic saying. That is, previously, the present essay had understood the saying to pertain primarily to the speaker or to the poet: the ethical dimension of language was then understood as *the poet's* abandonment of shelter and solipsism, *the poet's* venturing forth toward the other and proffering words in an ethical act of saying. What we see above, by contrast, is that the poetic saying likewise animates the event of art for *the reader*—the one, after all, for whom "things will appear" but as figures of the movement toward the other. It seems that reading, too, involves an ethical dimension, in the precise Levinasian sense, insofar as the reader is, at least potentially, carried toward the other, carried on the figures of proximity appearing in the guise of "the said of the poetic saying." Thus, if Levinas describes a kind of "seeking [*recherche*] dedicating itself, in the poem, to the other" (*Noms* 66f, 46e), this holds true for the reader no less than for the poet. The poem, as an arrangement of figures of the other, is equally an occasion casting the reader in a quest seeking proximity with alterity and the otherwise than being.

Such an ethics of readership suggests a whole new way to think of the event of art and the task of reading itself. Certainly, there will be instances where fictional texts of admirable craft offer themselves to fantasies and pleasures primarily narcissistic: there will always be the "bad novel" that "aims to please by flattering" as Sartre puts it in his *What is Literature?* essays (Sartre 70f, 67e). But just as certainly, Levinas suggests, there is another class of reading, in which the event of art stages an encounter between the reader and the proximity of the other in the saying of the poem. The reader, at least potentially, is carried along in the event of art, carried through the subterranean movement beneath the figures of the poem, to abandon the shelter of solipsism, open him- or herself to an encounter with alterity, and expose the subject to being affected by the other.

Irresistible: The Event of Art and the Call for an Ethical Criticism

The saying of the work of art opens upon the ethical for Levinas partly because, like any language event, it is motivated by an ethical saying that remains preserved within its said and partly because, moreso than ordinary language events, the saying of art scintillates to the degree that the reader too—perhaps centuries after the death of the artist—responds to the artistic saying and responds to the work specifically as an occasion for seeking the other. But the event of language in art also carries an ethical dimension in the way that it obliges the reader to take up the position of ethical speech. This is an ethics of criticism and it is an inseparable aspect of the work of art, as Levinas came to see it.

The poem, we might say, issues a saying that calls upon the reader to respond. Evidence of this call for an ethical response is not hard to find: the "prefaces, manifestos, titles or aesthetic canons" which constitute "a non-eliminable metalanguage" bear witness to it, testifying to a powerful "call for exegesis" (*Autrement* 71f, 41e). Hence, in the event of art, even an ordinary reader is "*not* content with being absorbed in aesthetic enjoyment" and feels therefore "an irresistible need to speak" (Réalité 124f, 1e; my emphasis). An exemplary critic, such as Levinas sees in Maurice Blanchot, must give himself over to the "irresistible temptation of commentary"—irresistible—ethically irresistible—precisely because, for the reader, in the text, "the *other* of the Image and the Letter rend the *same* of the Said" (*Sur* 58f, 158e). The reader must speak or write or create in response to the work of art. This critical response to the work of art is ethical, in a Levinasian sense, because it carries forward, from text to text, the rending of the order of representation and identities ("the same in the said") out of an encounter with alterity in the exoticism of the poem ("the *other* of the Image and the Letter"). Thus, the critical reader responds in words, offering saying to saying, offering him- or herself up to the cause of the other in the Letter. From this perspective, one might say that the ethical *raison d'être* of criticism is precisely the *autrement qu'être*, the otherwise than being in a poem that calls for the ethical critical response.

Art, as an event, must be considered inseparable from the "call" for exegesis and criticism that it issues. The said, we recall, is not a phenomenon absolutely apart from the pre-original saying on which it depends. The saying, as we have already noted, is both betrayed *and* preserved there in the said. So that while the linguistic system may absorb the saying, may claim a recuperation of the saying and a subordination of it to the thematics of the said, nonetheless, the saying—even *as* saying—remains there, as if asleep. The function of an ethical criticism is to "awaken" the saying within the said:

> [B]y interpreting the fact that essence exposes and is exposed, that temporalization is stated, resounds, is said, it is not to give priority to the Said over the Saying. It is first to awaken in the Said the Saying which is there absorbed. (*Autrement* 74f, 43e)

If art is an event inseparable from its call for interpretation,[10] then one important way that art opens onto the ethical lies in the way art issues this call and thereby places the reader or viewer or auditor under the obligation to respond critically.

The working of art is not inevitable. The cello performance or the poem that moves the subject today may leave the same person indifferent tomorrow; the statue that seizes the ethico-aesthetic subject may at another time make its appeal only at the level of ego or narcissism or mastery; a great work of literature may be read instead as if it were a mere tale for children or as a tourists' companion to the sites of a faraway city. An ethical criticism recognizes that the appearance of otherness within the said of the work of art may require a kind of care or midwifery. Criticism must somehow work to address itself to the relation with the other. If art is potentially an event of ethics, but potentially also a failure—failing to carry the subject forward in a movement toward the other, failing to give itself out in words offered to the other—then, as Levinas puts it, "this immobile statue has to be put in movement and made to speak" (Réalité 147f, 13e). Somehow, criticism must succeed in "interposing the perspective of the relation with the other—without which being could not be told in its reality, that is to say, in its time" (Réalité 148f, 13e). In aiming at the temporality of time and the beingness of being, at the "verbality" of being rather than at being as a sort of noun denominating an action, criticism might awaken that which enables being to be told in its reality: the relation with the other that constituted the pre-original saying foundational to the said. Thus, a criticism that would be ethically responsible in a Levinasian sense may well direct its immediate attention to the language and the figures and the themes of a given poem, but it would do so in order to reach beyond them to the event of art considered as ethical and ontological *work*, distinct from the mere artistic object and apart from the thoughts and emotions of the artist who produced the object.

It would seem to be a complicating factor that the critical response to art, like any philosophizing of the event of the other, poses itself within the field of cognition—that, in order to show itself, *the saying* must be shown *in the said*, the side of the manifestation and thematization of being. But thematization, writes Levinas,

> where the essence of being is translated before us, and theory and thought, its contemporaries, do not attest to some failure of Saying. They are motivated by the pre-original vocation of the Saying, by responsibility itself. (*Autrement* 18f, 6e)

For Levinas, philosophy and criticism themselves, despite presenting themselves to theme and to thought, may indeed be motivated by and responsible to the ethical event, to the sensibility and saying and temporality that interrupt rational thought and lie beyond its grasp. The saying, that is, persists even after the appearance of the said. Ethics may be figured in the ethical saying, but it is not restricted to that moment before the word. Ethics has a sort of afterlife as well, even as it is staged in criticism seemingly at the level of theme. The response of philosophy and criticism to the saying is, therefore, an ethical necessity, even if the theme can never exhaust the saying it strives to awaken:

> But, is it necessary and is it possible that the Saying on the hither side be thematized, that is to say, be manifest, that it enter into a proposition and into a book? That is necessary. . . . But it must also be that the *Saying* calls for philosophy in order that the light that occurs not congeal into *essence* the beyond of essence. (*Autrement* 75f, 43–44e)

To write criticism or to write philosophy in this sense is to enter into the ethical by bearing witness to an ethical saying. Despite the tendency of theme and thought to "congeal" the saying into essence, the philosopher or critic must write, must contend with the impossible yet irresistible call to awaken the saying, and must summon his or her art to retain some sense of a temporality alterior to the time of cognition and theme, some sense of the other beyond the solipsism of the ego, some sense of a saying issued in quest of the other.

Levinas's mature philosophy, then, sees in the work of art an event in which everyday solitude and ordinary, objective being is transcended to open upon an "otherwise than being" and an ethical proximity with alterity and the other. Unlike Heidegger, Levinas does not privilege art as a unique movement of the subject toward the ethical—in Levinas's view, prayer or reading the Bible or even a caress may also do this work. However, Levinas does make it clear that art is a special class of event, one apart from everyday language and most other kinds of discourse. It may be true, as the common view would have it, that art offers an especially vivid representation of the world and the movements of human emotion. But beyond representation, as Levinas shows us, art commands our interest for the very reasons that make it congenial to an ethics of alterity. First, art casts us out of our objective existence and into the temporality and verbality of being, overthrowing the egoistic solipsism of entities and identities, consciousness and perception. Second, as an essentially aesthetic event, as an event of sensibility in which one is touched by something beyond oneself, art befalls the subject in his or her vulnerability as a sensate corporeal subject and thus implies a subjectivity that is "for the other" and not for oneself. Third, among other things, art is an event of saying, a venturing forth toward the other, and to a greater degree than mere ordinary language, art preserves the ethical saying at the heart of language and calls for a critical response to somehow awaken that saying through an ethical commentary.

Our next chapter turns to Nathaniel Hawthorne's final romance, *The Marble Faun*, itself an event of art that, in its own way, both dramatizes and reenacts the crisis of the ethico-aesthetic subject faced with the alterity of time.

CHAPTER 6

Endings

Ethics, Enigma, and Address in *The Marble Faun*

Hawthorne's Final Romance

The last decade in the life of Nathaniel Hawthorne (1804–1864) seems something of a lost one for literary scholars. The years 1850–53 had seen the very pinnacle of Hawthorne's literary career with, in quick succession, his romances *The Scarlet Letter* (1850), *The House of the Seven Gables* (1851), and *The Blithedale Romance* (1852), together with two classic collections for children, *A Wonder-Book* (1851) and *Tanglewood Tales* (1853), plus two further collections of previously published tales and a presidential campaign biography for soon-to-be-elected Franklin Pierce. Pierce's election, however, brought Hawthorne mixed blessings in the form of an appointment as U.S. Consul at Liverpool. On the one hand, the 1853–57 appointment was very lucrative and enabled Hawthorne to travel around England, France, and Italy until he returned to Concord with his family in June 1860. On the other hand, the post severed him from his homeland, stranded him from his habitual sources of inspiration, and for seven years produced very little writing, save for several notebooks of travel impressions. In the final year of his travels around Italy and England and in the almost four years of his decline in Concord, Hawthorne worked on four final romances. Two of these, the roughly drafted Revolutionary War tale *Septimius Felton* and the more finely drafted trans-Atlantic *Grimshawe*, he abandoned before arriving at a satisfactory draft, and of the third, *The Dolliver Romance*, he completed a mere three chapters before his death in 1864. Thus, *The Marble Faun, or The Romance of Monte Beni* (1860), the strangest and arguably the most ambitious of all his completed romances, stands alone in Hawthorne's late period fiction[1] and finds the author not only nearing the end of his mortal span, but also at a moment of deep crisis in his art.

More explicitly than ever before in his oeuvre, Hawthorne's final romance finds the author turning to the crisis of human mortality. It is not, like *Septimius Felton*, a dark obsession seeking an escape from man's mortal doom; nor does it, like *The Dolliver Romance*, spin a fantasy of an old man who begins to shed his years and grow younger than his aged contemporaries. But when he again took up the pen to write *The Marble Faun*, after his long absence from American literary life, Hawthorne wrote in a melancholy mood, uncertain whether his words would any longer find their reader. In his Preface, for example, the old writer opens by remarking on the necessity of addressing a supposed sympathetic reader, of having faith that, somewhere, there was someone "more comprehensive of his purposes, more appreciative of his success, more indulgent of his short-comings, and, in all respects, closer and kinder than a brother" (853). At first playfully and then pensively, Hawthorne writes of this One Reader, whom he never personally encountered, nor corresponded with through the Post, but to whom alone his former publications were truly addressed—in spite of their wider publication:

> Unquestionably, this Gentle, Kind, Benevolent, Indulgent, and most Beloved and Honoured Reader, did once exist for me, and (in spite of the infinite chances against a letter's reaching its destination, without a definite address) duly received the scrolls which I flung upon whatever wind was blowing, in the faith that they would find him out. But, is he extant now? In these many years, since he last heard from me, may he not have deemed his earthly task accomplished, and have withdrawn to the Paradise of Gentle Readers, wherever it may be? . . . I have a sad foreboding, that this may be the truth. . . . If I find him at all, it will probably be under some mossy grave-stone, inscribed with a half-obliterated name, which I shall never recognize. (853–54)

It is a remarkably rich passage and we shall return to it later in the present essay, but let us note for now that here, in the grace and the gloom of the Preface, where one would expect to find the themes of the novel announced, Hawthorne directs our attention to the curious way in which writing, death, and the uncertain vagaries of address are bound together in his last romance. It will be the argument of this essay that, in its entanglement of these basic terms—death, the unknowable, and the problem of address—*The Marble Faun* begs us to consider a curious and fundamental dimension of ethical responsibility that this work of literature opens up.

In certain respects, it can come as no surprise that Hawthorne's text bears upon ethics. Hawthorne, after all, had always been concerned with moral issues in his writing and critics have long recognized that *The Marble Faun* is no exception in this regard. In the middle of the last century, for example, critical debate concerned itself with whether, through the novel, Hawthorne intended to affirm or to disapprove of the doctrine of the fortunate fall—since, "as every reader of *The Marble Faun* knows, the romance is a modern retelling of the Genesis story," with the character of Donatello making the key transformation from innocence to experience and the character of Miriam as the ambiguous temptress.[2] Be that as it may, we might nevertheless ask whether Hawthorne's announced ambition "to write a fanciful story, evolving a thoughtful moral" (854) truly finds its greatest force in the *felix culpa* moral theme proposed by the characters themselves. The present essay will argue that, beyond whatever the novel takes as its explicit theme, beyond its intellectual themes and prior to the values it may in fact promote (moral humility, say, or human sympathy), Hawthorne's final romance actually directs its artistic energy somewhere else, at some more foundational moment, prior to theme and thematics. The most remarkable quality of the novel, after all, is hardly its intellectual treatment of theological questions, or the moral transformation of Donatello, the least of its characters. Much more striking is how Hawthorne's novel works to suspend the reader on the verge of an epistemological abyss, captivated before the phenomenon of not-knowing—and specifically of not knowing something of utmost importance, something bearing upon life, death, and ethical necessity.

From the first to the last, *The Marble Faun* maintains a very powerful sense of this enigmatic presence. Set amid the wrack and ruin of contemporary Rome, it follows through galleries and churches three artists—Miriam, Hilda, and Kenyon—and their Italian companion—Donatello—as for a time they discuss their own art and the masterpieces they see around them. In the repose of the opening chapters, they find themselves drawn to consider the moral dimensions of various works from the past: the plight and pathos of Beatrice Cenci as given by Guido Reni, the struggle of Guido's archangel Michael in his victory over the demon, the ambiguous moral status of the classical faun as suggested by Praxiteles' statue (the figure of which, they say, bears uncanny resemblance to the character Donatello). Meanwhile, of the history of our central character, Miriam, we are told next to nothing—only that she works as an artist and that she is menaced by a mysterious man from her past. Hints are made, however, of some unspeakable crime, some terrible violence haunting Miriam's past, and knowledge of it (or complicity in it) appears to have delivered Miriam into her oppressor's power. Surprisingly, the novel never reveals the exact nature of this enigmatic past that constitutes the central mystery of the novel; we know for certain only that it involved the shedding of blood and that its enactment has bound together in bitter guilt Miriam and her dark shadow. When one night Donatello casts this man, Miriam's "Model," off the edge of a precipice, apparently with her glance of approval, the company of friends is shattered. Miriam, her admirer Donatello, and their two American friends find themselves caught in a confused web of responsibility that entangles them all according to their varying degrees of ignorance and complicity to the murder.

At its most direct level, the novel begs the reader to share and suffer the ethical quandaries at the heart of the characters' experience: What does it mean to be a witness? What is at stake in speaking rather than remaining silent? What does it mean to *share* responsibility? Can, indeed, responsibility be shared at all? With its insistent refusal to close and conclude such questions, *The Marble Faun* departs from the satisfactions and formal perfections of *The Scarlet Letter* and, as we shall see, shifts the ethical significance of these relatively direct questions away from the content of their possible answers, and into the brute weight of their unansweredness. Such a maneuver on the part of Hawthorne's text leads us to the central question of both the novel and the present essay: How is one to speak, or write, or respond, in the face of the radically enigmatic? It seems incumbent upon us, ethically and psychologically, to put the proper word to certain events and to address this word properly to a particular auditor or reader. But if the nature of the event remains as irretrievable as the past itself and as enigmatic as death and the limits of mortal existence, how are we to put it into language? If we are to speak, then to whom are we to address ourselves? When even the addressee of our words remains uncertain, we find ourselves—as Hawthorne finds himself in his Preface, and as the characters find themselves in the novel—perched on the verge of an abyss, suspended in relation to absence, ignorance, and death. We shall consider this enigmatic suspension first in terms of the novel's relation to time.

Time, the Eternal City, and the Disadvantage of History for Life

With the eternal city's debris of empire and its confluence of art and religion, Hawthorne's Rome proves a profound and powerful backdrop for the ethical concerns of the novel. Perhaps more than anything else, Rome stages a strange relation to time itself—and it does so not only for the characters, but tends to do likewise for the reader. The opening paragraphs of the narrative announce the writer's ambitious hopes:

> We glance hastily at these things—at this bright sky, and those blue, distant mountains, and at the ruins, Etruscan, Roman, Christian, venerable with a threefold antiquity, and at the company of world-famous statues in the saloon—in the hope of putting the reader into that state of feeling which is experienced oftenest at Rome. It is a vague sense of ponderous remembrances; a perception of such weight and density in a by-gone life, of which this spot was the centre, that the present moment is pressed down or crowded out, and our individual affairs and interests are but half as real, here, as elsewhere. . . . Side by side with the massiveness of the Roman Past, all matters, that we handle or dream of, now-a-days, look evanescent and visionary alike.
>
> It might be, that the four persons, whom we are seeking to introduce, were conscious of this dreamy character of the present, as compared with the square blocks of granite wherewith the Romans built their lives. (857–58)

The novel's interest in time, that is, far exceeds mere description of the sublime narrative world of the characters, together with their actions, perceptions, judgments, and dilemmas. *The Marble Faun* aims to complicate the distinction between what is staged inside the narrative (Rome) and what is staged inside the reader (the romance). Thus, as the narrator explicitly suggests above, if the *characters* in Rome are afflicted by an evanescent sense of the present, the narrative aims also to intervene in the *reader's* "state of feeling," to manipulate the reader's experience of time such that the reader's sense of the present likewise loses its consistency. More specifically, in Rome, and ultimately in the experience of reading the romance, one feels the persistent pressure of what Nietzsche would later call "the disadvantage of history for life": the sense of a Past so weighty and of such granite density as to overwhelm the Present and allow to it only the most fleeting and dreamlike presence, such that life itself seems to lose some essential degree of its substance and reality. One becomes existentially ungrounded from one's proper place in time and placed instead in the pseudo-presence of a time—the past—that is not, and cannot be, claimed as one's own.

The pathos of Rome thus issues from the tension between, on the one hand, the lived human sense described by Augustine that the present is where one dwells and where one has a claim to existence and one's mortal share of happiness and sorrow (*Confessions* XI.xvii–xviii), and, on the other hand, the Aristotelian or historical sense that it is precisely one's present that is devoured by a ceaseless, insatiable future and forever slipping away into an already overcrowded past (*Physics* IV.219a). Nor is this tension merely an atmospheric effect. It is, in fact, crucial to the moral life of the characters and lies at the core of the novel's ethical concerns.

Sometime after the murder, after Kenyon has left Miriam and Donatello in Perugia, and after Hilda has mysteriously disappeared into the Palazzo Cenci, Kenyon wanders Rome in a melancholy mood. The narrative voice again doubles itself, hinting at Kenyon's thoughts while at the same time directing itself to the reader's state of feeling, by remarking on the "ponderous gloom of the Roman Past" that crushes one down under its decay of marble and granite:

> You look through a vista of century beyond century—through much shadow, and a little sunshine—through barbarism and civilization, alternating with one another, like actors that have pre-arranged their parts— . . . until, in the distance, you behold the obelisks, with their unintelligible inscriptions, hinting at a Past infinitely more remote than history can define. Your own life is as nothing, when compared with that immeasurable distance; but still you demand, none the less earnestly, a gleam of sunshine, instead of a speck of shadow, on the step or two that will bring you to your quiet rest.
>
> How exceedingly absurd! All men, from the date of the earliest obelisk . . . have made a similar demand, and seldom had their wish. . . . But even while you taunt yourself with this sad lesson, your heart cries out obstreperously for its small share of earthly happiness, and will not be appeased by the myriads of dead hopes that lie crushed into the soil of Rome. How wonderful that this our narrow foothold of the Present should hold its own so constantly, and, while every moment changing, should still be like a rock betwixt the encountering tides of the long Past and the infinite To-come! (1196)

As one looks upon the long vista of centuries stretching back into the dim Roman past, one's vision comes to rest on the obelisks, "eldest of things, even in Rome" (941), beyond which one can see no further. For Kenyon, as for the reader (the second person "you" above), the obelisks stand as symbols of the limit of time, mortality, and human understanding. This is so in part because their antiquity and unintelligible inscriptions open upon a past so infinitely past that it finally defeats the grasp of the Augustinian present and the obelisks thus stand forth into the present as the insistent and inscrutable enigma of the past as such in historical time. It is also true because, as the quotation above suggests, there seems to be an absurd incommensurability between this sublime vision of the infinite past and one's own actual existence. To measure one's brief span against the infinite centuries is to think oneself and one's life "as nothing," and yet, as Descartes knew, this is impossible: to think oneself is necessarily to think oneself as something that exists. The sublimity of the obelisks, then, opens upon a kind of mortal or existential impossibility in which the present is obliterated and one's existence is cast into proximity with a kind of void, a mere step or two from death.

Time, we see, defeats the intelligible word. The word of the obelisk indeed lives on, but it speaks to us unintelligibly, as if the past as such could hold no communion with the present. And in the present of Rome and the romance, one's heart strives to read the mysterious inscriptions from a past beyond measure, but can finally only read one's own failure to decipher their meaning. In this failure that announces the brevity of life and the imminence of death, one struggles—and does not speak—but "cries out," like an infant, forceful yet inarticulate, clinging to the present, the only time one has.

Moreover, the enigma of the obelisks has already been attached at this point in the novel to the central mystery of the romance itself. In the days shortly before the murder, Kenyon and Hilda have been enjoying a stroll alone along the parapets of the Pincian, speaking of the peculiar attraction between Miriam and the young Italian count, and taking in the sights. They have already pondered the pre-Mosaic antiquity of the Flaminius obelisk in the foreground, gazed upon the distant immensity of Saint Peter's Basilica, and have turned their eyes once more to the scene below:

> Kenyon and Hilda again let their glances fall into the piazza at their feet. They there beheld Miriam, who had just entered the Porta del Popolo, and was standing by the obelisk and fountain. With a gesture that impressed Kenyon as at once suppliant and imperious, she seemed to intimate to a figure

> which had attended her thus far, that it was now her desire to be left alone. The pertinacious Model, however, remained immoveable.
>
> And the sculptor here noted a circumstance, which, according to the interpretation he might put upon it, was either too trivial to be mentioned, or else so mysteriously significant that he found it difficult to believe his eyes. Miriam knelt down on the steps of the fountain. . . . To other observers, if any there were, she probably appeared to take this attitude merely for the convenience of dipping her fingers into the gush of water. . . . But, as she clasped her hands together, after thus bathing them, and glanced upward at the Model, an idea took strong possession of Kenyon's mind, that Miriam was kneeling to this dark follower, there, in the world's face! . . .
>
> But—allowing that he had caught a true glimpse into the hidden significance of Miriam's gesture—what a terrible thraldom did it suggest! Free as she seemed to be—beggar as he looked—the nameless vagrant must then be dragging the beautiful Miriam through the streets of Rome, fettered and shackled more cruelly than any captive queen of yore, following in an Emperour's triumph. And was it conceivable that she could have been thus enthralled, unless some great errour—how great, Kenyon dared not think—or some fatal weakness, had given this dark adversary a vantage-ground?
>
> "Hilda," he said abruptly, "who and what is Miriam?" (942–43)

Hilda, of course, knows nothing and can tell nothing of her friend's past either. Thus, one is left, like Kenyon, trying to read and to correctly interpret the significance of a single, wordless image: that of Miriam kneeling in the shadow of the obelisk, fruitlessly appealing—perhaps—to the pertinacious Model for release. This image binds together the enigma of the past in both its historical and its personal dimensions. Against an ordinary, everyday presumption that the ethical sphere is defined by free moral choice and proceeds within the present, Kenyon intuits here the possibility that Miriam, at least, morally fettered to the past, cannot leverage her own narrow foothold in the present to attain anything like an autonomous moral stand—even as the ethical sphere maintains an urgency now more undeniable and more mysterious than ever. How, after all, is one to think of ethics if the ethical subject is not conceived as a free agent among other free agents? For Kenyon, whose vision is closest to that of the narrator and reader, the dimensions of Miriam's past suggest a terrible ethical sublime in parallel with the awful antiquity of the obelisks and the sublime vastness of Saint Peter's. That is, Kenyon and the reader here find themselves in the presence of a mystery so morally overwhelming that they dare not think it through—and one that is ultimately no less inscrutable than the ancient inscriptions on the obelisk. What Hawthorne's romance presents, then, is a central enigma, the dimensions of which extend beyond the limits of language and intelligibility, into time and the limits of human mortality, and ultimately into the dire problem of an ethics concentrated in the figure of fettered, shackled Miriam.

The sense of a profound moral mystery represented by Miriam only becomes more palpable on the night of the murder, shortly after the scene at the obelisk. On that night, after the visit to the Coliseum, and as the excursion lingers in the precincts of the Forum before ascending the Capitoline Hill, Kenyon recalls the story of Curtius. The legend recounts that in 362 BCE, the earth shook and a chasm opened up and the people of Rome trembled in fear. They called upon their soothsayers, who augured that the chasm would close only when Rome had sacrificed her greatest treasure into the void. Upon hearing this, Marcus Curtius, declaring that Rome's greatest treasure was a brave man, cast himself, mounted and fully armed, into the abyss. When gallant Curtius and his steed had vanished into the gloom, the earth again shook and the chasm closed up over them and the people of Rome were saved. Indulging his gothic imagination, Kenyon describes Curtius's chasm as the yawning void of time. "Imagine the great, dusky gap," he says,

> "impenetrably deep, and with half-shaped monsters and hideous faces looming upward out of it, to the vast affright of the good citizens who peeped over the brim! . . . Within it, beyond a question, there were prophetic visions—intimations of all the future calamities of Rome—shades of Goths and Gauls, and even of the French soldiers of to-day. . . ."
>
> "I fancy," remarked Miriam, "that every person takes a peep into [such a chasm] in moments of gloom and despondency; that is to say, in his moments of deepest insight."
>
> "Where is it, then?" asked Hilda. "I never peeped into it."
>
> "Wait, and it will open for you," replied her friend.—"The chasm was merely one of the orifices of that pit of blackness that lies beneath us, everywhere. The firmest substance of human happiness is but a thin crust spread over it,

> with just reality enough to bear up the illusive stage-scenery amid which we tread. . . . It was a foolish piece of heroism in Curtius to precipitate himself there, in advance; for all Rome, you see, has been swallowed up in that gulf, in spite of him. . . . All the temples have tumbled into it; and thousands of statues have been thrown after! All the armies and the triumphs have marched into the great chasm, with their martial music playing as they stept over the brink. All the heroes, the statesmen, and the poets! All piled upon poor Curtius, who thought to have saved them all!" (987–88)

While Kenyon can still, at this point in the novel, look into the past and regard its future calamities with a poet's or a tourist's fancy, and while Hilda, jealously guarding her purity, denies and evades the mortal threat of time altogether, Miriam can assume no such imaginary distance to the real, deathly void that lurks beneath the illusive stage-scenery of everyday Rome. Indeed, for her, the inexorable march of the centuries into the open grave of time is only a grander perspective on the abyss that already haunts her own existence. Marked by the untold violence in her past, and threatened by a calamitous future herself, she has already intuited a "dark chasm," a "voiceless gulf" separating her from even her closest friends (947). For Kenyon, the crisis of meaning in mortality, such as it appears to him, can still be cast into a moral schema to make sense, in the way that a narrative makes sense: as he reads the case of Curtius, this moral sense-making is a familiar narrative of heroic self-sacrifice. For Miriam, whose raw relation to the real permits fewer illusions on this score, the gulf is essentially "voiceless" and "dark" and finally defeats meaning, including the heroic narrative Kenyon would place upon Curtius and the void.

There are several reasons to think about this chasm in terms of death, time, and the possibility—or impossibility, as Miriam would have it—of rationalizing death into a moral schema. For one thing, the very nature of the abyss that Kenyon has summoned to imagination is historical in nature and works to bring other times—the future (when Kenyon adopts the perspective of Curtius's frightened fellow citizens) and the past (when Miriam looks back from her own epoch)—out of their proper temporal place and into the present. Moreover, the deathly nature of these other times is plain: the past is the time of ruin, the future is the time of death. Only the present can promise life and happiness. But Miriam, in a troubled mood, suggests that the "deepest insight," the insight that regards but that cannot illuminate the "dark chasm" underlying meaningful human existence, reveals even this present as but a fragile and precariously held position between the long past and the infinite to-come. Indeed, Miriam's ironic appraisal of Curtius's sacrifice shows her to be the only one of her friends to have rightly estimated the weight of the single human life that Marcus Curtius precipitated into the gulf "in advance." Where Hilda will speak blithely of heroic self-sacrifice and an excited Kenyon will carry on about a subterranean lake of Roman blood, Miriam alone remarks on the loss beyond meaning entailed in that single leap into the future.

The legend of Curtius is also important because it complicates the significance of the friends' discussion once they arrive at the edge of the actual precipice where the midnight murder will take place. At first, of course, the meaning of Curtius's bravery and self-sacrifice into the chasm near the Forum would seem to be opposed to that of the execution of traitors and political criminals who, according to Kenyon, were long ago cast from the heights of the Tarpeian Rock onto the stones below. But after the company has departed and Miriam and Donatello are left alone by the fatal gulf, Miriam's musings show her to be following her own line of association:

> "It would be a fatal fall, still!" she said to herself, looking over the parapet, and shuddering as her eye measured the depth. "Yes; surely, yes! Even without the weight of an overburthened heart, a human body would fall heavily enough upon those stones to shake all its joints asunder. How soon it would be over!"
>
> Donatello (of whose presence she was possibly not aware) now pressed closer to her side; and he, too, like Miriam, bent over the low parapet, and trembled violently. Yet he seemed to feel that perilous fascination which haunts the brow of precipices, tempting the unwary one to fling himself over, for the very horrour of the thing. . . .
>
> "Who were they," said he, looking earnestly in her face, "who have been flung over here, in days gone by?"
>
> "Men that cumbered the world," she replied. "Men whose lives were the bane of their fellow-creatures. Men who poisoned the air, which is the common breath of all, for their own selfish purposes." . . .
>
> "Was it well done?" asked the young man.
>
> "It was well done," answered Miriam. "Innocent persons were saved by the destruction of a guilty one, who deserved his doom." (994)

Given that moments later, Miriam's Model will detach himself from the shadows and, after a brief struggle, be cast into the darkness below, it is tempting to read this as a conversation premeditating his murder—which it may well be for Donatello, who has already begged Miriam's leave to initiate violence against the strange man poisoning the days of his beloved (928, 976). She, however, seems to be musing upon an altogether different death—namely, her own. The reader has already seen Miriam predict her own death from an overburdened heart (933), and if Donatello draws back hastily from the perilous fascination of the edge, she does not. In light of her conversations that night with Donatello[3] and Hilda[4] there is some reason to believe that Miriam, herself already on the brink of insanity, may fear that the crime in her past (and the burden it has placed upon her present) will poison the innocence and happiness of those she loves. Now that she finds herself on the edge of an actual precipice, the tale of Curtius told earlier that evening by Kenyon opens up new ways for her to figure her own private abyss. That is, by identifying herself in terms of Curtius's legend, she may indulge in a fantasy of her own self-sacrifice, a beautiful death, an escape from insight, and a way to tame the horror of her own chasm by situating it within a narrative of the necessary and ethical sacrifice of an individual for the greater good. His story would give her, if only in fantasy, a way to give recognized meaning to the private abyss of her past and present, as well as to the calamitous future she contemplates. Resonance with the fall of political criminals in old Rome suffices to develop her line of association, while simultaneously allowing Donatello to fatally read (or perhaps misread) the ambiguous tendencies of her thinking.

Then, in a dreamlike transformation of her own unspoken death wish, the precipitation is shifted from herself to her Model, and the idealized suicide is instead realized as an actual murder just at the moment when, unknown to Miriam, Hilda has peeped through the gate to find her friend:

> "What have you done!" said Miriam, in a horrour-stricken whisper.
>
> The glow of rage was still lurid on Donatello's face, and now flashed out again from his eyes.
>
> "I did what ought to be done to a traitor!" he replied. "I did what your eyes bade me do, when I asked them with mine, as I held the wretch over the precipice!"
>
> These last words struck Miriam like a bullet. Could it be so? Had her eyes provoked, or assented to this deed? She had not known it. But, alas! Looking back into the frenzy and turmoil of the scene just enacted, she could not deny—she was not sure whether it might not be so, or no—that a wild

> joy had flamed up in her heart, when she beheld her persecutor in his mortal peril. Was it horrour?—or ecstasy?—or both in one? Be the emotion what it might, it had blazed up more madly, when Donatello flung his victim off the cliff, and more and more, while his shriek went quivering downward. With the dead thump on the stones below had come an unutterable horrour.
>
> "And my eyes bade you do it!" repeated she. (996)

As much as the conversation they held an eternal moment before, in which Miriam fantasized of her own ideal self-sacrifice but was read to speak of the justice of her Model's real execution, the moment of the murder itself enacts a problem of reading. In the fatal breath or two of trial, Donatello addresses her with his eyes, and her eyes respond, he says later, with a death sentence pronounced upon her Model. Once again, Donatello reads Miriam otherwise than the train of her conscious thought—this time by reading her eyes primarily according to his own desires. Miriam, however, takes responsibility for the unknown wish of her heart, as if it had been her Model and not herself that she consented to see cast from the cliff: "Yes, Donatello, you speak the truth!" she says. "My heart consented to what you did. We two slew yonder wretch. The deed knots us together for time and eternity, like the coil of a serpent!" (997). Remarkably, this commitment of Miriam appears to resolve—in her own view, anyway—not just the matter of Donatello's accusation that evening, but also her singular relation to the all-too-real existential void. That is, having married her fate to that of another, to Donatello "for time and eternity," her relation to the real, no longer singular, is now mediated by the social sphere, by the supposition of a shared moral life, and by traditional moral narratives of fall and possible redemption. Whether this shift in Miriam's moral stance marks a true ethical engagement or else a very human retreat into what she once called the illusive stage-scenery of Rome, the romance itself does not immediately make clear.

The murder does, however, scatter the company of friends, and they never again meet as a foursome. Miriam and Donatello cannot sustain the passion of shared sin that binds them together. Hilda, overwhelmed by her encounter with death and moral fall, cannot find the strength—and in fact refuses—to comfort to her friend, and shares her misery and her secret burden of witness only in the confessional at Saint Peter's. Donatello, moody and dejected, repairs to his tower in the Apennines, followed later by Kenyon and (secretly) by Miriam. Over the next months, aided by Kenyon (who has intuited much of what passed on the precipice over Rome), a rapprochement is engineered between Miriam and Donatello so that they might painfully and fitfully build a new relationship based upon their shared moral burden. They seal their commitment in the main square at Perugia, and Kenyon returns to Rome with the intention of asking Hilda for her hand in marriage. Before he can find the proper moment, however, she suddenly vanishes without a trace. Kenyon searches fruitlessly, until he is finally given word from Miriam, who has unexpectedly appeared in Rome, that Hilda is safe and that she will be returned. Thus, on a balcony over the Corso at carnival time, Hilda reappears just as suddenly and just as mysteriously as she had vanished almost six months before. Donatello, by some secret arrangement unknown to us, is not seen again. Miriam, penitent and waiting for Donatello, is glimpsed only once. And so the narrative ends.

It is difficult to disentangle the strands of the present essay so as to treat the elements of its reading in isolation, but we should take a moment to gain perspective on where our meditation on *The Marble Faun* has brought us thus far. Primarily what we have seen is that Hawthorne's final romance stages a sublime encounter with the limits of death and mortal human existence. We have seen that, in some mysterious way, this encounter seems to bear upon ethics. This we understand in the first instance because the characters themselves read the situation in these terms and also because at stake in the plot is a murder (or, we suppose, two murders, if we also include an earlier one in Miriam's past) and the prohibition against murder has been understood as a foundational law of moral thought from Moses to Freud to Levinas. But we have also seen that the fragility of being here goes beyond the moment of murder and seems to derive as well from the strange nature of time itself. Questions of being and annihilation seem to belong to everyone in the Rome of this romance, even apart from matters of violence, simply because the Roman past is so weighty that it threatens to overwhelm the present and thus to unmoor all who live there (and all who read about it) from their proper time. The ruinous past, the calamitous future: these other times are the death of the present. But the actual murders, as well as the death implicit in the encounter with the other times, give themselves out not so much as specific dangers to be avoided if one could, but rather as something radically enigmatic and unknown, something that questions us at the level of ethics: How does one take responsibility for one's own fragile existence in the present? How does one take responsibility for the death of the other in the past? Death, as Emmanuel Levinas says in his late lectures, is a mystery, an enigma, a disquieting question—indeed a "pure interrogation mark"[5] that casts the subject into question and "causes [the subject's] identity . . . to burst open in the form of a question that arises in it."[6] In Hawthorne's final romance, death signals an analogous kind of crisis in Miriam especially, but also in almost everyone else. How, after all, is one to read ethics together with the radical enigma of real death, when the narrative of sacrifice proves inauthentic and cannot be sustained? Finally, and entangled amid all these strands, is the sense that what we are dealing with in *The Marble Faun* is something that persists at the limit of language, intelligibility, and interpretation, something that complicates, perhaps radically, how it is possible to speak of what must—but cannot—be put properly into words. In the next section of this essay, we will consider this last thread especially in terms of the problem of address, as we turn to the end of the novel.

The End of the Romance, the Death of the Reader, and the Impossible Address

The end of Hawthorne's final romance is well known for the gross lack of satisfaction that it offers to the reader. From the point of view of the twentieth-century critic, the novel has been, right up until chapter 50 and the postscript, a dazzling and delicately balanced refusal to reveal either the secret of Miriam's past or the rationale for Hilda's disappearance. There are still other untold aspects, of course, but these are mostly of the conventional sort one expects in building up to the conclusion of a novel—How will Hilda be found? Will she return Kenyon's love? What will become of Donatello and Miriam's feelings for each other? Will the murder be discovered and the police be involved? Or else they are philosophical questions one doesn't really expect to be answered outright—Is a moral fall (such as Donatello's) in fact necessary to awaken the soul and to spur one to a higher moral and intellectual state? How do we understand the moral and criminal culpability of various of the characters in relation to the murder and its aftermath? Or else, finally, they are merely fanciful questions whose urgency remains ultimately trivial—Are we, for example, to take Donatello as a real descendent of an ancient race of fauns?

The matters of Miriam's past trauma and of Hilda's disappearance, however, are extraordinary precisely because they seem so pregnant with real mystery and seem to promise a view into the secret order of things.[7] One doesn't expect a mystery in the divine sense, of course, but there are plenty of cues to suggest a mystery in the tradition of Eugène Sue's immensely successful *Les Mystères de Paris* (1842–43), which inspired scores of other such "urban mystery novels" in Europe and America throughout mid-nineteenth century, including George Lippard's very successful *The Quaker City, or the Monks of Monk Hall* (1845) and Ludwig von Reizenstein's extraordinary *Die Geheimnisse von New Orleans* (1854–55), to name only two of many American examples. With a novel set in contemporary Rome, and with the Edgardo Mortara affair of 1858 still fresh in the public imagination,[8] the largely Protestant readership in America and Britain might reasonably have looked for a scandalous glimpse into the putatively corrupt machinations and secret vices of the Vatican hierarchy. And indeed, Hawthorne teases the reader in this direction by implying that the mysteries at hand lie in the direction of the Roman Curia. One thinks here of the fact that Miriam seems unaccountably intimate with the corridors of wealth and influence, of the fact that her connections have apparently given her secret information regarding Hilda's captivity, and perhaps also of the persistent Beatrice Cenci motifs. But Hawthorne doesn't go much beyond such vague hints, and he keeps the door to the world of the Vatican and the Roman aristocracy finally closed against the reader's view.

Still, Miriam's mystery is the engine of the entire plot. It is because of this past that she is persecuted by her Model, whose murder is the centerpiece of the romance. It is because of this past that she has these particular relations with Hilda and her other friends: a reserve of the unspoken, a chasm of distance. It is because of this past that Miriam is who she is: the most fascinating character in the novel and one of Hawthorne's finest creations. And to the readerly questions of *Why?*—Why is Miriam being persecuted? Why must the murder take place? Why can't Miriam seek solace in her friends?—to these and other such questions, we look to her enigmatic past for a solution. But we look in vain.

As if to underline the provocation, Hawthorne's text repeatedly and directly insists that the reader is indeed in the presence of a mystery, but then, to a remarkable degree, it controverts literary convention and refuses to relieve the weight of the enigma with the satisfaction of revelation. The following passage, taken from the days leading up to the murder, is exemplary in this regard. In it, Miriam has sent Donatello away after their frolic in the Borghese grove and has conceded an interview to the mysterious man, the "shadow" who haunts her days in Rome and oppresses her spirit with burdens of the past:

> [T]here have come to us but a few vague whisperings of what passed in Miriam's interview, that afternoon, with the sinister personage who had dogged her footsteps ever since the visit to the catacomb. In weaving these mystic utterances into a continuous scene, we undertake a task resembling, in

> its perplexity, that of gathering up and piecing together the fragments of a letter, which has been torn and scattered to the winds. Many words of deep significance—many entire sentences, and those possibly the most important ones—have flown too far, on the winged breeze, to be recovered. If we insert our own conjectural amendments, we perhaps give a purport utterly at variance with the true one. Yet, unless we attempt something in this way, there must remain an unsightly gap, and a lack of continuousness and dependence in our narrative; so that it would arrive at certain inevitable catastrophes without due warning of their immanence. (929)

As a narrative moment, this is exceedingly strange.[9] It does not move the plot forward and it does not add to our information. Quite to the contrary. Vague whisperings, mystic utterances, fragmentary sentences—as readers, we demand that our author smooth over such "unsightly gaps" that can only add to our sense of anxiety. We demand a "continuous scene," as Hawthorne puts it, a fullness that would deny the gap and forget this lack and the dire uncertainty that seems to bear so mysteriously upon misfortune and crime, death and solitary suffering. But Hawthorne's narrator protests himself caught between doing a violence *to* the truth, in fabricating conjectural amendments, and risking a violence *of* the truth, in exposing his reader without "due" warning of the inevitable catastrophes of the text. So, without allowing his narrative to unravel into complete chaos, Hawthorne manages to weave an exquisitely balanced literary texture out of these fragmentary threads, and he exploits the frayed weft of his tale to force upon his reader an intuition of the brute nothingness concealed but almost visible beneath the tapestry. In the passage above, the reader is directly alerted to the fact that "possibly" the most important, most deeply significant words have been irretrievably lost. What is the reader to do in the inescapable face of such an aporia? This interview was to have revealed some clue to the man's identity; it was to have given some intimation of the dark crime haunting the past he shares with Miriam. Instead, the reader is afflicted with a renewed sense of obscurity. Moreover, as we see, the character of the reader's disquietude is entirely governed by the subject's relation to time—by the irrecoverable pastness of those words that have vanished on the winged breeze, and by the catastrophic future, which can be but imperfectly heralded. The distress of this and similar passages thus bears upon the present facing an intimation of its own limits, upon the abyss, the unsightly gap and lack of continuousness, that interposes itself between the present and the past and the future.

These are serious matters for this novel in particular, since the uncanny sense of some dark significance being enacted on another scene obscured from view—as unsettling and as fascinating as it is—gives its shading to every chapter of Hawthorne's moody romance, right up to the end. Hawthorne's romance is an essentially "moody" one in the sense that its undeniable fascination doesn't very much derive from its action or plot (which one may find a little thin for a novel of this length), and while it does successfully generate interest in character and in its discussions of works of art, these attractions get much of their power from how they bear upon the enigmatic unknowns of the novel, which remain the emotional center of the reader's experience. Thus, the experience of the novel is not primarily a crime novel or a philosophical novel or a sentimental education. Rather, it is first and foremost an experience of dwelling with the tension of an untold mystery. Right up until the end, that is.

What happens in the end, of course, is that Hawthorne yields, against his better judgment, to the demands of his reader. At least to a certain extent. Chapter 50 begins with a hint of unease in its tone, as the narrator pleads and protests the necessity of maintaining the carefully spun suspension before the enigma:

> The gentle reader, we trust, would not thank us for one of those minute elucidations, which are so tedious, and, after all, so unsatisfactory, in clearing up the romantic mysteries of a story. He is too wise to insist upon looking closely at the wrong side of the tapestry, after the right one has been sufficiently displayed to him, woven with the best of the artist's skill, and cunningly arranged with a view to the harmonious exhibition of its colours. If any brilliant or beautiful, or even tolerable, effect have been produced, this pattern of kindly Readers will accept it at its worth, without tearing the web apart, with the idle purpose of discovering how its threads have been knit together; for the sagacity, by which he is distinguished, will long ago have taught him that any narrative of human action and adventure—whether we call it history or romance—is certain to be a fragile handiwork, more easily rent than mended. The actual experience of even the most ordinary life is full of events that never explain themselves, either as regards their origin or their tendency. (1232)

The narrator may speak of the reader here in the third person and in an ideal sense, but the address of his appeal seems unmistakable—and no less so its aim: to cajole or maneuver the *actual* reader into the position of his "kindly" and "gentle" *ideal* reader. As the text makes plain, he wishes to get them to bear beyond the conclusion of the text the absences or the abyss that have characterized the romance from its very beginning. It's as if, in an almost literal way, he wants them to carry away "that indefinable nothing, that inestimable something" that distinguishes true art from the counterfeit (901). The essential, inestimable "something" about Hawthorne's final romance, then, emerges as an enigmatic, indefinable "nothing" that is urged upon the reader in the form of the persistent gaps, absences, and enigmatic elements of the unexplained and unknowable. Paradoxically, the "sagacity" of the wise reader thus consists in accepting the *lack* of elucidation and resting in an obscure state of *non*-understanding.

It would seem, however, that the narrator's words did not easily find the wise and gentle reader to whom they were addressed. Despite the fact that the chapter gives some very basic answers—we learn, for example, that Hilda (now released from her captivity) accepts Kenyon's proposal of marriage, that they intend to return to their native land, that Donatello is absent and that Miriam evidently awaits him while performing her penance in Rome—despite these answers, "everybody" complained of the ending as it stood at the conclusion of chapter 50.[10] And indeed, there is not much resolution to be had here. The chapter concludes with still *more* questions, leaving the reader, as ever, suspended before the abyss and with only the least trace of hope, as Hilda briefly ponders the future in the closing lines of the romance: "What was Miriam's life to be? And where was Donatello? But Hilda had a hopeful soul, and saw sunlight on the mountain-tops" (1238).

Those were to be the last sentences of *The Marble Faun*, and they were in fact the final sentences in its initial publication. However, Hawthorne's hopes for a kindly reader who would receive his work with indulgence and comprehension were very quickly disappointed and, from the demands of reader correspondence and early reviews, he felt compelled to add a postscript to later editions. The four-page postscript he reluctantly appended, however, only underlines the force of his earlier warning against the lack of satisfaction to be found in elucidations of the mysteries of a romance. While the postscript indeed "answers" several of the most pressing questions—yes, there's reason to believe that Miriam had family connections in the papal government, and yes, Hilda was held captive by the church—yet still it yields but little satisfaction. It is worth asking why this must be so. Certainly it is true that Hawthorne's postscript is uncharacteristically testy in its tone and refuses full disclosure. The answers he consents to give are brief and don't very "minutely" elucidate much of what we thought we wanted to know. Miriam's past crime, for example, her true identity, and the nature of the deal she made in exchange for the release of Hilda are left fully as enigmatic as ever. But can we really say that the lack of satisfaction offered by the postscript is really owing to its insufficient particularity? Perhaps, to the contrary, the failure of the postscript awakens the reader to the sense that the fascinating element of the romance—its disquietude at the limit of existence, its suspension before the face of time and death, its indefinable nothing—has all along been beyond the order of representation and must remain untouched by such answers as are offered at the conclusion of the novel. We are left with the sense that our suppositions of a sordid crime and a Vatican conspiracy—while perhaps justified within the terms of Hawthorne's narrative world—were nevertheless not the answer to the real question put to us by the text. That question remains, and remains untouched by the supposed revelations of the postscript.

The "real" ethical question posed of the reader lies instead, as we shall see, embedded within the structure of the novel's address. Ordinarily, when words are addressed to a person, implicit in the structure of the event is an obligation to respond on the part of the addressee. The addressee is obliged, for example, to act, to assent, to reply, to understand, to acknowledge, or to respond by doing something else of the kind. In this call for response, every address is in a certain sense also a question: *How will you respond?* When one reads that

> in the distance, you behold the obelisks, with their unintelligible inscriptions, hinting at a Past infinitely more remote than history can define. Your own life is as nothing, when compared with that immeasurable distance,

one responds properly by allowing the obelisks to appear before one's imagination and by suffering in consequence a state of feeling where one's own life recedes toward nothingness. Or when we read, in a somewhat less direct address, that "[t]he gentle reader, we trust, would not thank us for one of those minute elucidations . . . ," again we feel ourselves under obligation to respond, this time by placing ourselves in the position of the ideal gentle reader and by foregoing the desired revelation. But the more we consider the position of this *ideal* reader and the abyss that separates this position from that of any *actual* reader, the more complex and revealing becomes the problem of address and reader responsibility in Hawthorne's final romance.

This problem comes more clearly into view when one juxtaposes the failure at the end of the romance with the preface briefly considered at the start of the present essay. The necessity Hawthorne evidently felt to add the Postscript confirms the failure of his plea for the reader to forego elucidation. But that failure of address, one might argue, is due less to readerly obtuseness (as the narrator would have it) than to a structural impossibility in the situation of the reader. The address, in short, was destined to fail from the very beginning, as we might recall from the Preface:

> Unquestionably, this Gentle, Kind, Benevolent, Indulgent, and most Beloved and Honoured Reader, did once exist for me, and (in spite of the infinite chances against a letter's reaching its destination, without a definite address) duly received the scrolls which I flung upon whatever wind was blowing, in the faith that they would find him out. But, is he extant now? In these many years, since he last heard from me, may he not have deemed his earthly task accomplished, and have withdrawn to the Paradise of Gentle Readers, wherever it may be? . . . I have a sad foreboding, that this may be the truth. . . . If I find him at all, it will probably be under some mossy grave-stone, inscribed with a half-obliterated name, which I shall never recognize. (853–54)

The writer has placed his reader in an impossible position all along. Even though the actual reader is living and reading the narrative in the present time, all the text conspires against this position proper to the reader, and attempts instead to coerce the reader into occupying the position of the dead, a place in the past. While the structure of address is thus indeed in place, calling upon the actual reader to respond, the ideal reader has nevertheless been situated in the place of no response. The reader, then, is split between two times: the *present* of responsibility—given that one is actually reading—and the *past* of no response—given that the "most Beloved" reader (with whom one is obliged to identify) reads from the position of the dead. Thus, the ideal (dead) reader will *not* thank the author for an explanation, will *not* insist at looking at the wrong side of things, will *not* tear the fabric of the tapestry, and so forth, but the actual reader cannot bear the impossibility of responding—cannot bear the impossibility of, for example, straining to give one's understanding to the text. Hawthorne seems to be asking for a radical passivity in which the ethical reader will take the romance and "accept it at its worth," a worth that requires one to suffer the unintelligibility beyond meaning which addresses the subject across an abyss of time. Not every reader will submit to such terms.

We see that, in a certain sense, Miriam and the reader face the same problem: they are both obliged by external forces—Miriam's pertinacious Model, the crushing weight of Rome, the sublime unintelligibility of the obelisks, Hawthorne's own gap-riven text—to bear a singular relation to the void of the real—that is, to the limits of mortal life and death, the abysses of time and address, and the complex nature of an ethical responsibility that does not present itself as such to an autonomous, thinking subject. Against this void and its very profound sense of enigma and unknowablility, there is an almost irresistible, all too human tendency to retreat from the relation to the real into the familiarity of the quotidian and the comforts of convention—to retreat, in other words, to the illusive stage-scenery of everyday life that Miriam once saw through. If Hawthorne's narrator seeks to coerce his reader into occupying an impossible position between the living and the dead, if he urges his reader to forego the comforts and conventions of pulp mysteries, if he forces an uncanny and alienating truth upon the reader, then one might reasonably hope that he would forgive this same reader for failures of ethical heroism, given that Miriam, too, forsakes the real for the more easily borne weight of conventional moral sin and its narrative of potential redemption.[11]

Our next chapter will turn to Alain Badiou, a contemporary philosopher who tries to develop, more explicitly and more thematically than Hawthorne's romance could, a true ethics capable of contending with the unintelligible void.

CHAPTER 7

Riven

Badiou's Ethical Subject and the Event of Art as Trauma

"Can we be delivered, *finally* delivered, from our subjection to Romanticism?" asks the French philosopher Alain Badiou (b. 1937), with an evident sigh.[1] A peculiar question, it would seem, for an epoch often eager to declare itself at once post-Romantic and postmodern. For Badiou, however, Romanticism denotes not a historical moment now long past, but a philosophical gesture whose reach extends through both analytic and continental philosophy as well as through contemporary theory: an almost fatal and complete "disentanglement" of philosophy from mathematics,[2] coupled with the rise of the "age of the poets," wherein philosophy was sutured to *art* as the only possible "body of truth."[3] For the first tendency, Badiou cites G. W. F. Hegel; for the second, Friedrich Nietzsche and especially Martin Heidegger, its acme. We should not misinterpret Badiou's sigh, however. When he seeks to overcome Romanticism through the reengagement of philosophy with mathematics and set theory, when he seeks to desacralize the Romantics' Infinite through its mathematization, he is not thereby seeking to bury Romanticism's rediscovery of poetry as a mode of thinking. Certainly it is true that Badiou's project strives to re-entangle philosophy and mathematical ontology.[4] He succeeds, I think, and in this respect, Badiou may indeed be said to have overcome Romanticism. Nevertheless, as we shall also see, poetry is essential to Badiou's thinking of truth and remains at the very heart of his project, whether he is writing of mathematics or Mallarmé, ethics or aesthetics. So, while Badiou would contest any claim that poetry *alone* has a purchase on truth, in important ways his own project reaffirms the Romantic schema in art: poetry and truth are not to be disentangled. One term implies the other.

My aim here is not to elaborate a full philosophical description of Badiou's relation to Romanticism—Justin Clemens has already begun such work in his admirable book on the Romanticism of contemporary theory. Nor do I wish to quibble over the use or usefulness of "Romanticism" as a label to describe a historical tendency of thought. Rather, what I would like to do in the present essay is to trace out a series of propositions concerning art, ethics, and subjectivity, which do in fact derive from the Romantics and which Badiou places at the heart of his own project. Badiou is important to considerations of art, ethics, and subjectivity, because, among other reasons, his work stands as the most serious effort by a dedicated philosopher to develop a philosophy consistent with the fundamental insights of Lacanian psychoanalysis.[5] As our guiding thread, we will follow the way Badiou uses *trauma*, conceived in a Lacanian sense, as a trope in thinking about art and its relation to ethics. Thus, my discussion broaches two key questions: In what way does it make sense for Badiou to think of the event of art in terms of trauma, and, furthermore, what does this imply for the nature of ethics in Badiou's philosophy? We shall begin with a general consideration of art and ethics derived primarily from two of Badiou's books of the 1990s: his *Ethics* (1993) and his *Handbook of Inaesthetics* (1998). As we move further into Badiou's thought, we will turn to two somewhat earlier writings, to *Being and Event* (1988) and to a 1989 essay on Beckett, in order to highlight why trauma was a useful trope for Badiou in particular—that is, for a post-Heideggerian, post-Lacanian thinker informed by set theory and striving for a post-Romantic philosophy of the event. As we will see, the matter is an interesting one not only for how it opens up Badiou's description of an ethic of art, but also for suggesting a larger trend in the history of aesthetics since the Romantics that locates the force of art as bearing upon a traumatic subjectivity—a force thus at once ethical and existential.

Finally, Badiou is often positioned, by himself and by others, as a thinker at odds with the mainstream of continental and Anglo-American thought. This he certainly is in many respects—as in his remarkably compelling elaboration of set theory as the cornerstone of his philosophy. But, if we trace out the logic of his tropes, we are reminded that he is, after all, situated within a tradition of thinking about art, ethics, and subjectivity—whatever we might wish to call this tradition, whether Romantic or post-Romantic, Lacanian or post-Lacanian, Heideggerian or post-Heideggerian—and that he shares certain strands of this tradition not only with his older contemporaries such as Emmanuel Levinas, Maurice Blanchot, and Jacques Derrida, but also with thinkers at the origin of Romantic thought: Friedrich Schiller, Friedrich Schlegel, Percy Shelley, Ralph Waldo Emerson, and others.

The Event of Art: The Hole of Truth and the Punctured Subject

We will begin, then, with Badiou's conception of the work of art. Despite the several novels and plays he has written,[6] it is evident that Badiou's ultimate commitment is to philosophy, so it is not altogether surprising that for him, as for Heidegger and many other philosophers, *art* is a matter of *truth*. Badiou, however, has a rather idiosyncratic notion of "truth," and since it refers neither to the veridicality of propositions nor to Heidegger's *aletheia*, this claim requires a little unpacking.

Badiou opposes what he calls "truth" to the domain of objectivity and ordinary knowledge. Indeed, truth, in the very essence of its operation, "constitutes a *hole* [*un trou*] in forms of knowledge," as he puts it in several places,[7] and he associates it with the Lacanian real. Thus, truth, for Badiou, is the name of an exceptional event[8] and a process that forces a break with the everyday course of knowledges and situations and consequently brings into being a "subject" where there was formerly just a human animal, a mere inhabitant of a given situation. We will consider some of Badiou's examples or images later, but for now let us note that a truth in the first instance is an event, a flash, an irreducible singularity, and then subsequently is marked by the continued fidelity of the subject who constitutes the site of that truth. This second moment of the truth, the fidelity, is understood as a continuing commitment by the subject to bear witness to the event that was its first moment and to relate henceforth to his or her particular situation from the perspective of that event, to think according to its radical truth, and to invent, in consequence, a new way of being and acting in the situation (*L'éthique* 61f, 41e). It is a crucial point for Badiou: for him, truth is productive, inventive, creative, anticonservative;[9] it is "the coming-to-be of that which is not yet" (*L'éthique* 45f, 27e).

There are, for Badiou, four fundamental procedures of truths: art, science, politics, and love. Or, to put it more in terms more typical for Badiou: the poem, the matheme, the politics of emancipation, and the encounter with the disjunction of sexuation (*Conditions* 79f, *Manifeste* 141e). Badiou gives a number of images of an event of truth, and these help illuminate the matter. In the *Ethics* book, his favored examples of such events in art come from the history of music and, less frequently, from theatrical experience. Elsewhere, he writes of modern poets, from Hölderlin, to Mallarmé, to Pessoa and Celan. But in the *Ethics* book, he returns repeatedly to Haydn's invention of the classical musical style and in discussing it, he remarks that it is characteristic of any event of truth that it

> is both *situated*—it is the event of this or that situation—and *supplementary*, thus absolutely detached from, or unrelated to, all the rules of the situation. Hence the emergence of the classical style, with Haydn . . . concerns the musical situation and no other, a situation then governed by the predominance of the baroque style. It was an event for this situation. But in another sense, what this event was to authorize in terms of musical configurations was not comprehensible from within the plenitude achieved by the baroque style; it really was a matter of *something else*.
>
> You might then ask what it is that makes the connection between the event and that "for which" it is an event. This connection is the void [*le vide*] of the earlier situation. What does this mean? It means that at the heart of every situation, as the foundation of its being, there is a "situated" void, around which is organized the plenitude (or the stable multiples) of the situation in question. Thus at the heart of the baroque style at its virtuoso saturation lay the absence [*vide*] (as decisive as it was unnoticed) of a genuine conception of musical architecture. The Haydn-event occurs as a kind of musical "naming" of this absence [*vide*]. For what constitutes the event is nothing less than a wholly new architectonic and thematic principle, a new way of developing musical writing from the basis of a few transformable units—which was precisely what, from within the baroque style, could not be perceived (there could be no knowledge of it). (*L'éthique* 92–93f, 68–69e)

The Haydn-event, as Badiou calls it, inaugurated the configuration of classical style, from Haydn himself through to its saturation point with Beethoven; it inaugurated a truth that, whether consciously or subconsciously, whether more or less articulately, befell the composer in the first instance, and then also listeners and subsequent composers who had been likewise situated within the baroque, but who thereafter found themselves seized by this same revolutionary truth concerning musical architecture as the hitherto unnamable vanishing point or void of the baroque. It is a "truth," precisely, in that this truth of the Haydn-event is the same for all, even as it unfolds or proceeds within differing particular compositions or performances of music. Within a given situation (and all truths are so situated), there is no one truth for person α and a different truth for person β. For that matter, within a given situation, there is no one truth for culture γ and a different truth for culture δ. And, yet again, there is no objective truth out there in the world, waiting to be discovered by any who would see it. As the Haydn example illustrates, truth is an event that proceeds *in* a given situation (*L'éthique* 63f, 42e), here the symbolic field of the musical baroque, but this truth is the *same* truth for all who bear witness to it (*L'éthique* 46f, 27e).

For Badiou, this event of truth implies an ethics in the way it calls upon the subject whom it befalls to continue to bear witness to this truth by engaging one's life, one's decisions, and one's existence, in a continuing reinterpretation that is through this event and according to its truth. Badiou refers to this second moment in the process of a truth as a *fidelity*. "To be faithful to an event," he writes, "is to move within the situation that this event has supplemented, by *thinking* . . . the situation 'according to' the event" (*L'éthique* 62f, 41e). Alban Berg and Anton Webern, to take another of Badiou's examples, were faithful to the event that was Arnold Schoenberg's invention of the twelve-tone technique in musical composition. Thus, they "[could] not continue with *fin-de-siècle* neo-Romanticism as if nothing had happened" (*L'éthique* 62f, 42e). Likewise, as he also notes, much contemporary art music really constitutes a fidelity to the great Viennese composers of the early twentieth century. The fidelity, in which the subject continues the truth process beyond its initial event, accepting the obligation "to *invent* a new way of being and acting in the situation" (*L'éthique* 62f, 42e), is the ethical decision to which the subject must continually commit him- or herself (or not).

The course of an artistic truth thus has three moments. The first moment is the inaugural event of art, which then, in the second moment, persists through the choice of continuing, in the subject's fidelity to the event. The truth comes to an end, in the third moment, only when its configuration has become saturated and it has exhausted its own infinity, as Badiou puts it (*Petit Manuel* 89f, 56e). In the exhaustion of a truth, its component works succeed less and less in inquiring into the truth in which they themselves participate. A configuration, as he puts it in his *Handbook of Inaesthetics*, "thinks itself in the works that compose it" (*Petit Manuel* 28f, 14e)[10] and when it ceases to think itself, when its component works no longer succeed in inventively inquiring into the procedure of that configuration, then that truth comes to a certain end.

What I especially want to highlight here in Badiou's description of the event and process of a truth, and in the ethic of truths that follows from it, is the position of the subject,[11] who, we might say, is called upon to dwell with a trauma. Committing oneself to Schoenberg's tonal innovations may not seem such an onerous ethical calling, and hardly traumatic in the everyday sense, but we might recall that truth, for Badiou, is essentially a hole. It pierces a given order of knowledge, as we have said, but, to those who are faithful to it, it pierces them too. Someone who bears witness to an event of truth can, for example, "be *this* spectator whose thinking has been set in motion, who has been seized and bewildered by a burst of theatrical fire [*un éclat théâtral*], and who thus enters into the complex configuration of a moment of art" (*L'éthique* 66f, 45e).

The subject's seizure in the work of art is an old theme for philosophy, but here there is no repose, no lingering in the restful contemplation of the beautiful, no subjective harmony as in Kant's third critique.[12] Instead, our spectator has been seized and bewildered by—what?—a burst of theatrical fire (!), and thereby enters into the complex configuration of a moment of art. Theatre spectators on the edge of their seats, he writes,

> demonstrate a prodigious interest in what they are doing—in the advent of the not-known Immortal in them, in the advent of that which they did not know themselves capable of. Nothing in the world could arouse the intensity of existence more than this actor who lets me encounter Hamlet. . . . Nevertheless, as regards my interests as a mortal and predatory animal, what is happening here does not concern me; no knowledge tells me that these circumstances have anything to do with me. I am altogether present there, linking my component elements via that *excess beyond myself* induced by the passing through me of a truth. But as a result, I am also suspended, broken, annulled, dis-interested [*suspendu, rompu, révoqué: dés-intéressé*]. For I cannot, within the fidelity to fidelity that defines ethical consistency, take an interest in myself, and thus pursue my own interests. All my capacity for interest, which is my own perseverance in being, has *poured out* . . . into what I will make of my encounter, one night, with the eternal Hamlet. (*L'éthique* 71–72f, 49–50e)

In Badiou's theatergoing subject above, we see a curious tension between, on the one hand, the subject's being "altogether present" in a way that seems familiar to Romantic and Heideggerian thinking about the promise of art, and, on the other hand, in the very same moment, the subject's being "suspended, broken, annulled, dis-interested"—and, earlier, "*riven*, or punctured [*imperceptiblement et intérieurement* rompu, *ou troué*]" (*L'éthique* 67f, 46e; Badiou's emphasis). For Badiou the subject is, in the very instant of the its coming to be, already in "eclipse," as if the subject itself, in the event of art, were to appear essentially in the flicker of its own vanishing or void. Thus, a poem, for example, summons one—but summons one to give oneself over to, or dispose oneself to, *its* poetic operations and it commits one to think according to *its* thought, instead of according to the pursuit of one's own interest (*Petit Manuel* 51f, 29e). Thus, the reader of a poem, as he writes in relation to Celan, must "will his or her own transliteration" (*Petit Manuel* 58f, 34e), as if the letters of one's aesthetic subjectivity, the "letters of one's body," as Willy Apollon calls it,[13] were to be offered up to the event and cast into a foreign idiom. For Badiou, the fidelity to the event may involve a conscious willing, but the first instance of the truth event seems distinctly traumatic in his trope. "To enter into the composition of a subject of truth," as he puts it, "can only be something that *befalls you*" (*L'éthique* 74f, 51e; trans. modified). Insofar as the will may later enter into Badiou's ethics, fidelity is a commitment, whether knowingly or unknowingly, to sustain oneself in a certain relation to that originary traumatic eclipse of the subject.

A Thing of Nothing: Ethics and the Phantom Excess

To be clear, "trauma" is not a word Badiou himself employs; as we have seen, he uses an array of others to describe his subject—riven, punctured, ruptured, severed, broken, annulled, and so forth. These terms, if we consider them in a Lacanian register, suggest physical trauma in the "imaginary" sense of the *corps morcelé*, the fragmented body that implies a notion of trauma as a sort of mirror-stage in reverse. But how, more precisely, do these tropes, which we group under the rubric of *trauma*, bear upon Badiou's theory of the *subject*, especially upon the subject in the event of *art*—and why does it make sense to place all of this under the heading of *ethics*? The answers have something to do with the theoretical edifice elaborated by Jacques Lacan, who is significant for Badiou for four principal reasons: for initiating a modern thinking of love,[14] for insisting on the importance of the category of the subject in philosophical thought (*Manifeste* 24f, 44e), for developing a conception of the real at the heart of human subjectivity,[15] and for repeatedly asserting that mathematics is the science of the real (*Conditions* 185f; *Theoretical Writings* 107). We will see that insofar as Badiou develops his theory of the subject consistent with the Lacanian subject instituted through trauma, for Badiou, the stakes of this "trauma" will ultimately be read not in the imaginary, but at the limit of the symbolic and the real. But let us approach these questions of the subject and what we are calling trauma a little more deliberately, since Badiou is approaching these matters not from the exigencies of the analytic clinic, but rather from the interest of philosophy—and specifically of a very particular philosophy grounded in mathematical set theory.

We can begin by considering more carefully and more particularly the structure of the subject implied by Badiou's description of the theatergoer who encounters in Hamlet both the utmost intensity of existence as well as, in the same instant, a certain annulment. As Schoenberg was an event for composers and audiences of the late Romantic style typified by Mahler, Hamlet may equally be considered an event in the history of literature—for example by demonstrating the possibility of a modern, post-Attic tragedy, or by turning to national or nonclassical sources as fit topics for tragedy, or by more explicitly locating the real event of the play in the obscure existential drama of a character's deepest interior. But, as we saw in Badiou's description, Hamlet is also, at the same time, an event situated within an I—that is, within Badiou's theatergoer in his or her particularity:

> I am altogether present there [*Je suis là tout entier*], linking my component elements via that *excess beyond myself* [*l'excès sur moi-même*] induced by the passing through me of a truth. But as a result, I am also suspended, broken, annulled, dis-interested. For I cannot, within the fidelity to fidelity that defines ethical consistency, take an interest in myself, and thus pursue my own interests. All my capacity for interest, which is my own perseverance in being, has *poured out* . . . into what I will make of my encounter, one night, with the eternal Hamlet. (*L'éthique* 71–72f, 49–50e)

Structurally speaking, the key aesthetic event for Badiou here is an encounter between, on the one hand, the presence and finite "altogetherness" enjoyed by the theatergoer, wherein his or her component elements are linked into One, and, on the other hand, an excess beyond this altogetherness, the infinity of the eternal Hamlet, that passes through the subject, annuls the theatergoer in his or her situation, and demands some kind of accounting of what the subject will "make of the encounter." Is there not something paradoxical about this altogetherness which encounters an excess beyond itself—for how can someone be, precisely, *all*-together, if there is some other element that remains in excess of the *all*?

Badiou's *Being and Event* (1988) is devoted to a much more technical and complete description of "situations" generally and, by implication, of the seemingly paradoxical structure of the situation in which the theatergoer's encounter with Hamlet takes place. We might take the theatergoing individual him- or herself as a "situation," a structured whole composed of a set of component elements or terms: here, especially, the particulars of one's history, one's sense for family and romantic obligations, one's taste, one's regard for literary and theatrical history, one's openness on a given night to the drama of Shakespeare's *Hamlet*, and a whole multiplicity of other elements chance has thrown together. Any or all of these elements may be highly complex, but they are "consistent" in the sense that, however complex they may be, they are included in how one represents oneself to oneself (in what Badiou calls "the state"), or, more basically, they simply belong to one's situation, present but prior to any question of representation. They compose that of which the situation consists. One's taste, for example, may be composed of a vast array of sometimes-conflicting influences and voices coming from one's culture, one's circle of friends, one's reading, the quirks of one's personal history, both conscious and subconscious, and so forth. Whatever their origins and however internally incoherent they may be, they are all counted as being situated in the theatergoer as elements of his or her own taste. In this sense, the situation is defined by its *all*, the Oneness of one's multifarious elements. Moreover, each of these elements, insofar as it counts as belonging to the situation, has been acted upon by some kind of a logic, a regime or rule that produces the situation by determining what counts as belonging to it. By contrast, the occurrence of an *event*, which in Badiou's sense is always an event *for a given situation*, poses the question of what lies outside the jurisdiction of this regime, when, according to the law of the situation, everything that counts, everything presentable, lies within it—hence its Oneness, its all-togetherness as we have called it.

Badiou argues that, in an event such as the event of art (or science, or politics, or love), the Oneness of the situation is indeed disrupted by some unpresentable, supplementary *thing* that, within the law of the situation, counts as no-thing. Intriguingly, Badiou also claims, in *Being and Event*, that this void, or "nothing" of the situation, lies at the very heart of poetic movement in particular as a kind of impasse or impossibility:

> Naturally, it would be pointless to set off in search of the nothing. Yet it must be said that this is exactly what poetry exhausts itself in doing. . . . [P]oetry propagates the idea of an intuition of the nothing in which being would reside when there is not even the site for such intuition . . . because everything is consistent. The only thing we can affirm is this: every situation implies the nothing of its all. But the nothing is neither a place nor a term of the situation. For if the nothing were a term that could only mean one thing; that it had been counted as one. Yet everything which has been counted is within the consistency of presentation. It is thus ruled out that the nothing . . . be taken as a term. There is not a-nothing, there is "nothing" [*Il n'y a pas un-rien, il y a « rien »*], phantom of inconsistency. (*L'être* 67–68f, 54–55e)

While every situation "implies the nothing of its all," the situation itself cannot, by definition, provide a way to bring this void point into knowledge, since there is no consistency to the void of the real, and since even intuition lies under the rule of the situation which, by definition, has no law capable of discerning (or "counting") anything in excess of itself. In the face of this encounter with alterity, poetry since the Romantics has been driven to say what cannot in fact be said, to present what cannot in fact be presented—as if, impossibly, a fullness of being might be approached, the phantom of inconsistency banished, by causing the indiscernible "nothing" supplementary to the situation to assume a visible consistency.

This, then, is what justifies the term *traumatic* as a general trope for Badiou's description of the ethical subject in the event of art. It is not just that the coherence of the situation is punctured or riven by something radically alterior to itself, something that threatens to undermine or reorganize the entire configuration of the existing situation—this might be a commonsensical, imaginary description of trauma—but that this radical alterity constitutes a real hole in the order of language. Indeed, from a Lacanian perspective, Badiou's event is precisely "traumatic" insofar as it marks an encounter with the irreducible real at the heart of the signifier and the symbolic order.[16] Badiou's "nothing" or void assumed by the subject shares a number of key structural features with Lacan's concept of the traumatic encounter with the real: its "extimacy" to the subject, its essential resistance to signification, and its radical potential for introducing something new. Lacan's real is located in "extimate" relation[17] to the subject (*Le Séminaire VII*, 167f, 139e) in that the real is at once situated as the "traumatic nucleus" governing the syntax of the subject (*Le Séminaire XI* 66f, 68e), utterly interior and intimate to it, and, at the same time, radically supplementary, that is, exterior and excluded from it. So when, in his *Ethics* seminar, Lacan describes that which, in the real, suffers from the signifier (150f, 125e), he situates it "at the center precisely in the sense that it is excluded . . . strange to me while being at the heart of this 'me' " (87f, 71e; my translation). Moreover, because the real as such cannot be assimilated to the order of the signifier (*Le Séminaire XI* 55f, 55e), the "trauma" of an encounter with the real is witnessed precisely in its "opacity" and its "resistance to signification" (*Le Séminaire XI* 118f, 129e). Finally, due to the very fact that the real constitutes an impasse in the logic of the signifier, the encounter with the real "admits something new, which is precisely the impossible" (*Le Séminaire XI* 152f, 167e)—admits, that is, something impossible in the order of the signifier as it has hitherto been governed. For these reasons, surely, and perhaps others, Badiou himself describes, at the heart of his event of art, an ethic of a truth that is also, in a precise Lacanian sense, "an ethic of the real" (*L'éthique* 74f, 52e).[18]

Badiou is not, ordinarily, one to follow philosophical trends that place language per se at the center of philosophical inquiry, but there seems no way to escape this problem of language in thinking the event. One believes that there has been an event, that something new has happened, that there *is* something beyond the One of the situation, and yet, from within the horizon of the situation where one discerns, thinks, and speaks, one cannot place a true proper name to the event, one can only surmise an appropriate "generic" procedure that would faithfully work to incorporate the event into the situation, and even the particular nature of this "something new" remains yet indiscernible:

> [A] subject, which realizes a truth, is nevertheless incommensurable with the latter, because the subject is finite, and the truth is infinite. Moreover, the subject, being internal to the situation, can only know, or rather encounter terms or multiples presented (counted as one) in the situation. Yet the truth is an un-presented part of the situation. Finally, the subject cannot make a language out of anything except combinations of the supernumerary name of the event and the language of the situation. It is in no way guaranteed that this language will suffice for the discernment of a truth, which, in any case, is indiscernible for the resources of the language of the situation alone. It is absolutely necessary to abandon any definition of the subject which supposes that it knows the truth, or that it is adjusted to the truth. Being the local

> moment of the truth, the subject falls short of supporting the latter's global sum. Every truth is transcendent to the subject, precisely because the latter's entire being resides in supporting the realization of the truth. The subject is neither conscious nor unconscious of the true.
>
> The singular relation of the subject to the truth whose procedure it supports is the following: the subject believes that there is a truth, and this belief occurs in the form of a knowledge [*un savoir*]. I term this knowing belief *confidence.* (*L'être* 434–35f, 396–97e)

The subject is called upon to support the realization of a truth. He or she has "confidence" that there *is* in fact a truth and that something new *has* happened in the situation. But, from the standpoint of the situation itself, the subject can speak only a kind of nonsense in relation to this event, knitting together a language out of existing, inadequate terms of the situation and "the supernumerary name of the event." The name of the event, "Hamlet" in our example, or "Schoenberg," is supernumerary in the sense that it has no conceptual referent within the situation. Of course, Hamlet, as a proper name, designates a Danish prince, a character, and a play (to say nothing here of Hamlet's phantom father), but it is also used antonomastically to refer to an event—yet this it does in the most nebulous fashion, as if "Hamlet" were neither name nor signifier, but a kind of conceptless signifier-surrogate used to indicate the whatever-it-was-that-happened one night at the theater. Likewise, "Schoenberg" may be used as an antonomasia for innovations in musical composition such as atonality, dodecaphony, and serialism, which may in turn be more precisely described, but fidelity to the truth of the "Schoenberg event" surely exceeds the instance of even its inventor, running its course through Olivier Messiaen, Pierre Boulez, and György Ligeti, to younger and more recent composers such as Kaija Saariaho, Erkki-Sven Tüür, and Helena Tulve—each of whom has departed from anything like atonal, twelve-tone, or serialist orthodoxies, while still, arguably, being faithful to the Schoenberg event and, certainly, committed to composing within a tonal space made possible by Schoenberg's work. In this sense, "Schoenberg," too, is used in place of a signifier to indicate the nebulous whatever-it-was-that-happened to the tonal system in classical composition with the appearance of *Pierrot Lunaire* (1913). These names, Hamlet and Schoenberg, together with the signifiers one associates with them, strive to refer to something that exceeds the situation. In order to do so, the subject must rework or redirect existing terms to "*displace* established significations" and thereby support a truth for a situation that at present cannot discern it (*L'être* 437f, 399e). If, for Badiou, a truth makes a hole in knowledge, it likewise marks a babble-point in relation to the present possible language of the situation.

The fidelity of the subject, then, is exposed to chance, grounded in nothing, unsupported by knowledge, and nonsensical to the eyes and ears of outsiders. It calls for a decision to commit to an interpretation of an event and it requires the ethical subject to assume a course of action (a "procedure") faithful to that event from among choices that, within the best knowledge of the situation, are strictly undecidable. This is true because, from within the situation where he or she is located, the subject has no recognized way to decide whether there has even been an event, no way to adjudicate whether one interpretation of the event (supposing there to have been one) is superior to another, and no way to judge with certainty whether a given procedure is a proper and faithful response to the event that the subject supposes took place.[19] In the face of such a differend, then, one commits oneself on a chance, a wager, and, like Badiou's Mallarmé, casts one's die. As Badiou writes,

> If poetry is an essential use of language, it is not because it is able to devote the latter [language] to Presence; on the contrary, it is because it trains language to the paradoxical function of maintaining that which—radically singular, pure action—would otherwise fall back into the nullity of place. Poetry is the stellar assumption [*l'assomption stellaire*][20] of that pure undecidable, against a background of nothingness, that is an action of which one can only *know* whether it has taken place inasmuch as one *bets* upon its truth. (*L'être* 213–14f, 192e)

Against Heidegger's nostalgia for lost presence, and surpassing the presence and altogetherness of his own theatergoer, Badiou asserts that poetry and art find their true and ethical task in supporting a pure action: the coming into being of a subject and, with it, the truth that occasions the subject. Poetry is itself, in the poet as in the reader, the casting of a die among undecidables, set against a background of nothingness. Hence, *poetry* is intimately aligned with the *subject*, which Badiou defines as "that which decides an undecidable from the standpoint of an indiscernible" (*L'être* 445f, 407e) and with *ethics*, which, similarly, comes down to an imperative: "Decide from the standpoint of the undecidable" (*L'être* 219–20f, 197e).

In his *Ethics* book, Badiou gives his ethical imperative a more Lacanian ring. Lacan's "ethics of psychoanalysis" is well known, both through his great 1959–1960 seminar of that name and through the writings of the brilliant philosopher and critic Slavoj Žižek, who has recurred to it throughout his career.[21] Lacan formulates his ethical dictum with a characteristic, concentrated simplicity: *do not cede ground on your desire* (*Le Séminaire VII*, 368f, 319e; my translation). For Lacan, this ethics bears upon symptom formation: giving up on one's desire, forsaking this one Good, produces the Evil of symptoms and the insistence of death in the body. In his own *Ethics* book, Badiou echoes Lacan, his "master" as he calls him (*L'éthique* 121e), when he articulates his own ethic of truth as *do all that you can to persevere in that which exceeds your perseverance. Persevere in the interruption. Seize in your being that which has seized and broken you* (*L'éthique* 69f, 47e). Both Lacan's ethic of psychoanalysis and Badiou's own ethic of truth, as we have seen, are an ethics of the real and call for a certain persistence in one's relation to that real. Truth and ethics bear upon a certain relation with the real of language: the indiscernible truth of music beyond musical syntax, the unnamable truth of a poem beyond communication and hermeneutic concerns of reference and interpretation. This truth event, which has broken and seized the subject, requires the subject to commit to a decision regarding what cannot be decided, articulated, or known. One must give oneself over to the event, contend with the situational anxiety of the void, and persevere in this relation to chance and the real. And if, through this process, one is obliged to cast one's lot with something that ruptures the very situation in which one lives, this is surely all well and good for a philosopher who, after all, defines the Good as "the internal norm of a prolonged disorganization of life" (*L'éthique* 82f, 60e).

Badiou on Levinas, Love, and the Poetic Naming of Ethics

Badiou's use of trauma as a trope aligns him not only with Lacan's ethics of the real, as we have just seen, but also, to a more limited extent, with the work of Emmanuel Levinas, who in his late years often also employed trauma as a trope for describing the ethical encounter with the face of the Other.[22] Badiou's own thinking of ethics arrives at a moment when the conceptualization of ethics in the academy has been brought decisively under Levinas's name, first through the sponsorship of Jacques Derrida, Luce Irigaray, and Jean-François Lyotard, and then through its appropriation by the rhetoric of contemporary multiculturalist politics. The *Ethics* book is evidently among Badiou's best-selling volumes and clearly his most sustained statement on ethics, and, though he might there seem to claim a counter-Levinasian position, in actual fact, the polemical thrust of that book belies his closeness to the Jewish thinker. Even in the *Ethics* book, his brief account of Levinasian ethics as an ethics of difference, or an ethics of the other, stands as a moment of scrupulous care and respect, before he turns to address the misappropriation of Levinasian thought by multiculturalism, which, Badiou argues, is committed to a conventional conception of "otherness," one cast in ethnographic or demographic terms, rather than in properly phenomenological terms (or pre-phenomenological terms, one might say), as with Levinas. One might think, for example, of Levinas's claim that "the best way of encountering the Other is not even to notice the color of his eyes" (Levinas. *Éthique* 79f, 85e). If Levinas's philosophy describes an encounter with alterity that takes no account of eye color, then presumably, by extension, it likewise has no commitment to the basic categories—race, class, sexuality, and gender—within which multiculturalism typically situates its elements. Later, when Badiou highlights (and distances himself from) Levinas's theological grounding of the ethical alterity of the other in the infinite alterity of God, still, his pique lies with what he sees as the easy moralism of multiculturalist ideologues and the fashion they have made of the "ethics of the other" as, precisely, a pious discourse divorced from true, Levinasian piety (*L'éthique* 41f, 23e). In short, Badiou's reader must make a careful distinction between his polemical adversaries in the *Ethics* book, since his true quarrel lies elsewhere than with the "coherent and inventive" (40f, 23e) work of Levinas. Levinas's work may disappoint Badiou for orienting itself ultimately via religious axioms, but he defends it as "strikingly distant" from the "catechisms" of multiculturalism (37f, 20e).

Badiou makes a more interesting and direct claim for Levinas's importance in an offhand remark found in his *Manifesto*. There, in writing of the history of philosophy since Hegel, he claims that philosophy has come to misapprehend the nature of its own work and has ceded its task, at various moments, by "suturing" itself to one of its four conditions: hence, according to Badiou, Anglo-American philosophy has sutured itself to the promise of positivist *science* as the sole procedure of truth, Marxism has sutured philosophy to the promise of emancipatory *politics* as the sole procedure of truth, and, faced with philosophy's sutures to science and to politics, Nietzsche and Heidegger gave philosophy over to the *poem*.[23] Now, just as the attentive reader begins to wonder whether there were no overly enthusiastic philosophical partisans of *love*, Badiou offers a strangely phrased afterthought: "It may even be added," he writes, "that a Levinas [*un Levinas*], in the guise of the dual talk on the Other and its Face [*visage*], and on Woman, considers [*envisage*] that philosophy could also become the valet of its fourth condition, love" (*Manifeste* 48f, 67e). This is certainly a curious statement and one wonders what is meant by it, since love is not usually considered a central term for Levinas. What, for Badiou in particular, can be the relation between love and Levinas, the preeminent thinker of ethics? What is love as, precisely, a condition or truth procedure for philosophy? Why, finally, do some of Badiou's most sustained discussions of love as a condition of philosophy appear amid discussions of art—for example in discussion of the works of Samuel Beckett,[24] or in his intriguing remarks on the novel as an art form essentially coupled to love?[25]

Badiou, whose most serious philosophical work is thought through mathematics, perhaps unsurprisingly describes the course of an amorous truth as supporting a subjective movement through three distinct "numericalities." The numericality of love, according to Badiou, is counted thus: one, two, infinity. That is, love is essentially the production of a truth about the Two (*Manifeste* 64f, 83e), pertaining ultimately to difference as such (*Theoretical Writings* 146e). Stated yet again, love is a riving of the One of solipsism in an encounter with the Two of the sexuated amorous couple that opens, like a passage, upon the plethoric Infinite of the sensual world:

> In love, there is first the One of solipsism, which is the confrontation or duel between the *cogito* and the grey black of being[26] in the infinite recapitulation of speech. Next comes the Two, which arises in the event of an encounter and in the incalculable poem [*le poème incalculable*] of its designation by a name. Lastly, there is the Infinity of the sensible world that the Two traverses and unfolds, where, little by little, it deciphers a truth about the Two itself. This numericality (one, two, infinity) is specific to the procedure of love. We could demonstrate that the other truth procedures—science, art, and politics—have different numericalities,[27] and that each numericality singularizes the type of procedure in question, all the while illuminating how truths belong to totally heterogeneous registers. (L'écriture 363f, 33e)

Prior to the pure encounter of love, there is only solitude: the everyday situation of the ego and, as Levinas argues, "the very structure of reason" (*Le temps* 48f, 65e). The Two of love, by contrast, inaugurates an extraordinary *event*, in Badiou's sense of the term, insofar as it is a

> hazardous and chance-laden mediation for alterity in general [*une mediation hasardeuse pour l'altérité en general*]. It elicits

> a rupture or a severance of the *cogito*'s One; by virtue of this very fact, however, it can hardly stand on its own, opening instead onto the limitless multiple of Being. We might also say that the Two of love elicits the advent of the sensible. The truth of the Two gives rise to a sensible inflection of the world, where before only the grey-black of being had taken place. Now, the sensible and the infinite are identical. . . . (L'écriture 358f, 28–29e)

Badiou's descriptions are remarkable for the way they combine two unusual features. The first are the aesthetic tropes of Badiou's description—not just his evocation of the Infinite of love through citation of sensual scenes from the oeuvre of one of the great literary writers of the twentieth century, but Badiou's own affirmation that such scenes are, in themselves, "poems," regardless of their prose form (L'écriture 359f, 29e). The second is the language, so strongly reminiscent of Levinas, when Badiou writes of the Two-ness of love not as the imaginary completion of romantic fantasy, but rather as an encounter with alterity itself, a "rupture" of the cogito's solitude, together with the sense that the ethical consists in persisting, in being faithful, to this evental encounter with alterity.[28] Let us examine these two points about Badiou's language more closely.

Badiou's use of aesthetic tropes can be understood if we recall the almost impossible role of language necessary for the faithful elaboration of a truth within a situation that cannot discern or name it. When, therefore, we read above that the Two, the heart of the amorous event and the opening of the ethical subject to the alterior and the infinite, "arises in the event of an encounter and in the *incalculable poem* of its designation by a name," or when we read in a different essay that "one must be *poetically* ready for the outside-of-self [*il faut* poétiquement *être prêt au hors-de-soi*]" (Le Recours 100f, 75e; Badiou's emphasis), we must suspect that Badiou is not here indicating a unique role for poetry in the elaboration of an amorous truth. Rather, Badiou is suggesting a special role for poetry in the elaboration of *any* kind of truth. We might think of this as somewhat akin to the insight of Poe's Dupin, who says, referring to the Minister who has purloined the royal letter, that "as poet *and* mathematician, he would reason well; as mere mathematician, he could not have reasoned at all" ("The Purloined Letter" 691). Regardless of the truth procedure in effect, whether scientific, political, artistic, or amorous, fidelity to a truth event requires a naming that, in turn, can only proceed indirectly, through the language resources of the poetic act, which Badiou suggests are uniquely capable of introducing alterity into the language of a situation:

> For the nomination of an event— . . . an undecidable supplementation which must be named to occur for a being-faithful, thus for a truth—*this* nomination is *always* poetic. To name a supplement, a chance, an incalculable, one must draw from the void of sense, in default of established significations, to the peril of language. One must therefore poeticize, and the poetic name of the event is what throws us outside of ourselves, through the flaming ring of predictions [*ce qui nous lance hors de nous-mêmes, à travers le cerceau enflammé des prévisions*]. (Le Recours 100f, 75e)

The poem, then, is more than the heart of the artistic event, whatever its medium. It is also the composition of a supernumerary name for the unnamable and undecidable event of truth, composed out of the void of the language of the situation. More than this, it is poetry that "throws us outside of ourselves" to surpass in subjectivization the solipsism of the One and to open upon the Two of love and the true Infinite of the sensible world. One might venture it as a new formulation of Badiou's ethical maxim: *One must poeticize.* That is, one must exceed one's situation and assume an ethical relation to the event by striving to name it through the resources of the poetic word. As the Romantics intuited and as Badiou's philosophy formulates much more precisely, poetry and ethics, like poetry and truth, are not to be disentangled.

The unique role of poetic language in Badiou's philosophy—surpassing solipsism, bringing one into proximity with alterity, opening upon the infinite—thus shows Badiou's ethic of truths much closer, in certain respects, to Levinas than his commentators usually allow. But to get a fuller, somewhat more technical sense for *why* one must poeticize, let us consider the role of poetic language in a different way, one that shows Badiou, like Lacan in his theory of the Thing, sketching a theory of the subject who assumes an ethical relation to the void of the real through the proxy of the poetic signifier.

Badiou's subject of truth, we recall, exists as a subject only in the bearing of that truth and is otherwise just a human animal, more or less happily situated, as the case may be. But to be a subject of truth also implies, as we will see, what Badiou calls an "imperative of saying" (*Petit* 141f, 91e)—that is, an ethical obligation to carry a truth in language and in poetic language in particular. Part of this is certainly a tactical problem: if Aeschylus (or some tragedian still earlier) invents a new way to stage the songs and rites of dismembered Dionysos, or if Cervantes single-handedly invents a novel set of conventions for writing fictional prose narrative, it is not hard to see that these new artistic truths won't succeed in revolutionizing their respective artistic situations if their inventors keep their insight to themselves, or if those who would follow cannot interpolate tragic or novelistic values and modes of composition into larger conversations about what constitutes value in artistic work. Part of "the imperative of saying," however, reaches beyond tactics to the essence of truth within Badiou's philosophy, and specifically in its aspect of the Lacanian real—that is, as unspeakable, unthinkable, and ungraspable.

If the subject must speak to being, to what *is*, in truth, and if truth is aligned with the Lacanian real, then the subject cannot, ultimately, be speaking to this or that particular being, such as we might recognize it and situate it within our existing regimes of legitimacy and knowledge. Rather, the subject's ethical saying is motivated by pure Thing-like being itself, as Badiou explains in an essay about "Worstward Ho," a late text by Samuel Beckett:

> The imperative of saying is immediately correlated to that about which there is something *to* say, in other words, the "there is" [*le « il y a »*] itself. Beside the fact that there is the imperative of saying, there is the "there is."
>
> The "there is." or pure being, has two names and not just one: the void and the dim [*la pénombre*].[29] (*Petit* 141f, 91e)

We can see, after Heidegger and after the early Levinas of *Existence and Existents*, that the "there is . . ." gives the ground of being, as if it were the setting or the site of beings. At the same time, we must also, after Badiou, recognize this "there is" as also the void of being, in that there can be nothing there that legitimately counts as actually existing. This is because a situation, as the setting for coherent thought, identifies being with what is presentable. Pure being, the being of nothing, in which nothing in particular is presented, is thus indiscernible from within the situation. Hence, our earlier problem restates itself: there is an imperative of saying, an obligation to poeticize, but the imperative requires us to speak on that about which there is both something to say and at the same time *nothing meaningful to be said*, from the standpoint of the situation.

It is poetic language in particular that, according to Badiou, offers the subject a way of contending with this impossible imperative to approach the void of being and to speak about that which cannot be spoken. Certainly, as has been well appreciated since the Romantics especially, there is something uncanny or mysterious at work in poetic language, and, indeed, in art more generally, insofar as art is understood to pertain ultimately to something quite other than what it represents. We might introduce, by way of brief example, Stephen Crane's short lyric from *The Black Riders and Other Lines* (1895):

> Should the wide world roll away
> Leaving black terror
> Limitless night,
> Nor God, nor man, nor place to stand
> Would be to me essential
> If thou and thy white arms were there
> And the fall to doom a long way. (Crane 1302)

What is this poem "really" doing, from the perspective of Badiou's philosophy? Without pretending do justice to this remarkable little piece, and exploiting it merely as an example, we might still pause a moment to savor the fascination of its images (the rolling away of the wide world, the revelation of black terror and limitless night, the long fall to doom enclasped in the white arms of the beloved); we might marvel at its pleasing musicality, its alliteration, its odd polysyndeton and shifting rhythms; we might puzzle briefly over its unsettling ambiguity of attitude (to what extent is this a love poem announcing a desperate devotion against the backdrop of an existential void, and to what extent a bitter confession of helpless seduction and inevitable ruin?); and we might appreciate the precarious asymmetry of its oppositions for situating the reader's thought (the specific material whiteness of the arms set against the disembodied blackness of terror; the transitory finitude of sensuous life set against the illimitable dominion of the void; the countering of the infinite of non-being with the infinite of love). We might even observe that the representational content of the poem suggests certain Badiouian themes. Nonetheless, Badiou's own theory of poetic language would claim that in a given poem any allegorical potential for Badiou's philosophy is merely fortuitous. A poem might as properly concern the fanciful ravings of a poet faced with an uncanny raven or the bravado of an old poet besieged by his blue-eyed banditti—or, for that matter, concern literally anything or nothing at all. True poems are not defined by the content of their themes any more than they are defined by lineation and rhythm.[30] Indeed, as Badiou describes it, the images, ambiguities, and themes of the poem, together with the musicality of its rhythms, alliterations, and repetitions, *retreat* as the poem enters a relation to the void, a relation that is not one of conceptual representation. Whatever a poem may be *about*, Badiou suggests, a poem is always *also* this relation to the void.

In his work on Beckett, Badiou describes a certain "disobjectification" in poetic language, in which the poem disencumbers itself of particular beings to open upon the void ground of being itself. Hence, in the mysterious action of poetic language, substantive objects—here, the sound and the music of the poem—*and* objects of thought—here, *representations* of white arms and *concepts* of the pure "there is" that remains after the wide world is rolled away—"disobjectify" to indicate the place of a truth:

> The poem introduces the following question into the domain of language: what is an experience without an object? What is a pure affirmation that constitutes a universe whose right to being, and even probability, nothing guarantees?
>
> The thought of the poem only begins after the complete disobjectification of presence.
>
> This is why we can say that, far from being a form of knowledge, the poem is the exemplary instance of a thought obtained in the retreat and subtraction from everything that sustains the faculty of knowledge.
>
> No doubt this is why the poem has always *disconcerted* philosophy. (*Theoretical* 238e)

Language is absolutely powerless to speak directly of the void and can do nothing more than append a name to it, because the void as such cannot be inserted into meaning and knowledge. But poetic language, in Badiou's account, can indicate proximity to the void through the disappearance and disobjectification of objects and, through the action of just this disappearing or giving way, can yield the palpable "sense" of a truth beyond objectivity and unrecognizable from within the logic of the situation. One may indeed enter into the poem because of the seduction of its images, themes, and rhythms, and one may of course reflect on the range of objects of thought offered by the poem, but, whatever the form and content of the poem, as the poem begins to do its work *as* poetic language, it offers another drama—namely, the vanishing of these objects as they escape toward the void of being in the sensible, *aesthetic* thinking of a truth. These objects—these white arms, this limitless night, that delightful rhythm—are at first present at the level of the said, but then, somehow, in the transmutation of art, they no longer count, as the force of a truth seizes the subject. The objects, we might say, fade in the light of brighter aura, the aura of a truth beyond objects and knowledge, an aesthetic truth pertaining to being and the void: sensible, but strictly unthinkable in thought.

In this sense, poetry essentially and necessarily represents a failure and a retreat from the faculty of knowledge. There is the "there is" about which the subject must speak, but about which it can say nothing. The proximity indicated in the disappearance of the objects in the poem gestures toward the threshold of the void of the real and the true, toward the very least degree of being, but it cannot touch the void itself. Language then, fails to achieve absolute plenitude—as in the fantasy of a perfect adequation of word and thing—but it likewise fails to achieve an absolute void that would obliterate the possibility of the subject.

One is reminded of Lacan here, whom Badiou cites and who remarks of the truth in one of his late seminars that truth is never whole, that it can never be wholly said (*Petit* 41f, 23e).[31] Something of the real remains ever irreducible. It is precisely this fact which poetic language respects with a kind of "delicacy" (Theoretical 235e). Badiou is writing of both Lacan and Mallarmé when he writes that

> The poem's revelatory power turns around an enigma, so that marking out the very *point* of this enigma is the powerless Real of the power of the true. In this sense, [Mallarmé's] "mystery in letters" is a genuine imperative. When Mallarmé argues that "there must always be enigma in poetry," he inaugurates an ethic of mystery founded on the respect, by the power of a truth, of its own point of powerlessness.
>
> The mystery is, strictly speaking, that every poetic truth leaves at its own center what it does not have the power to bring into presence. (*Petit* 41f, 23e)

This delicacy with respect to a certain powerlessness in relation to the power of a truth is why Badiou says, apropos of Beckett, that the essence of poetic saying is ill-saying (*Petit* 153–54f, 100e). If poetry is "a thought which is nothing aside from its act" (*Theoretical* 241e), and if this act reflects the "imperative of saying" to say what must be said, then one says it as perfectly as one can, but, still, it must be acknowledged, one says it badly. So far as Badiou is concerned, the subject must contend with this fact that the saying of the truth is destined to futility, but he or she must bear this failure not with the self-lacerations of guilt, but with courage: the courage to endure and to recommence the saying which must be said, but which cannot be wholly said and which must therefore conclude again (and again) in a kind of failure. Hence, the courage Badiou finds in the last lines of Beckett's novel, *The Unnamable* (1953): I can't go on, I'll go on.

The imperative of saying and the ethic of mystery Badiou locates in poetic language may remind us not only of Blanchot, as Gabriel Riera observes (Riera 82), but also of Levinas. Nonetheless, this is one instance where the shared language between the philosophers obscures some important differences. For both Levinas and for Badiou, the ethics of saying involves an opening of the subject, in respect, onto ungraspable alterity. But whereas the ethics of saying that Levinas describes in his *Otherwise than Being* involves primarily an ethics of attending to the saying of the other and only secondarily an ethics of the subject's own saying (as in criticism), for Badiou, closer to Lacan, the ethics of saying is primarily an act to which one commits oneself. For Badiou, as we have seen, it is one's own act of saying that is imperative, even if one is, like Webern and Berg following Schoenberg, or like Sophocles following Aeschylus, faithfully following the saying and said of another inventor's truth.

And indeed, generally one would not wish to overstate the similarity between the ways Badiou and Levinas conceive of the ethical. Badiou, for his part, considers himself resolutely committed to a *Greek*—philosophical, mathematical—mode of thinking ethics, whereas Levinas, for his part, is very self-consciously committed to a non-Greek, *Jewish*—theological—mode of thinking the ethical. Thus, Badiou's mathematical grounding and conceptualization of alterity, his "numericalities" of solipsism and the Infinite, his set-theoretical elaboration of the event, and his insistent recourse to the category of *truth* as the grounds for the specifically *ethical* force of alterity and the infinite—all this is quite foreign to Levinas's sensibility. And, as we have already seen, Badiou displays little sympathy for Levinas's grounding of the ethical nature of alterity within Jewish tradition, so that Levinas's often Abrahamic sense of alterity, with its potential caprice and persecutory command, is absent when Badiou writes of the subjective commitment to forsake the pursuit of one's own interest, will one's own "transliteration," and live and think according to the alterior truth of the event that has befallen one. Finally, where Levinas concentrates his thinking at the intersection of phenomenology and theology, writing little on love as such, less on literature and politics, and nothing at all on science, Badiou, through the entirety of his oeuvre, makes it a matter of principle to circulate his thinking among the four procedures of truth he himself has defined: the scientific (as in *Being and Event*), the artistic (as in the *Handbook of Inaesthetics*), the political (as in *Metapolitics*), and the amorous (as in the essays on Beckett and on the Lacanian description of sexuation). This also gives Badiou a broader scope for thinking the ethical in places—art, science, politics—where Levinas's writings do not often venture.

Nonetheless, we have also seen that both Badiou and Levinas, when they present their work on ethics, write through tropes of *trauma*, as a way of thinking subjectivity as the rupture of the solipsism of the cogito in an encounter with alterity, difference, and the infinite. This is indeed very significant. If Badiou stands together with the Romantics (and Lacan) to posit, at the heart of the work of art, a subject who contends with a constitutive void or "nothing" or hole, Badiou and Levinas (and again Lacan) stand together against hundreds of years of philosophical thinking by imagining at the core of ethics a subject who has been riven and punctured in relation to a singular, traumatic event. When Badiou salutes Levinas as a thinker of love,[32] as he does in his *Manifesto*, he is recognizing Levinas's rigor in thinking the event of love as an ethical movement from the One of solipsism, through the encounter with alterity (the Two), to the Infinite, even if Badiou is also, at the same time, working from an Infinite conceived through mathematical ontology (not theology), and also underlining his own critique that Levinas's suture of philosophy to the condition of love unduly neglects other possible procedures for truth—the political, the scientific, and the artistic.

Badiou's implicit critique of Levinas's thinking of ethics—that it correctly elaborates certain essential structures of an ethical event in one procedure (love) only to turn a blind eye to the event in any other procedure (artistic, political, scientific)—is analogous to his critique of Romantic philosophies of art. Romantic theories of art, in Badiou's view, correctly locate the position of *truths* as immanent to the work of *art*—so that, for the Romantics, art is not thought to point to a truth that exists outside of art, as when it is called upon to illustrate a truth situated in politics, science, or love. Rather, the truth of art is intrinsic or internal to the artistic effect of works of art. As Badiou and the Romantics agree, art is not *about* a truth; art *is* a truth. However, the Romantics, in Badiou's view, fail to recognize the singularity of the truth produced by art; they fail to see that the particular truth activated in the artwork is specific to art alone, and thus "irreducible to other truths, be they scientific, political, or amorous" (*Petit Manuel* 21f, 9e). We will grant Badiou his point here: it is hard to imagine any thinker, Romantic or otherwise, who would fully prefigure Badiou's declaration that there are four procedures of truth and that every truth is the truth *of* a given situation strictly within one of these four procedures, either artistic, political, scientific, or amorous. These are surely among the most fundamental and original features of Badiou's own philosophy.

But I would argue that there is another debt, unacknowledged, that Badiou's thinking of art owes to the Romantics: the description of art as addressed to a subject constituted through a foundational, traumatic, encounter with a "nothing" or void of the real. This seems to me the key Romantic gesture in the thinking of art: from Schiller's irremediable "dismemberment of being"[33] and Emerson's declaration in "The Poet" that man "is only half himself" and must therefore poeticize to address his fundamental void of being (448), to Heidegger's later view that one must bear poetic witness to being to attain to a greater degree of being oneself,[34] to Lacan's claim that the work of art renews the subject's relation to the real (*Le Séminaire VII*, 169–170f, 141e). Romantic theories of art, like Badiou's own, proceed from the given of a subject facing the void and elaborate a theory of art specifically as addressing that unspeakable ontological hole.

What Badiou contributes to Romantic philosophies of art is a new rigor in elaborating the event of this situated void, and especially in thinking it through the innovations of mid-twentieth-century set theory. Thus, where the early Romantic thinkers of the event of art work more or less intuitively, as both poets and theoreticians of poetry themselves, where Heidegger works out of dormant linguistic possibilities, and where Lacan works through empirical observation and practical clinical interest,[35] Badiou gives a much fuller, more truly philosophical grounding to those earlier developments toward a Romantic theory of art.

Additionally, by formalizing his event of art in set theory, Badiou is able to further prise apart the theory of a subject constituted in traumatic relation to an originary event from the melancholic pathos or horror customarily associated with trauma and loss. This matter has already caused some misunderstanding in Badiou's critical reception. Perhaps because of his narrow focus on Badiou's book on Saint Paul, or perhaps because he is quick to appreciate manifestations of horror, but in any case missing the sense of horror in Badiou's work,[36] Žižek overstates the case when he claims, in *The Ticklish Subject*, that Badiou's "main point" in his elaboration of the subject is to "avoid identifying the subject with the constitutive Void of the structure."[37] In fact, Žižek and Badiou would agree that the experience of the void is always an experience of horror (*Le Siècle*, 36f, 20e)—but horror is only a part of that experience, and to overemphasize this aspect risks losing sight of the essentially generative potential of the void for the subject. So, certainly, it would be wrong to minimize the extent of Badiou's actual theoretical engagement with the traumatic real. As we have already seen, although Badiou spends much effort describing the second moment of an evental truth (its poeticization in the subject's fidelity), he also gives a full description of the subject in that first moment of facing the void or the "nothing"—a fact highlighted by those many terms suggesting physical trauma: "suspended, broken, annulled," "riven or punctured," "a rupture or a severance," and so forth. In *Being and Event*, he is quite plain: while "a truth alone is infinite" (*L'être* 433f, 395e), "the subject is finite" (*L'être* 434f, 396e). Indeed, this very incommensurability faced by the finite subject gives it its specific sense: overwhelmed, annulled, inarticulate—and persistent nonetheless.

Yet Žižek's argument, even if overstated, nevertheless points to an important difference in tone that distinguishes Badiou from his more Romantic theoretical forebears in thinking the real of art. Thus, the whole thrust of Badiou's philosophy resists attaching any melancholic, Romantic *pathos* to this trauma of the finite subject as he or she contends with the void and the incommensurable, infinite truth. To be sure, the traumatic structure of the subject is not a dry fact for Badiou—the very passion of his writing on the topic recognizes its drama. But, in contrast with the pathos or nostalgia inherent in Emerson and Heidegger when they present the fundamental absence at the heart of human subjectivity, and in contrast to the rawness and destitution of Antigone when Lacan presents the subject's ethical bearing of the real, for Badiou the traumatic structure of the subject is part and parcel of the very event he celebrates for being inventive, creative, "the coming-to-be of that which is not yet" (*L'éthique* 45f, 27e), indeed the only way for something new to appear within a situation. The point is that, in the event of truth, the subject, which is indeed finite and, yes, traumatically riven and babbling, is nevertheless able to participate in a fidelity to something that exceeds his or her own finitude and is thereby able to accede to an ethical, more properly human, subjectivity. So, Badiou's ethics and his theory of art bear upon an effort to surpass the suffering body, surpass the animal, surpass the contemporary organization of moral life around the figure of the victim,[38] and to instead articulate a properly human ethics. If we speak of trauma with Badiou's subject, then, it is neither to rally the reader's pious sympathies nor to invoke his or her horror on behalf of the subject or any "other." Rather, as we have seen, "trauma" highlights certain features of Badiou's subject to place his theory of art in limited relation with that of the Romantics, to display his debt to Lacan's traumatic real in particular, to clarify his critique of Levinasian ethics, to highlight the role of the poetic naming of the void in any procedure of truth, and to offer a vision of the subject who is at once riven and finite as well as heroically, creatively, persistent in the face of the real.

Epilogue

Word After Word

Let us say then, with Hawthorne's Miriam, that there is a void haunting the dreams and imaginings of humanity in its moments of deepest insight. Irving's Sleepy Hollow dreams dreams of a monstrous, headless void hurrying along in the gloom of night, stalking its byways, and spiriting away, it may be, its itinerate schoolmaster. The Romantics' Beatrice gazes back over her shoulder from the threshold of darkness, perfectly composed and radiantly beautiful, but always already half obscured in the shadows of death. Brown's Clara Wieland writes her narrative, wending her way toward the inevitable gulf of death and oblivion, longing to cast herself from its verge, beyond remembrance and beyond hope, restrained only by the literary word. On the day of her suicide, Antigone's triumph is measured by the utter uncanny destitution of her existence. Hawthorne's Miriam Schaefer intuits a pit of blackness lurking beneath every aspect of the "illusive stage-scenery" of existence, a great chasm of time ceaselessly devouring history's parade of heroes, statesmen, and poets. Crane's subtle lyric of love and desperation, casts its poet into the void itself, plunging through limitless night, enclasped (one likes to think) in the white arms of his beloved, but falling to his doom.

This spectral void haunting the heart of human existence is sensible under different guises. It has appeared in our literary texts most typically in the human enigma of death: how to make sense of the fact that something so seemingly momentous as a single human life can be destroyed in the freak chance of a battle, where one person dies and another survives to tell the tale; how and in the name of what purpose one must live when one's beloved companions have perished in passion and violence; how and to what extent one is responsible for the life and the death of others—even of strangers and those who seek to persecute. Death thus opens upon the struggle to create an ethics and a meaning for life out of the very incommensurability between the fragile mortal finitude of the flesh and the very infinitude of the thought dwelling there. It represents, then, both a void of being (as the event whereby the subject or the other vanishes from being) and, at the same time, a void of knowledge (as in *What is the ethical significance of death? How, conversely, is one to fashion a meaning for mortal life?*). But while the void seems linked to mortal finitude—to the deaths that did or didn't happen in the Revolution and its aftermath in Sleepy Hollow, to the suicide of Wieland and the death out of which Clara writes herself, to the murder of Miriam's model and the death of Hawthorne's reader—there have been other semblances of the void, too, less directly related to death. These we have seen in the enigma of the events in Sleepy Hollow and in Miriam's past, in the ethico-existential solitude of Miriam and Hilda as they carry alone their moral burdens, in the Kierkegaardian paradoxes in the fault lines of Wieland's faith, in the wild void that motivates the passion and words of Clara and Miriam, in the indeterminate romantic and spiritual fate of Crane's poet, in the voiding of the present in Hawthorne's Rome, and elsewhere.

The Romantics, and the post-Romantic continental thinkers that followed in their wake, were hardly the first to thematize the radical void as a defining feature of human being and subjectivity. Lacan looked to Aristotle for a classical source explicitly postulating an essential deficit of being suffered by humanity (*Le Séminaire XX* 91f, 99e). Heidegger looked back still farther, to Sophocles, as we saw, and to the pre-Socratics, to describe an uncanny humanity never quite properly at home in its own being. One might equally look to ancient Semitic myths telling of humanity's fall into language, lack, and death. What the Romantics and the post-Romantics did develop in original ways, however, have been three ideas: (1) that a being defined in relation to the void as such is subject to a kind of foundational ethics, (2) that this ethics calls upon the subject to enter into a particular relation to language, and (3) that "poetry" is the name—or, more modestly, *one* name—for this kind of language. Consequently, as we have seen in our Romantic texts and as we have developed through our post-Romantic thinkers, there is a fundamental ethics at the heart of the event of art, insofar as, through the purity and power of its language, art brings the subject to a more ethical relation to his or her being.

Brown's Advertisement, Irving's Postscript, and Hawthorne's Preface all explicitly signal the key interest of each text in "the illustration of some important branches of the moral constitution of man," in the question of "the moral of the story," and in the evolution of "a thoughtful moral"—and this they declare even as, "sensuously, passionally, they all attack the old morality," to recall D. H. Lawrence's description of the American Romantics. Whatever the actual commitments of the writers biographically considered, these texts find no final satisfaction in Christian systems and sentiments, in the sufficiency of moral conscience as a guide, in moral orders founded upon the social contract, or in the categorical imperative of enlightened practical reason. Where, then, lies the declared ethical interest of these texts, if not in the old morality? This book has argued, moderating Lawrence's claim, that these texts leave the old moralities unattacked and relatively undisturbed to aim instead at an ethics more fundamental than the everyday, social sphere of these more contingent moralities. As our readings showed, the ethical urgency of the texts by Brown, Irving, and Hawthorne bears upon the subjective relation to the void and to language as such. We saw how each, in its own way, stages tale-telling as an ethico-psychological imperative to put into words the traumatic encounter with the void and to offer these words properly to another person. Hence, in Irving's tale, the babble of the Sunday morning crowd considering Ichabod's empty hat by the roadside and hence too the lengthy chain of narration testifying that this is a tale to pass on. Hence, in Brown's novel, Clara Wieland's persistence in penning her tale, before—as she expects and craves—she may lay down her head in the lap of death. Hence, in Hawthorne's final romance, the bereavement and bitterness of the narrator, casting his frayed, gap-rent text to the wind, knowing its one reader has preceded him to the grave.

Our theoretical readings have proposed that these American texts merely make more explicit what is in fact the case with literature and art more generally: that whatever its thematics, whatever its tropes and its imagery, whatever might be claimed in its prefaces and afterwords and advertisements, insofar as there is an event of art, there is a subjective encounter with a radical void that calls upon the subject, ethically, psychologically, and existentially, to give him- or herself over to the work of language and thereby to enter into a more ethical relation to being and subjectivity. Our theoretical readings (like, in their own ways, our literary readings), have displayed different understandings of what, precisely, it means to be a "subject of language"; they have, moreover, figured the void variously—as death, enigma, paradox, absence, nothingness, trauma, the real, the thing, the abyss, gap, night, radical alterity, discontinuity, and so forth; and they have, finally, had varying understandings of what it means, within the context of art, to strike a relation (or a specific non-relation) to the void. The differences of emphasis, development, and values among thinkers such as Heidegger, Lacan, Levinas, and Badiou lead, as we have seen, to distinctive elaborations of these terms and their mutual relations within a given system of thought. But, though their differences are not trivial, we should not let them obscure the fact that their disagreements are staged on the site of significant common ground. For they have all committed themselves to what this book has described as a post-Romantic aesthetics: a conception of art and literature as created out of, and addressing themselves to, a subject of language who emerges in essential relation to an existential void or lack. And they have all elaborated a foundational ethics, coupled to this peculiar conception of art, to describe how the split-subject comes to take up or surpass his or her own limited being through an engagement with art and the poetic word.

Notes

Introduction

1. At any rate, Horace's own point in the famous passage of *Ars Poetica* is that the two—doing good *and* giving pleasure—are *combined* in the most successful compositions.

2. Cited in Heidegger, *Poetry, Language, Thought*, 136–37.

3. In his admirably researched and judiciously written intellectual biography of Nietzsche, the Swedish scholar Thomas Brobjer claims that Emerson was Nietzsche's "very first important encounter with philosophy," before both Plato and Schopenhauer, and that Nietzsche reread Emerson almost every year from 1862 to his mental collapse in 1889, making Emerson likely Nietzsche's "most read and reread author" (Brobjer 22–23). Also, according to Brobjer, Emerson's overall influence on Nietzsche was "enormous" and a translation of Emerson's *Essays: First and Second Series* probably the most heavily annotated book in Nietzsche's library (Brobjer 24). Nietzsche also owned (and annotated) a number of other books by Emerson, mostly in German translation: *The Conduct of Life*, the Goethe and Shakespeare essays from *Representative Men*, a privately commissioned translation of "Historic Notes of Life and Letters in Massachusetts," and more (Brobjer 119n11).

4. Walter Harding has compiled a very useful list of books in Emerson's library, *Emerson's Library* (1967), which displays Emerson's very full interest in German intellectual life. In addition to the early Romantic writers mentioned above, Emerson's library also included titles by Lessing, Kant, Fichte, Hegel, Schleiermacher, de Staël, the Grimm brothers, Heine, Grillparzer, and others, as well as various commentaries, histories, and biographies in German philosophy and literature. Most of these titles are in English translation; many of them, however, are in the original German.

5. The Germans were translating Shakespeare even before his death in 1616, but the translations made from 1797- by August Wilhelm Schlegel (Friedrich's brother) and edited by Ludwig Tieck are considered the classic translations of Shakespeare, surpassing earlier renditions, including the twenty-two plays translated by Christoph Martin Wieland in the 1760s. Other translations of interest, from the perspective of the Romantics, include Lenz's *Love's Labour's*

Lost (1774), Schiller's *Macbeth* (1801), Goethe's *Romeo and Juliet* (1812), and various fragments by Herder in his long *Shakespeare* essay (1773). Friedrich Hölderlin's translations of Sophocles (1804), unhappily reviewed at the time, have found more appreciative readers in Heidegger and Philippe Lacoue-Labarthe. They are unusual, among other reasons, for having themselves been translated into French and English, as a curious and compelling work of art, even apart from their Sophoclean source.

Chapter 1. Sleepy Hollow

1. The critical literature on history and trauma is now vast. In its conceptualization of trauma and its strange historicity, however, the present essay is specifically indebted to two foundational texts, Freud's *Beyond the Pleasure Principle* (1920) and *Moses and Monotheism* (1938) and to the important critical work represented by Cathy Caruth's *Unclaimed Experience: Trauma, Narrative, and History* (Baltimore: Johns Hopkins University Press, 1996). See also Kai Erikson's article on community trauma and Robert Jay Lifton's remarks on trauma by proxy in *Trauma: Explorations in Memory*, Cathy Caruth, ed. (Baltimore: Johns Hopkins University Press 1995). Nadine Fresco's fascinating article "Remembering the Unknown," *International Review of Psychoanalysis* 11 (1984), on the intergenerational transmission of trauma in families of Holocaust survivors, was especially useful in thinking about how trauma may come to be shared among a community and not remain simply the possession of an individual.

2. Cathy Caruth, [Part II] Introduction, *Trauma: Explorations in Memory*, Cathy Caruth, ed., 153.

3. I remark on Katrina's plumpness ("plump as a partridge," 1065) for its contrast with Ichabod's own figure ("the genius of famine descending upon the earth," 1061). She—together with her bounteous dowry—seems the only object (unless the tales of the Hessian be an object) that promises to satisfy the monstrous appetites of Ichabod Crane, who eats and eats without ever getting full. This essay shall return in the third section to the matter of excessive appetites.

4. Indeed, in 1824, "The Adventure of the German Student" (from Crayon's *Tales of a Traveller*) would feature another headless (and now plainly supernatural) ghost situated provocatively between love and history.

5. Hawthorne and Brown do not make the case so explicitly as Irving does in this passage, but Brown's "To the Public" in *Edgar Huntly* (1799) and Hawthorne's "Preface" to *The Blithedale Romance* (1852) both display a certain anxiety with regard to the European narrative advantages of history and cultural tradition. There were certainly other examples of this claim coming from both sides of the Atlantic.

6. This is indeed a hallmark of the Knickerbocker narrator persona. See for example, "To the Public" in *A History of New York*, 377–81; the preface to

the Dolph Heyliger stories in *Bracebridge Hall*, 300–303; and the early remarks in "The Money Diggers" section of *Tales of a Traveller*, especially 647–655.

7. This 1839 reminiscence from *The Knickerbocker Magazine* was published as simply "Sleepy Hollow," and is not to be confused with the 1820 tale, "The Legend of Sleepy Hollow."

8. "Cowboys" were bands of highwaymen and freebooters who roamed the Neutral Ground between the British-controlled New York City and the American-held West Point. They claimed loyalist sympathies and confiscated the property of patriots who fell into their hands. Highwaymen with patriot sympathies were called "Skinners." See Robert E. Cray Jr.'s very informative article on cowboys and skinners and on especially John Paulding, Isaac Van Wart, and David Williams, the three men who stopped the disguised Major André on the road near Sleepy Hollow, evidently with the idea of robbing him: "Major John André and the Three Captors: Class Dynamics and Revolutionary Memory Wars in the Early Republic, 1780–1831," *Journal of the Early Republic* 17, no. 3 (Fall 1997): 371–97.

9. Henry Steiner, "Re: Question: Sleepy Hollow during the revolution," e-mail to the author (June 13, 2001).

10. Major John André was the staff officer in charge of intelligence for the British Commander-in-Chief, General Clinton. André had opened negotiations with the disgruntled American Major General Benedict Arnold, and in September 1780 was behind American lines, completing negotiations for Arnold's treason, when his sloop was forced back down the Hudson, stranding him behind the lines. André attempted to reach British lines by land, but was caught by an irregular patrol near Tarrytown, out of uniform, under a false name, and carrying papers relevant to Arnold's treason. Arnold received the news and quickly escaped to New York City. André's gallantry during his trial and appeal (to be reclassified, despite his disguise and his conveyance of classified documents, from spy to prisoner of war) earned him broad sympathy (1081). Nevertheless, he was found guilty and was hanged as a spy, some miles down river from Sleepy Hollow and on the opposite shore, at Tappan. Had the unfortunate major but remained in British uniform, he would have survived and instead been interned as a prisoner of war.

11. Pease, *Visionary Compacts: American Renaissance Writings in Cultural Context*, 16–17.

12. One narrator claims the tale of Ichabod to have been "some thirty years since" (1060); the discussion of the survivors at the Van Tassel's makes it clear the war has already reached its "happy termination" (1078). We might locate Ichabod's fall, therefore, with some precision, in the late 1780s.

13. Poe 140 (recycled 1445), 460, 1381.

14. *Bracebridge Hall* (1822): "It seems, in fact, to be a part of our nature, like instinct in animals, acting independently of our reason" (103).

15. Freud, "The Uncanny," 238, "Das Unheimliche," 251.

16. Van Wyck Brooks, *The World of Washington Irving* (New York: E.P. Dutton, 1944), 205.

17. See the "Strange Stories" part that opens *Tales of a Traveller* (1824) for a similar gentleman who asks all the wrong questions of pleasurable tales (392, 394, 406, 409, 424, 438).

18. *A History of New York* 389. Similarly also 397–98, 405, 409–10.

19. Following a sketch of a traditional, English, Christmas dinner, Crayon reflects upon the moral field of literary writing as one of *pleasure* rather than *knowledge*. Through pleasure, more certainly than through knowledge, one may hope to "penetrate through the gathering film of misanthropy" (961–62).

Chapter 2. Lacan and the Beyond of Language

1. Lacan, *Seminar VII* 129f, 107e. Note that page numbers followed by "f" cite the French language editions; those followed by "e" refer the reader to the published English translation. Translations from *Seminar VII* are my own; other citations follow the commercial English translations.

2. Lacan gave public yearly seminars between 1953 and 1980. Although the seminar was open to the public (and formed a focal point of Parisian intellectual life), it was "not addressed in its initial impulse to philosophers" but rather to analysts in training (*Autres écrits* 204f, 108e). The seminars were transcribed at the time by a stenographer, and then, beginning in the 1970s, edited into published form by Jacques-Alain Miller.

3. Zupančič and Jaanus arrived at this striking formulation independently of each other.

4. The present essay will leave aside the arguable degree to which Lacan's theories remain truly "Freudian," when Freud himself wrote of art with a very different agenda and when, after all, Heidegger seems in many respects a more important interlocutor for the theory of art that Lacan elaborates in this seminar. Still, Lacan is always plainly working within the psychoanalytic register (more than a philosophical one), and he is undeniably "Freudian" to that extent.

5. Since the Bible isn't ordinarily understood to have quite the same status as other, nonreligious, texts, one doesn't quite know what to make of the inclusion of biblical passages among more traditional examples of aesthetic objects. Possibly, Lacan is simply following a tradition in philosophical aesthetics, from Hegel to Nietzsche, which views art and religion as existing together on a continuum, either historical (such as Nietzsche's Dionysian origins of tragedy) or else conceptual (both expressing and striving toward Hegelian *Geist*). Possibly too, for the patients Lacan speaks of, the particular biblical passages don't have (or had only in childhood) a religious significance and now instead enjoy a status more akin to poems or literary narrative.

6. Lacan's editor often (but not always) capitalizes Lacan's idiosyncratic use of *la Chose*. The Kantian and Heideggerian resonances of *das Ding* are suggestive, and Lacan plays on them, but Lacan himself claims as his fundamental point of reference Freud's technical use of the term in the *Project for a Scientific Psychology* and the essay on negation (58f, 45–46e). Lacanians will note the

affinities between Lacan's 1959–1960 concept of the Thing, and what he later conceptualized under the barred A.

7. Lacan, *Seminar VII*, 67f, 54e; 78f, 63e; 85f, 70e; 150f, 125e.

8. The *Ethics* seminar alludes briefly to several essays by Heidegger: "The Origin of the Work of Art," "The Thing," and an essay that Lacan himself translated in 1956, "Logos." Heidegger's essay on "The Thing" (1951) appeared in French translation just the year before Lacan's seminar and describes a jug (*der Krug*, not quite *un vase*) as defined in its thingness essentially by a void or emptiness (*Poetry Language Thought* 166–67). Lacan, as we shall see, is very clearly borrowing from Heidegger, despite mildly aestheticizing the jug as a vase. Significantly, too, both Lacan and the late Heidegger think the experience of art in terms of an encounter with language as such, though this claim will have different significance for Lacan than it did for Heidegger.

9. It strikes me that this supposition of a lost natural world is less a rhetorical or pedagogical trope of Lacan's own than suggestive of the way that subjects generally mythologize loss—a nostalgia observable in the clinic and giving its structure to the fundamental myths of culture.

10. Freud's etymological musings in "Das Unheimliche" suggest much this same unsettling quality in the uncanny: a homely intimacy coupled with a strange exteriority.

11. The examples Lacan gives in his seminar seem chosen to illustrate this emptiness visually: the vast cathedral, the empty vase, the depth of a perspectival painting, the space implied by the baroque experiments with anamorphosis. However, I would argue that these selections are intended pedagogically, not prescriptively. Lacan certainly isn't saying that true art is restricted to the literal representation of space. Cézanne's apples, for example, are another touchstone for Lacan and yet, from a classical standard of perspectival geometry, Cézanne is distinguished for a *flattening*, not a deepening, of perspective. One critic, Michel Hoog, remarks that, from the mid-1890s, with such paintings as *The Forest* and *Women Bathers*, Cézanne "totally abandoned traditional perspective and modeling with shade. At times, space simply ceases to exist; all elements constituting the picture are placed on a single continuous plane without depth" (Hoog 102). To large degree this is true also of Cézanne's famous apples and oranges. Lacan's selection of Cézanne for an example suggests, then, that regardless of its subject material or the specific techniques it exploits or refuses, art aims at some other dimension.

12. *là où on ne sait plus donner de la tête.*

13. Oddly, the Norton translation of *Seminar VII* omits this last sentence entirely.

14. For a comprehensive, elegant, and theoretically astute account of Lacan's relation to literature in particular, readers are referred to Jean-Michel Rabaté's superb study *Jacques Lacan: Psychoanalysis and the Subject of Literature.* Rabaté's chapter on the *Ethics* seminar focuses on Lacan's discussion of Antigone, showing how she can be "both sublime and beautiful in her 'blinding way' precisely because she does not sublimate her own desire, rather she heightens it and charges it with libidinal intensity, even when this desire is a desire for death" (79).

15. For a modern account of the attribution of this painting, as well as a modern historian's account of the murder and the trial, see Charles Nicholl's informative article, "Screaming in the Castle."

16. *The Cenci* was published by Shelley in 1819, but not performed until 1886. "Les Cenci" was published anonymously in 1837, then collected posthumously in 1855 as one of Stendhal's *Chroniques italiennes.* One might also mention Harriet Hosmer's 1856 sculpture and Julia Margaret Cameron's artful 1870 photographs. In the twentieth century, Antonin Artaud mounted his own version (1935) to launch his "theater of cruelty"; and, in addition to this, there have been at least five film versions (1910, 1926, 1941, 1956, 1969) and four operas, by Brian (1952), Battistelli (1953), Ginastera (1971), and Goldschmidt (1994).

17. Most notably in *Pierre* (407), but also in his journals (3 Mar 1857) and in the poem *Clarel* (3.7.16–24).

18. My account here of the Cenci tale is derived from Stendhal's telling. There would seem to be some disagreement among latter day scholars on various of the details of the story, the most serious of which is a debate on the veracity of Beatrice's allegation of paternal incest. Such debates, however, like the current art historical consensus that the portrait is neither by Guido Reni nor of Beatrice Cenci, are largely immaterial to the present argument, since the matter at hand regards the very powerful claim of beauty made by Hawthorne and the Romantics, who understood the circumstances of the painting as I present them here.

19. *Il se passe quelque chose encore au-delà* . . . If we recall that the French text originated as an oral presentation, we hear that what happens in the subject's encounter with beauty is not only an encounter with a mysterious "something else beyond," as I translate the primary sense of the French text, but also *quelque Chose en corps au-delà*—an encounter with the Thing that constitutes the beyond of the body.

20. In the spirit of a comparative Romanticism, looking at the aesthetics that originated with Schiller and the Jena Romantics in the 1790s, developed further with the American Romantics of the early and mid-nineteenth-century, and reached its fullest theoretical elaboration with Heidegger and the French poststructuralists in the mid-twentieth century, it is interesting to note that Lacan's theory here also finds a certain resonance in the writing of Edgar Allan Poe. In "The Philosophy of Composition," Poe aligned beauty with melancholy—that is, we might say, with the pathological attraction to death—and then went on to assert that, "unquestionably," the combination of beauty and death composed the most legitimate domain of poetry. The death of a beautiful woman, he claimed, was "the most poetical topic in the world" (16–19). It might be further noted that the visual arts were not a special interest of Poe's, and there seems to be no mention in Poe's essays of Beatrice's portrait.

21. For a fuller treatment of Lacan's theory of beauty, readers are referred not only to Rabaté's fine reading of *Antigone* in *Jacques Lacan: Psychoanalysis and the Subject of Literature*, but also to Philippe Van Haute's lovely essay "Death and Sublimation in Lacan's Reading of *Antigone*."

22. When this essay conceives of the symbolic field as the site of being (or of everything possibly discernible as being) and, by extension, of the real as the site of nothing and non-being (what cannot be counted as being), it follows the work of the Lacanian philosopher Alain Badiou in his *Being and Event* (1988). Badiou's work, and his theory of the subject as situated between being and event, between the symbolic and the real, is the topic of the final essay in the present book.

23. Briefly stated, Lacanian theory proposes that it is the inauguration into language that gives birth to the subject as a desiring subject. Prior to language—and thus prior to the gap it introduces in the order of being—there can be no "desire" for the subject, properly speaking. Moreover, this intertwining of desire and language persists. On the one hand, the experience of desire will forever refer the subject to that real lack introduced by the signifier; on the other hand, to address this lack, the subject will commonly attempt to fill that gap by producing more signifiers.

24. In a certain sense, *jouissance* does suggest pleasure, but this pleasure might better be thought of as excitement in the body—one that can be positive and pleasurable, certainly, but also disruptive or deadly. Lacanians think of the symptom, for example, as the pathological persistence of jouissance in the body. Importantly, insofar as we love our symptoms, jouissance can be both pleasurable *and* deadly.

25. In her deeply admirable book *Ethics of the Real*, Alenka Zupančič sees here an opening from Lacan's ethics of desire onto something like an ethics of the drive. Zupančič is striving to account for Lacan's increasing recognition of the centrality of the drive as (in some sense) the goal of an analysis, even if desire remains the path one travels *en route*. See especially 238–45.

Chapter 3. Brown's *Wieland* and the Ethical Circumscription of Death

1. The presumed journalistic source hinted at in Brown's Advertisement is "An Account of a Murder committed by Mr. J— Y— upon his Family, in December, A.D. 1781," which appeared almost fifteen years after the murder, in *The New-York Weekly Magazine; or Miscellaneous Repository* and (in a reprint one month later) in *The Philadelphia Minerva*.

2. Two familiar early American examples of this would be Hannah Foster's *The Coquette* (Boston, 1797) and Susanna Rowson's *Charlotte Temple* (Philadelphia, 1794).

3. Christoph Martin Wieland (1733–1813) was a major German poet and translator (of Shakespeare) who wrote most of his work just before the *Sturm und Drang* period of young Goethe and Schiller. His work was certainly known in American literary circles at the time of Brown's writing. His youthful epic, *Der geprüfte Abraham* (1753), had been published in Boston in 1764 as *The Trial of Abraham*; his late verse romance, *Oberon* (1780), was being translated by

John Quincy Adams at the time Brown was composing his novel; and Brown's *Wieland* explicitly describes the title character as related to the family of Christoph Martin Wieland (6). The point of connection between Brown and the German writer would appear to be a shared interest in Abraham and Isaac, as well as Brown's general admiration for the German writer's "fertile genius" and the poetical quality of his prose (Brown, *Literary Essays* 140). Also, it might be said that the New York Friendly Club, including Brown, Elihu Hubbard Smith, and William Dunlap, took a special interest in German literature generally (Brooks 162). Dunlop translated several Kotzebue plays, Smith was a devoted enthusiast of Schiller, and, according to Bryan Waterman, the eminent (and very helpful) scholar of the Friendly Club, Brown himself took German lessons from a Swiss immigrant named Roulet.

4. Brown adds the Carwin and Pleyel characters, invents the prehistory, and changes the post-history of the murders. Brown does retain from the newspaper account the basic scenario of a devout and respected man who murders his wife and four children in response to a divine (and insatiable) voice; he also retains the female narration framing the murderer's own confession, although the newspaper narrator is *not* identified as the murderer's sister, as in the novel. Also, the murderer is a more sympathetic character in Brown's less brutal telling. Tomhanick is today called Tomhannock and lies about twenty miles northeast of Albany, near the Vermont border.

5. *Wieland* had gone through several London editions in the early nineteenth century, and Brown had a strong reputation among the English Romantics, who were greatly enthusiastic about his work—Percy Shelley and Hazlitt in particular, though also Godwin, Keats, Scott, and Peacock (Cowie 342; also Brooks 23–25). On the continent, there is less evidence I can find of Brown's readership, but at least one Paris translation of *Wieland* had appeared (as *Wieland, ou la Voix mystérieuse*, 1841) by the time Kierkegaard wrote and published *Fear and Trembling* in 1843, and there may have been an even earlier French translation. Brooks asserts that there was a German translation of *Wieland* made in the nineteenth century—and this seems not unlikely—but I have been unable to verify any such published translation until Polakovics's in the 1970s (as *Wieland, oder die Verwandlung*). Whether the English or French versions were known to Kierkegaard by reputation, or whether he himself had access to a German translation, I've not found any surviving record that Kierkegaard was familiar with the novel or its reputation.

6. Derrida. *Donner la mort.* On the unknown 57–60f, 55–58e; on silence 60–62f, 59–60e; on the gift 64f, 63e. Note that page numbers followed by "f" refer to the original French version; those followed by "e" refer to the English translation.

7. Aristotle finds family murders especially productive of tragic affect: "Let us, then, take up the question of what sorts of incidents strike us as terrible or pitiable. . . . What tragedy must seek are cases where the sufferings occur within relationships, such as brother and brother, son and father, mother and son, son and mother—when one kills (or is about to kill) the other, or commits some other such deed" (1453b).

8. We might accept Clara's conclusion that Wieland understands that he is a man of errors, but the fallibility of her powers of interpretation has been one of the continuing motifs of the novel.

9. The quotation comes from *Macbeth* (Act I, scene v). The essence of the passage there is Lady Macbeth's prayer to the "spirits" that, against all nature, she find the necessary cruelty to commit the murder and bring her husband's ambitions to fruition. And further, that the thick of night and the smoke of hell hide her deed even from her own knife, even from heaven itself, which would surely intervene in such a monstrosity by crying forth "hold, hold!"

10. For the horrific image and the limits of language in *Macbeth*, we might think of Macduff's discovery of King Duncan's murder: "O horror, horror, horror! Tongue nor heart cannot conceive nor name thee. . . . Approach the chamber, and destroy your sight with a new Gorgon: do not bid me speak; see, and then speak yourselves . . ." (Act II, scene iii).

11. Isaiah 53:3: "He is despised and rejected of men; a man of sorrows, and acquainted with grief."

12. It is striking how persistently *Wieland* is described in terms of the forceful presentation of a traumatic image. William Dunlap, Brown's friend and biographer wrote, again, in nearly the same terms as Cooper and Clara herself: "Few novels or romances have been written, which seize so strongly upon the imagination and feelings of the reader, hurry him from the realities which surround him, bury in oblivion his joys or sorrows, and fix his whole attention on the images which the author presents before him, as Wieland" (Dunlap 12).

13. This bracketed gloss belongs to the Hong translation of *Fear and Trembling*.

14. The narrator of Brown's best short story, "Thessalonica: A Roman Story" (1799), gives his testimony under the same conditions, only this time in witness to the bloody reprisals of imperial Rome against a rebellious province: "To expatiate upon the scene . . . is a task to which I am unequal. Language sinks under the enormity and complication of these ills. I was a witness and partaker; the images still exist in my imagination as vividly as when they were presented to my senses; my blood is still chilled, my dreams are still agonized by dire remembrance; but my eloquence is too feeble to impart to others the conceptions of my own mind. . . . The period of forgetfulness, or of tranquil existence in another scene, is hastening to console me. Meanwhile, my task shall be, to deliver to you, and to posterity, a faithful narrative" (51–52).

15. Michel Foucault, alluding to Maurice Blanchot (250f, 89e).

Chapter 4. Heideggerian Ethics

1. For a fascinating discussion of Levinas's citation, see Jill Robbins's *Altered Reading*, 117–31.

2. This essay follows the practice of Joan Stambaugh in decapitalizing "being" and in hyphenating *Da-sein*. For her rationale, see the Translator's Preface (1996) to *Being and Time*.

3. For citations in the present essay, page numbers followed by "g" refer to the German language text. Page numbers followed by "e" refer to the English translation. Also, unless specifically noted otherwise (as in this case from "Logos"), the German texts I cite from *Vorträge und Aufsätze* are collected in English translation in *Poetry, Language, Thought*. Throughout the essay, I have modified a number of the translations or retranslated passages entirely to give more literal renderings.

4. Heidegger's German (*das Gegen-einander-über*) sounds rather less Levinasian than the perfectly conventional Hertz translation might suggest to contemporary readers of theory (*Unterwegs* 211g, 103e). *Das Gegen-einander-über* suggests the full array of things opposing the primary thing in question, collectively facing it or standing "over and against" it.

5. This is not to understate the differences between Heidegger and the nineteenth-century American thinker. To take only the most obvious of these, Emerson stages his entire discussion in terms of genius, a Romantic investment in the author that Heidegger would claim to be essentially irrelevant: "That he [Georg Trakl] is the poet remains unimportant here as with every other greatly favored instance of a poem. The great fortune consists precisely in this, that it can deny the poet's person and name" (*Unterwegs* 17–18g, 193e). Still, in the spirit of Paul de Man, one might question Heidegger's actual commitment to such a claim, given his reliance in his late philosophy upon the figures of Hölderlin and various pre-Socratic thinkers such as Heraclitus. See de Man's "Heidegger's Exegeses of Hölderlin" for observations in a similar vein. Moreover, Heidegger and Emerson seem much closer in spirit than other enlightenment and Romantic writers (one thinks of Herder and Rousseau) who likewise speculate on the essentially *poetic* qualities of the earliest language, but who do so without linking it to the specifically *world-opening* potential of poetry intuited by Emerson and Heidegger. See Herder (103–104) and Rousseau (11).

6. Heidegger makes it clear that the force of his essay pertains especially to "great" art (*Holzwege* 26g, 19e)—in addition to van Gogh, the essay mentions, characteristically for Heidegger, classical Greek works (*Antigone*, a temple, the Aegina sculptures) and German poets of high standing (Hölderlin and C. F. Meyer).

7. Julian Young, in his book *Heidegger's Philosophy of Art*, laments the "obsessive" attention lavished by the secondary literature upon this essay and upon the van Gogh meditation in particular (5). Certainly it is true that the essay is among the central texts of contemporary continental aesthetics. Young's complaint, however, is also partly attributable to the way his book highlights Heidegger's 1930s interest in the communal function of ancient Greek art—paradigmatically the Greek temple as it gathers together an entire culture to witness the presencing of world (65). This emphasis has its great payoff in Young's very interesting and valuable discussion of the communal aspect of Heidegger's thinking of art during the Nazi period and in Young's helpful accentuation of shifts in Heidegger's thinking from the 1930s to the 1950s (both of which the present essay has left aside). On the other hand, Young's interpretation leaves him without satisfactory options for discussing the van Gogh painting, which is arguably the best known and most striking feature of the entire essay, but which

Young must call "almost completely irrelevant" (5) and "an anomaly" (65) in Heidegger's thinking of the period, since van Gogh is far too modern to share this communal aspect. As we shall see, the van Gogh meditation shows that, even as early as 1936, Heidegger was developing a compelling theory of art that could positively account for modern painting and poetry, even amid the private conditions prevailing with most art after the great age of the cathedrals.

8. We leave aside here the Meyer Schapiro debate, pursued in *The Truth in Painting* by Jacques Derrida, of precisely which van Gogh painting Heidegger is referring to, and whether the painting in fact represents a *pair* of *peasant woman's* shoes (and not, say, two mismatched left shoes, or else perhaps the shoes of van Gogh himself).

9. Oddly, the English translation of the essay published in *Off the Beaten Track* omits this short sentence.

10. It would be interesting to read the tropes of Heidegger's language here—the prosopopoeia of a painting that stares and speaks—through the lens of Maurice Merleau-Ponty's profound (and very beautiful) final essay, "Eye and Mind" (1961). There, Merleau-Ponty writes of the painter's vision and of a reflexivity of the visible in painting, such that it becomes impossible to distinguish who sees and who is seen, who paints and what is painted (32f, 129e). This ambiguity, or potential reversal in the role of the painter and the visible, the see-er and seen, opens upon Merleau-Ponty's reconsideration of ontology through the experience of vision. The primacy of the visible over the linguistic surely marks a point of contest with Heidegger's orientation around language, but, perhaps despite himself, even Merleau-Ponty will find that a painting can speak. As he says, "[T]here is nothing to prevent the painter from going back to one of the emblems he has shied away from—making it, of course, *speak* differently [*parler autrement*]" (88f, 148e; emphasis mine).

11. Another of Heidegger's examples in "The Origin of the Work of Art."

12. Once again, we might note here an affinity between Emersonian and late Heideggerian thought. For Emerson, too, a life lived in poetic fullness re-presents, with greater or lesser fidelity, not, say, the song of the one's heart, but rather the singing of the phenomenal world itself: "[T]he soul of the thing is reflected by a melody. The sea, the mountain-ridge, Niagara, and every flower-bed, pre-exist, or super-exist, in pre-cantations, which sail like odors in the air, and when any man goes by with an ear sufficiently fine, he overhears them, and endeavors to write down the notes, without diluting or depraving them" (Poet 458–59).

13. Beaufret was the French philosopher most instrumental to the rehabilitation of Heidegger's postwar reputation. He was also, as it happened, an analysand of Lacan's between 1951 and 1953, and would later, over Easter 1955, introduce Lacan to Heidegger in Freiburg. Several months after that, the Heideggers stayed with the Lacans for a few days at La Prévôté, in France. Lacan gave them a speedy tour of the countryside and a look around Chartres Cathedral. Elisabeth Roudinesco gives an informative account of the relations between the three men in her *Jacques Lacan* (1993).

14. Ultimately, it may be that the key difference between the Freudian and Heideggerian accounts of the uncanny lies in their authors' differing emphases in presenting this absence at the heart of subjectivity or human being. For Freud, the absence, or lack, bears upon sociality: in Lacanian terms, upon one's dependence on the jouissance of the Other for the satisfaction of need and upon one's subjection to language and the law of the father. For Heidegger, the absence, or nullity, bears ultimately upon what he calls "thrownness": the fact that human beings find themselves "thrown" into existence without themselves having willed it—which, as he says, means "*never* to have power over one's ownmost Being from the ground up" (*Sein* 284g, 330e).

15. Heidegger's earliest work on the uncanny comes in a phenomenological investigation of dread, just before *Sein und Zeit* (1927), in his 1925 summer lecture course, the *History of the Concept of Time: Prolegomena* (see §30 for the relevant passages). Here, in a way that somewhat anticipates Levinas's analyses of Macbeth's dread before the irremissibility of being (in *De l'existence à l'existant*, 1947), Heidegger analyzes *Angst* as Da-sein's uncanny dread of itself and for itself, its uncanny dread of being-in-the-world as such. He reprises this point about Da-sein in *Being and Time*, again in a discussion of angst and the uncanny (*Sein* 188g, 233e).

16. Yet again, we might recall Emerson, who, in his essay on the "The Poet," proposes that humans are essentially incomplete and that they must strive to complete themselves through speaking or singing their experience in an act of poetic testimony: "[M]an is only half himself, the other half is his expression" (448). In the German tradition, one might recall the work of Hölderlin's occasional sponsor, Friedrich Schiller. In the Sixth Letter from *On the Aesthetic Education of Man* (1795), Schiller remarks, amid tropes of physical violence, on the "dismemberment of being" (586g, 43e), the loss of fullness and harmony afflicting man. See also the Fourteenth Letter on the ultimate irreparability of this state of being (612g, 73e). Like Schiller, Emerson, and Lacan, Heidegger finds this lack to be an irremediable, existential fact of human being bearing essentially on ethics (and also on art and literature and beauty), but unrelated to the loss thematized in the myth of the Fall of Adam or in the Augustinian theology of original sin.

17. This is one of the few places where Heidegger's thinking of the uncanny opens onto history, politics, and ideology, in the familiar sense of these terms. To be sure, the seminar he gave between April and July 1942 displays more than his usual irritation with the Americans, who joined the war against Germany several months earlier, in December 1941. Additionally, one might find it more than merely coincidental that Heidegger turns to *das Unheimliche*, or unhomeliness, for the second half of his course just as, at the end of May 1942, the Royal Air Force's first 1,000 bomber raid devastates the city of Köln, forcing more than one hundred thousand residents from their homes (to say nothing of the massive human dislocations of the war more generally). Still, it is easy to see such traces of history in the seminar as peripheral to Heidegger's meditative accompaniment to Hölderlin's river hymns. To bring the matter closer to the center of Heidegger's concerns, we might note that while humanity must

seek its proper place within relations to world, earth, and divinities—and this is the "pre-political" essence of Western humanity that engages Heidegger's philosophical thought (*Hölderlins* 102g, 82e)—every historical humankind, every actually given culture, must configure these relations differently, and thus must become homely in a different way, as Heidegger himself observes (*Hölderlins* 153g, 123e). In other words, while we all must bear unhomeliness at the center of our being, our being unhomely and our becoming homely are actualized according to historically inflected configurations of the relations between human and divine, master and slave, sacrifice and battle, honor and glory, and so forth. Thus, the classical Greek configuration of Sophocles is necessarily and intrinsically foreign to the Christian, postenlightenment German configuration that Hölderlin and Heidegger were born into. As Heidegger puts it, "[W]hat is proper to the Greeks and what is foreign to them is other than what is proper and what is foreign to the Germans" (*Hölderlins* 154g, 124e). In terms of his own project (or that of his poet, Hölderlin), Heidegger remains undismayed by the foreignness of Greek historicality, since he holds that all "coming to be at home," as we read earlier, is "a passage through the foreign." For the views of a critic who reads Heidegger's discussion of *Antigone* with more acute political suspicion, see Charles Bambach's discussion in *Heidegger's Roots: Nietzsche, National Socialism, and the Greeks* (especially 143–59). Bambach considers the discussion of *Antigone* in *Introduction to Metaphysics* within the context of Heidegger's other writings of the mid-1930s.

18. Heidegger makes this point in *Being and Time* in one of his treatments of uncanniness there. Uncanniness, he writes, "puts Dasein's Being-in-the-world face to face with the 'nothing' of the world; in the face of this 'nothing,' Dasein is anxious with anxiety about its ownmost potentiality-for-Being" (*Sein* 276g, 321e). In the uncanny, Dasein "calls" to itself, as if alien to itself, to care for its own potentiality for being.

19. Hölderlin published his complete translation of Sophocles' *Antigone* in 1804.

20. Heidegger concedes the unconventionality of his translation of το δεινον as *das Unheimliche* or "the uncanny." He justifies this translation ("incorrect" yet "more true," *Hölderlins* 78g 64e), which is indispensable to his most important claims about the play, by asserting that there are three commonly accepted translations for δεινον: the *fearful* that shows itself likewise in horror and in awe, the *powerful* that may be violent or else that everywhere looms over us, and the *inhabitual* that is either the extraordinary or else the universally skilled. As Heidegger observes, Hölderlin himself wavered in translating the term for the choral ode of *Antigone*, rendering it first as *gewaltiger* or "powerful," and later as *ungeheuerer* or "extraordinary." Heidegger, who chooses neither of these, does not claim that the Greeks themselves had a conceptual grasp of δεινον as the uncanny. Rather, he claims that "uncanny" is a term that succeeds in thinking the three terms (fearful, powerful, inhabitual) in their "unity"—that is, in the ground of their belonging together as δεινον (*Hölderlins* 83g, 68e).

21. Robert Fagles, a respected contemporary translator of Sophocles, translates the lines thus:

Of course I did. It wasn't Zeus, not in the least,
who made this proclamation—not to me.
Nor did that Justice, dwelling with the gods
beneath the earth, ordain such laws for men.
Nor did I think your edict had such force
that you, a mere mortal, could override the gods,
the great unwritten, unshakable traditions.
They are alive, not just today or yesterday:
they live forever, from the first of time,
and no one knows when they first saw the light. (Sophocles 82)

22. Here again is Fagles's translation, with "dreadful" doing the work of Heidegger's "uncanny":

Ismene: So fiery—and it ought to chill your heart.
Antigone: I know I please where I must please the most. . . .
Ismene: You're wrong from the start, you're off on a hopeless quest.
Antigone: If you say so, you will make me hate you,
and the hatred of the dead, by all rights,
will haunt you night and day.
But leave me to my own absurdity, leave me
to suffer this—dreadful thing. (Sophocles 64)

23. The heart of Heidegger's discussion of the uncanny in *Being and Time* in fact concerns conscience. There, he declares that *Unheimlichkeit* is "the basic kind of Being-in-the-world" (*Sein* 277g, 322e) and he describes how Da-sein (or human existence, we might say), is grounded in *Unheimlichkeit*. In the ordinary course of things, however, Da-sein is lost in everydayness, covering over its thrownness, obscuring the contingency of its being. In the uncanny call of conscience, in the angst of existential guilt, Da-sein summons itself both to face up to its thrownness and to assume its own potentiality for being. Note that Heidegger's discussion of conscience and guilt here is non-normative, in the sense that these concepts refer not to external ideals, but rather derive from Da-sein's sense of its own potentiality for being. See §§54–58 for a much fuller, more technical discussion of conscience, guilt, and uncanniness.

24. Susan Bernstein's fine article, "It Walks: The Ambulatory Uncanny," is helpful in describing why the uncanny, with its essential violation of the law of noncontradiction, "puts into question the possibility of definition itself" (1112).

Chapter 5. Levinas

1. Leaving aside the personal offense that Levinas often expressed at Heidegger's Nazi party affiliation and his dissatisfaction with Heidegger's unapologetic postwar silence, the principal *philosophical* point of tension in

Levinas's relation to Heidegger rests in Levinas's insistence that ethics, not ontology, properly holds priority in philosophy. There is much to be said on this matter, though the present essay is not quite the venue for it (interested readers might begin with Peter Gratton's excellent treatment in "Heidegger and Levinas on the Question of Temporality"). Within our narrow consideration of the intersection of ethics and aesthetics in poetic language, Levinas and Heidegger were not so very far apart, as we will see—and perhaps closer than Levinas himself sometimes wished to admit. Arguably, Levinas was not always the best judge of his own work's relation to Heidegger. One might think, for example, of the laudatory 1972 essay on Paul Celan where one senses a certain confusion, a wavering of judgment, as Levinas pauses to account for the fact that "Heidegger had known, nonetheless, to celebrate [Paul Celan]" after a visit from the Jewish poet (*Noms* 60f, 40e). Levinas seems uncertain here how to reconcile his habitual view of Heidegger (presumably as an unregenerate Nazi) with the Heidegger whose visits from Celan "nonetheless" almost incredibly, "altered him profoundly," according to "unquestionable testimony" (*Noms* 187n1f, 174n1e). On the matter of art, Levinas's most judicious comparison between his own more Blanchotian views and Heidegger's late philosophy comes in an essay on Maurice Blanchot, where Levinas concedes "the very great proximity between the Heideggerian notion of being and that realization of unreality, that presence of absence, that existence of nothingness that, according to Blanchot, the work of art, the poem, allows us to express" (*Sur* 21f, 136e). At the same time, Levinas firmly resists what he takes to be Heidegger's position, namely that "all that is human can be said, in the final account, in terms of truth, be described as a disclosure of being" (*Sur* 21f, 136e). For Levinas as for Blanchot, literature uncovers a darkness or a shadow, something upon which the category of truth, understood as a disclosure of being, can gain no purchase. Note that, here and throughout this essay, I have modified a number of the translations.

2. Interested readers should look no farther than Jill Robbins's *Altered Reading: Levinas and Literature*, an admirable and erudite book in a thousand respects, which highlights Levinas's view of literature as generally "dismissive" early in his career (Robbins xxi). If, despite the excellence of her book, the present essay must take a different view, perhaps this is owing to a different selection of favored texts, a different focus within the evolution of Levinas's thought, and a different sense for which texts constitute the exceptions in evaluating Levinas's thinking on art. For her argument, Robbins relies especially on a particular reading of "Reality and its Shadow" (1948) and she has little to say in *Altered Reading* about *Otherwise than Being* (1974). She does indeed take some interest in Levinas's readings of Blanchot and other writers and she recognizes that "a more positive appreciation" emerges in these texts from the sixties and seventies (Robbins 75); nonetheless, in terms of her main argument, these for her are exceptions. The interest of the present essay, by contrast, lies precisely in these later texts where, I would say, Levinas's thinking on art has matured. But even in the early texts, I think there is much to support a more generous view of art: Levinas's devotion to *Macbeth*, for example, to the point where Levinas muses whether "the whole of philosophy is only a meditation of

Shakespeare" (*Temps* 60f, 72e), as well as the literary allusion rife throughout his early work. Altogether, I would argue, his early writings might better be described as ambivalent concerning the work of art. And if I would caution against committing Levinas more extremely on the basis of these early texts, this is partly due to the later, less ambiguously positive consideration of art Levinas developed from the mid-1960s, but also partly due to vacillations visible even in the early texts themselves. Finally, at the level of biography, it would be surprising if a philosopher with a genuinely severe regard for art would raise a son to be a professional pianist and a composer of national stature in France. Michaël Lévinas was born in 1949.

3. Levinas's neologism is *la verbalité* in French, which his American translators have rendered variously: Cohen as *verbality* (*Éthique* 38e) and Lingis as *verbalness* (*Autrement* 34–35e). Readers will see from what follows that the root of the word is to be taken as expressing something about grammar (i.e., about verbs, in contrast with nouns), not about orality (i.e., not about the verbal in contrast to the written or the visual).

4. For influential early discussions of the structure of "Nomos Alpha," see Vandenbogaerde's "Analyse de 'Nomos Alpha' de I. Xenakis" as well as Xenakis' own explanations in "Towards a Philosophy of Music."

5. Siegfried Palm's performance of the work is especially fascinating for highlighting the sense of an event unfolding just beyond the grasp of cognition. Palm was an outstanding cellist and a champion of new music in the 1960s. He was also the dedicatee of Xenakis' "Nomos Alpha" and he premiered the work in Bremen, 1966. His 1974 performance was first released on LP by Deutsche Grammophon in 1975. In the energy of his performance and in his labored breathing, Palm gives to the listener an image of the cellist as absolutely committed, body and soul, to this difficult and very physical piece: not passively absorbed but rather utterly focused on the production of sound demanded by the score. The sounds are so precise, so carefully played, and yet so surprising, that Palm himself gives the impression of dwelling, like the listener, fully in the particular sound of the moment, rather than in the larger architecture of the composition.

One can only speculate how the piece came to Levinas's attention, given that (so far as this writer knows) there were no recordings of "Nomos Alpha" available to Levinas during the writing of *Otherwise than Being*. Xenakis was, however, a composer of rising prominence, a writer and publisher of essays on the philosophy of music, and a resident of Paris during much of this period. Indeed, by October 1968, concerts of his music (including a performance of "Nomos Alpha") were selling out in Paris. If Levinas attended the Royan Festival, in Bordeaux, 1969, he may have seen a choreographed performance of "Nomos Alpha." Levinas's son, Michaël, born 1949, was himself a rising young composer by the time of *Otherwise than Being* (1974) and (one speculates) may have brought Xenakis' work to his father's attention. Michaël Lévinas's first important composition, "Arsis et Thésis" was premiered at the Royan Festival in 1972.

6. One thinks here of Levinas's widely reprinted early essay "Reality and its Shadow" (1948), which is ambivalent in its consideration of the status of art

insofar as it sometimes appears to condemn art—for causing the subject to get so completely carried away and for reducing the subject to silence—and yet at other times appears to reach exactly the opposite conclusion—namely, that the temporality of art confronts the subject with his or her existence as, precisely, a *responsible* subject and, moreover, that art calls for a specific type of interpretive response and not for silent satisfaction. The present essay will return to some of these issues in its final section.

7. It may well be, as both Pierre Hayat and Alphonso Lingis imply, that "the image" in Levinas's philosophy owes something to Jean-Paul Sartre's work on the intentional structure of the image in *The Imaginary* (Réalité 15f, 5n4e). Levinas's conceptualization does share several points of contact with Sartre's—a certain immediacy, a certain wholeness or fullness. Nonetheless, Levinas makes the term so thoroughly his own that one might turn more advisedly to other writings in Levinas's oeuvre in trying to get a handle on its sense here. In *Otherwise than Being*, Levinas describes truth as consisting in "the exposition of being to itself." The "image" is the image of the whole necessary for the exposition of being to itself: the image is the part that counts for the whole. Levinas describes two moments of the image relevant to our purposes here. In the first, the *sensible* image is "immediately welcomed without undergoing modifications." In the second moment, the structural inadequacy or divergence, between the whole and the part that is supposed to reflect it, forces the image to assume a *symbolic* dimension that opens upon the field of knowledge, ideas, and theme, and thereby represses the immediacy and passivity of the image qua sensible image (*Autrement* 100–101f, 61e). We might propose that, since sensation as such can have no object, the image is what sensation welcomes in lieu of an object, before the second moment of the image, when sensation lapses into perception and the sensible image lapses into a graspable object.

8. We will see that Levinas's use of the term *saying* here is distinct from the use Heidegger puts it to (as *die Sage*) in his writing on language. For more on Heidegger's usage, see especially the essay, "The Way to Language" (1959) in *Unterwegs zur Sprache*. It would be interesting project to compare the two thinkers on this term (or indeed three thinkers, since Lacan also uses the term in the early 1970s, in *Seminar XX: Encore* and in "L'étourdit" in *Autres écrits*), since saying is a concept that helps each of them articulate the relation between ethics and language. Such a comparison, however, lies somewhat outside the scope of the present essay and must await another occasion. We might briefly note, however, that Levinas's own contention was that Heidegger ignored the saying in his efforts to make the said resonate poetically. See the *God, Death, and Time* lectures for more on Levinas's claim (especially 175f, 151e).

9. For an outstanding general treatment of Levinas's relation to Blanchot, readers are referred to Gabriel Riera's essay, " 'The *Possibility* of the Poetic *Said*' in *Otherwise than Being* (Allusion, or Blanchot in Lévinas)." Paul Davies, in his valuable article "A Fine Risk: Reading Blanchot Reading Levinas," shows that influence between Blanchot and Levinas went in both directions. In particular, Davies shows how various of Blanchot's later writings (for example *The Writing of the Disaster*) were responses to Levinas's *Otherwise than Being*, taking up its

vocabulary (for example, "the saying") and engaging with philosophy through the lens of Levinas's description of responsibility as a response to alterity and the other.

10. In *The Differend*, Lyotard captures well this aesthetic call for ethical response in language. There, Lyotard describes the appearing of the other as "an event of feeling" (164f, 111e) that signals a "differend," a radical dissymmetry in which there is at once an *impossibility* of translating between the two sides of the abyss and a concomitant *obligation* to bear witness to this dissymmetry in language. Cf. §22–23: "The differend is the unstable state and instant of language wherein something which *must* be able to be put into phrases *cannot* yet be. . . . What is at stake in a literature, in a philosophy . . . is to bear witness to differends by finding idioms for them. In the differend, something 'asks' to be put into phrases, and suffers from the wrong of not being able to be put into phrases right away" (29–30f, 13e; my italics).

Chapter 6. Endings

1. *The Marble Faun* was Hawthorne's last book save one—*Our Old Home* (1863), a collection of graceful English travel sketches and reminiscences from his tenure as U.S. Consul in Liverpool.

2. Sidney P. Moss, "The Problem of Theme in *The Marble Faun*," *Nineteenth-Century Fiction* 18, no. 4 (March 1964): 393. The present essay does not contest that the characters read their own tale in light of the *felix culpa* theme. Miriam (1215) and Kenyon (1236), after all, each propose it explicitly as the moral of their story (or perhaps more narrowly as the moral of Donatello's story). On the other hand, their experience of events is not quite identical with the text of Hawthorne's romance. Donatello, for example, is an important part of their small circle of friends—and at the very center of the *felix culpa* theme they describe. For Hawthorne's reader, however, he is a virtual non-character, with very few spoken lines and but little psychological depth or real drama. Unlike each of the other three characters, for example, we never follow Donatello when he is alone and we are rarely invited to consider his thoughts or feelings. From this perspective, it seems hard to sustain the claim that the theme of the romance as a whole centers on the least of the four main characters, even if Hawthorne might seem to anoint Donatello's marble semblance in the title. For a different treatment of the matter, see Merle E. Brown, who argues that the moral theme of Hawthorne's final romance is the same one he always writes about: the necessity of recognizing one's "already existent sinfulness" and taking one's place in the community of human beings who are bound together by sin and dependent upon each other through their inadequacy: "The Structure of *The Marble Faun*," *American Literature* 28, no. 3 (Nov. 1956): 312.

3. "Donatello," said Miriam, coming close to the young man and speaking low, but still with the almost insanity of the moment vibrating in her voice, "if you love yourself— . . . Get you gone without another word."

"I tell you," Miriam went on, "there is a great evil hanging over me! . . . It will overwhelm me as utterly as if this arch should crumble down upon our heads! It will crush you, too, if you stand at my side! . . . Cast me off; or you are lost forever!" (983–84).

4. "I frighten you, you say. For heaven's sake, how? Am I strange? Is there anything wild in my behaviour?" (991).

5. *God, Death, and Time* 23f, 14e.

6. Ibid., 133f, 117e.

7. Gordon Hutner's outstanding study, *Secrets and Sympathy: Forms of Disclosure in Hawthorne's Novels*, offers a strong, alternative reading of *The Marble Faun* to that of the present essay. Hutner focuses on Hawthorne's repeated emphasis on *sympathy* as the way in which the subject is able to enter properly into the work of art and thus intuit, in an act of interpretation, the merely suggested answers that the author of the romance leaves in a state of secrecy. For Hutner, and for his Hawthorne, reading is "a collaborative activity of finding a work's most resonant possibilities, most precise attainments of perfection, the fulfillment of a work's suggestiveness, the apprehension of its deepest secrets" (152). As will be seen, the present essay argues, rather, that sympathy is important as a way for the reader to strive *and fail* to rationalize the mystery of the text, so that the sympathetic reader is ultimately brought, like Kenyon vanishing under the granite weight of Rome and like Miriam surveying the chasm, to face the void of the real: the *impossibility* of its final disclosure and the *failure* of its apprehension. One might take issue with Hutner's emphasis on interpretation as the self-evident end of reading, but Hutner's entire study offers many points of interest and is highly recommended.

8. Edgardo Mortara was born to a Jewish family in Bologna. After he was secretly baptized by his nurse, however, the six-year-old boy was seized from his parents and raised in the household of Pope Pius IX—an abduction sanctioned by Vatican law, which then held that any baptized child must be raised within a Catholic household. The scandal that then erupted inspired controversy all over Europe and America, and even became the subject of topical dramas such as *La Tireuse de cartes* (1859), by the New Orleans–born playwright Victor Séjour, and *Mortara, or The Pope and His Inquisitors* (1860), by the Cincinnati playwright, Herman Moos.

9. Critic Michael T. Gilmore, in his lovely *Surface and Depth: The Quest for Legibility in American Culture*, writes that Hawthorne signals a "swerve of high or elite literature from the popular pressure toward legibility" (80). We see in *The Marble Faun*, however, that Hawthorne's "swerve" is even more radical than Gilmore claims. At hand above, and throughout the novel, is no mere privacy-protecting refusal of disclosure, something that might (hypothetically) be impolitely wrested from the narrator or a given character, or else freely offered in a kind of confession. Rather, what we see above is the simultaneous insistence that the mystery is crucial for understanding everything of importance about the novel, and, at the same time, a declaration that its revelation is irrecoverable. There is an answer, the romance seems to say, but discovering it is a structural impossibility.

10. This, at any rate, is what Hawthorne told his American publisher, George Ticknor, according to the editors of the Library of America edition of the novel. See the note on page 1271. The same note remarks that early reviewers of the novel also complained of the open ending.

11. As it happens, and as Susan Williams reminds us, the biographical Hawthorne was in fact rather bitter and unforgiving of those readers and critics who attacked the novel's ending (Williams 156). Nonetheless, as Williams also notes, the novel found plenty of readers—albeit readers who perhaps treasured the book especially as a tourist's literary companion to the sights of Rome and its art galleries—certainly a transparent retreat to the "illusive stage-scenery" of Rome, if this was the extent of the readers' engagement with the more literary qualities of the romance.

Chapter 7. Riven

1. Badiou, *Conditions* 158f, *Theoretical Writings* 22e. Note that page numbers followed by "e" refer to the English translations; those followed by "f" refer to the French language edition.

2. Badiou, *Conditions* 159f, *Theoretical Writings* 22e.

3. Badiou, *Petit Manuel* 12f, 3e. Jacques Rancière, in his "Aesthetics, Inaesthetics, Anti-Aesthetics," rightly contests ascribing to the German Romantics (as Badiou seems to do) any claim that art alone is capable of truth (Hallward 220).

4. Many of the issues in the present essay are recast from a more mathematically engaged standpoint in Arkady Plotnitsky's excellent article "Badiou's Equations—and Inequalities: A Response to Robert Hughes's 'Riven.' " Plotnitsky's article is a very rich one, but a special point of interest is his careful description of Badiou's relation to mathematics, reminding readers that Badiou is, in the final analysis, working with mathematical ontology (not mathematics) and his stance is a philosophical one (not a mathematical one): Badiou, in Plotnitsky's reading, is most essentially a philosopher of discontinuity and the ontologically multiple. In some ways, then, Plotnitsky's article forms an important complement to the present essay by insisting both upon the centrality of mathematics and upon the multiple as a vital pole in the larger context of Badiou's thought, a larger context set aside in the present essay's focus on discontinuity and art.

5. Badiou names Lacan himself an "anti-philosopher," but his estimation of the importance of Lacanian thought for contemporary philosophy is nevertheless the very highest. As he writes in his *Manifesto*: "The anti-philosopher Lacan is a condition of the renaissance of philosophy. A philosophy is possible today, only if it is compossible with Lacan" (*Manifeste* 64f, 84e).

6. *Almagestes* (1964), *Portulans* (1967), and *Calme bloc ici-bas* (1997); also a short story, "L'Autorisation" (1967), and a romanopéra, *L'Echarpe rouge* (1979), according to Peter Hallward's very helpful bibliography in the English translation of *Ethics* (151–59e). Badiou's plays include *Ahmed le subtil* (1994),

Ahmed se fâche, suivi par Ahmed philosophe (1995), and *Citrouilles* (1995); the writing of the first of these seems to have been underway as Badiou was writing his *Ethics* in the summer of 1993. Evidently there are other theatrical pieces, too: in the prologue to his book on Saint Paul, Badiou mentions one from the early 1980s called *The Incident at Antioch* (1f, 1e).

7. See his *Manifesto* (60f, 80e), also *L'éthique* (63f, 43e) and *Conditions* 201f, *Theoretical Writings* 123e. The relation between truth and knowledge is a complex one for Badiou. For present purposes, we might think of knowledge as something like the degraded and distinct afterlife of a truth—*degraded* since, following Lacan, Badiou asserts that "a truth is essentially unknown" (*Conditions* 201f; *Theoretical Writings* 123e) and that "what we *know* of truth is merely knowledge" (*Conditions* 192f; *Theoretical Writings* 114e), and *distinct*, since, as this paragraph makes plain, knowledge as such no longer enjoys the status of truth and is precisely what is disrupted and reorganized by the appearance of a new truth.

8. Correspondingly, as Badiou notes in his interview with Lauren Sedofsky, "most of the time, the great majority of us live outside ethics" ("Being by Numbers" 124).

9. One might read Peter Hallward's introduction to his *Think Again* collection for an illuminating and concise presentation of the essential anticonservatism of Badiou's thought (Hallward 7–12). For a much fuller treatment of Badiou's effort to think the possibility of novelty, see Adrian Johnston's outstanding piece, "The Quick and the Dead: Alain Badiou and the Split Speeds of Transformation," and its sequels: Žižek's essay, "Badiou: Notes from an Ongoing Debate," and Johnston's reply, "Addendum: Let a thousand flowers bloom!—Some Brief Remarks on and Responses to Žižek's 'Badiou: Notes from an Ongoing Debate,' " all found in the same issue of the *International Journal of Žižek Studies* (1, no. 2).

10. Regarding Badiou's relation to the Romantics, it might be observed that Badiou's claim here echoes the very influential description of "the literary" made by Friedrich Schlegel: that literature is an interrogation of its own status (for example, in *Athenaeum Fragments*, numbers 116 and 255). Badiou may be familiar with this claim from the work of his colleagues, Philippe Lacoue-Labarthe and Jean-Luc Nancy, whose well-known work *The Literary Absolute* is concerned with the aesthetics of Schlegel and the Jena Romantics. Badiou cites Lacoue-Labarthe and Nancy's book (but does not name Schlegel) in his *Ethics* (112f, 84e).

11. For Badiou there is the possibility (the necessity, really, since no truth procedure is solipsistic) for a collective subjectivity. In brief, all those who bear witness to a given truth event enter into the composition of *one* subject (64f, 43e). Hence, Berg and Webern, for example, together with other witnesses to the Schoenberg event, compose but one subject. Badiou (and Hallward, his translator for the *Ethics*) write of the subject in the singular (however multiple its composition in terms of human individuals); I shall follow suit.

12. In the *Critique of Judgment* (1790), Kant is, of course, writing of the beautiful very generally, not specifically of beautiful *art* (indeed his examples are

natural ones: flowers, birds, crustaceans). See the General Comment on the First Division of the Analytic for a compact description of subjective harmony in the beautiful and §27 for remarks on "restful contemplation" in the beautiful.

13. Apollon elaborates his concept of the "letters of the body" in several essays included in the *After Lacan* collection, most explicitly in the chapter of that name, "The Letter of the Body" (103–15).

14. Lacan is the thinker of love named most frequently by Badiou: "I moreover know of no theory of love having been as profound as [Lacan's] since Plato's, the Plato of the *Symposium* that Lacan dialogues with over and over again" (*Manifeste* 63f, 83e). The final section of the present essay returns to Badiou's conceptualization of love.

15. Here is how Badiou describes the Lacanian real in an interview with Peter Hallward that serves as an appendix to the English translation of *Ethics*: "What especially interested me about Lacan was his conception of the real. . . . And in particular, this conception of the real as being, in a situation, in any given symbolic field, the point of impasse, or the point of impossibility, which precisely allows us to think the situation as a whole, according to its real" (121e).

16. See Jacques Lacan, *Le Séminaire XI*, 51f, 52e and 54f, 55e, where Lacan describes "the real as trauma," as his editor, Jacques-Alain Miller, writes in the topical subheading. Lacanians in general tend to regard the key theoretical insight of the talking cure as the intuition that language, always and inevitably, carries some supplement of trauma at its core. For a fascinating discussion of how it is that language—in certain respects absolutely heterogeneous to the unrepresentable real—nonetheless implies an element of the traumatic real, readers might usefully consult three essays by the Gifric analysts in Québec: Willy Apollon's "The Letter of the Body," Danielle Bergeron's "Violence in Works of Art, or, Mishima, from the Pen to the Sword," and Lucie Cantin's "The Trauma of Language," all available in their *After Lacan* collection.

17. A neologism.

18. One point of genuine contrast between the ethics of Lacan and Badiou: for Badiou the *object* of ethics (that which his ethical subject pursues with faithful tenacity) matters much more than for Lacan, for whom the subject's particular object of desire is less important than the subject's "access to desire" generally—that is, apart from the particularity of this or that object (*Le Séminaire VII*, 370–71f, 321e). Also, while everyone seems to agree that Badiou's real is Lacanian in most important respects, there is some question as to precisely how far the similarity extends—that is, how Lacanian Badiou's real really is. The present essay, like Alenka Zupančič's *Ethics of the Real*, treats the Lacanian real and the Badiouian real as basically correspondent within the specific context of a particular discussion of literature and ethics (for Zupančič, see especially 234–38). Arkady Plotnitsky, in his "Badiou's Equations—and Inequalities: A Response to Robert Hughes's 'Riven,' " finds Badiou has developed the Lacanian real in a direction perhaps more open to the political than Lacan's; one hopes Plotnitsky will find future occasion to clarify and develop this claim. The outstanding Lacanian critic, Juliet Flower MacCannell, a more critical reader of Badiou, finds that the place of the real in Badiou's philosophy reflects an untenable fantasy of seizing the

energies of the drive for other purposes, as if to compel the real-as-impossible to become possible (MacCannell 153–54).

19. Distinguishing truth from opinion (or from mere simulacrum of truth) appears to be a key point of difficulty in the elaboration of Badiou's project thus far. Badiou himself commits the problem to the care of philosophy and regards it as the central task of philosophy—the ethical task of philosophy—to seize the truths that appear in art (and in science, love, and politics) and to announce them and distinguish them from mere opinion (*Petit Manuel* 28–29f, 14–15e). In this way, philosophy, too, faces the real, but it also contributes to the elaboration of truths within sense. Ernesto Laclau, in his incisive essay on Badiou, seems not to be comforted by the aid of philosophy in sorting out the success of such wagers. As Laclau puts it, one can hardly look to the logic of the situation itself to identify its true void as in fact an event of truth; nor, in the case of a pseudo-event, can one really look to the pseudo-event to declare itself as mere simulacrum. In short, as we have also seen above, there seems to be no place within Badiou's theoretical edifice from which to decisively enunciate a truth/simulacrum distinction (Hallward 123–26).

20. In this "Mallarmé" chapter from *Being and Event*, Badiou does not explicitly develop his thoughts on Mallarmé's stellar imagery in the poem, "Coup de dés," but it seems plain that, here as elsewhere for Badiou, "stellar" carries a Mallarméan resonance (see also *Deleuze* 11f, 4e and *Petit Manuel* 89f, 56e).

21. Žižek's best-known essay on Badiou, "The Politics of Truth, or, Alain Badiou as a Reader of St Paul," is largely staged in terms of Lacan's *Seminar VII: The Ethics of Psychoanalysis*. See *The Ticklish Subject* (127–70). Žižek specifically cites Lacan's ethical formula (*ne pas céder sur son désir*) at least twice in the same volume (153, 297).

22. Levinas employs the term throughout his late masterwork, *Otherwise than Being* (1974), where "trauma" appears in a number of contexts, from the way the transcendent encounter with alterity *befalls* the chosen ethical subject prior to will (10f, xlii-e and 95f, 56e), to the ethical exposure of the subject to sensibility and to pain in particular (82f, 48e), to the violence and unrepresentability in the "non-relation" of subject and other (196–97f, 123e and 195n1f, 197n27e), to the general problem of an ethics which strikes one from a place outside of being (225f, 144e). One might also recall Levinas's answer to Philippe Nemo's first question ("How does one begin thinking?") in the *Ethics and Infinity* (1982) interviews: "It probably begins through traumatisms or gropings to which one does not even know how to give verbal form . . ." (11f, 21e).

23. Gabriel Riera's essay "For an Ethics of Mystery: Philosophy and the Poem" describes and develops Badiou's claim that philosophy has abdicated certain aspects of its task and that, in what Badiou calls the "age of the poets," poetry has assumed aspects of thought that belong more properly to philosophy. In particular, Riera highlights Badiou's effort to articulate a new relation between philosophy and the poem, one that would, as against Heidegger's suture, work from the position that the truths of the poem belong to the work of art while nonetheless being included within philosophy.

24. "L'écriture du générique: Samuel Beckett."

25. "Qu'est-ce que l'amour?" On this point regarding the novel, see 254f, 264e.

26. This is a reference to Beckett's short prose piece entitled "Lessness" (1970), which describes the endlessness of a landscape, ash grey under a grey sky, which Badiou associates as "the place of being" (L'écriture 334f, 6e).

27. In the last chapter of his book on *Metapolitics*, Badiou elaborates more fully on the numericality of politics and gives some brief hints concerning the numericalities for *science*, and for *art* (whose first term is a *finite number*). Regarding art in particular, he remarks, somewhat cryptically, that "Art presents the sensible in the finitude of a work, and the infinite only intervenes in it to the extent that the artist destines the infinite to the finite" (*Abrégé* 143e; also *Theoretical Writings* 154e).

28. Peter Dews, in his essay "States of Grace," also remarks, briefly, on the similarity of such structures in the thought of the two thinkers, insofar as Badiou and Levinas share a contrast between "the immanence of the domain of natural life and its transcendent interruption" (Hallward 114).

29. The "dim" is another of Badiou's references to Beckett's "Lessness" and the "grey black" place of being.

30. Badiou's own readings of poets such as Mallarmé, Pessoa, and others, show him to be very attentive to matters of theme, image, and language. This section of the present essay, then, does not make claims on how one ought to read a poem (Badiou makes no prescriptions on this point); rather, it aims to suggest how Badiouian philosophy situates poetry and poetic language in relation to a truth and its elaboration.

31. Lacan may well say this in *Le Séminaire, Livre XXIII: Le Sinthome* (1975–76), as Badiou indicates, but this claim is more readily available in the opening lines of Lacan's 1973 *Television* broadcast: "I always speak the truth. Not the whole truth, because there's no way, to say it all. Saying it all is literally impossible: words fail. Yet it's through this very impossibility that the truth holds onto the real" (Lacan. *Autres écrits* 509f, 3e).

32. Given his particular philosophical perspective, it makes sense that Badiou also regards psychoanalytic theory after Lacan as, above all, an elaboration of the Two of sexuation—and love, as Badiou writes, "is that from which the Two is thought" (*Manifeste* 63f, 83e). Hence, for Badiou, psychoanalysis after Lacan "is the modern treatment of the condition of love" (*Manifeste* 24f, 44e).

33. In the Sixth Letter from *On the Aesthetic Education of Man* (586g, 43e). Curiously, Ralph Waldo Emerson, in his essay "The American Scholar," uses a similarly vivid trope, describing man as a sort of monstrous amputee (53–54).

34. *Erläuterungen* 36g, 54e. To be clear, I am not claiming that Heidegger, any more than Lacan or Badiou, is a thoroughgoing Romantic; only that Heidegger's views specifically *on art* derive from the tradition initiated by the Romantics (though of course, in Heidegger's case, poetry is no small part of his later thought).

35. One might say that Lacan's entire theory of art, as it appears in the *Ethics* seminar he gives his clinical trainees, aims to work through a practical

puzzle: Why is it that, in the course of an analysis, when the analysand approaches something he recognizes as "aggressive towards the fundamental terms of his subjective constellation," he will, with predictable regularity, make reference to some work of literature or music (*Le Séminaire VII,* 280f, 238–39e; my translation)?

36. Badiou's clear sense that horror is but one aspect of the void or hole of the real, is shown when he discusses the inaugural trauma of the subject in a 1991 paper presented to the Department of Psychoanalysis at the Paul-Valéry University: "We are so accustomed to thinking of castration in terms of horror that we are astonished to hear Lacan discussing it in terms of love . . ." (*Conditions* 197f; *Theoretical* 120e).

37. Žižek 159. For a superb treatment of Žižek's relation to Badiou (and an outstanding treatment of Badiou's relation to materialist thought in the tradition of Althusser), see Bruno Bosteels's careful two-part essay in *Pli*, "Alain Badiou's Theory of the Subject: The Recommencement of Dialectical Materialism?" See also Žižek's rejoinder to Bosteels, "From Purification to Subtraction: Badiou and the Real" (Hallward 165–81), a much stronger essay than his earlier venture in *The Ticklish Subject.* In the newer essay, Žižek offers a more appreciative account of Badiou's engagement with finitude and the real, though he misstates the case when he writes that the

> ultimate difference between Badiou and Lacan thus concerns the relationship between the shattering encounter of the Real and the ensuing arduous work of transforming this explosion of negativity into a new order. For Badiou, this new order "sublates" the exploding negativity into a new consistent truth, while for Lacan, every Truth displays the structure of a (symbolic) fiction, i.e. no Truth is able to touch the Real. (Hallward 177)

It is not clear to me that Žižek has located a genuine dispute here. Badiou's subject may indeed be tasked with "sublating" the truth into a new order of language, logic, and sense, but Badiou also seems well aware that the status of the truth *as real* is lost in that very process and has instead lapsed into mere knowledge—albeit a new knowledge with (if one may put it this way) a still vibrant relation to the truth as real. Readers may recall a claim this essay cited earlier: "What we *know* of truth is merely knowledge" (*Conditions* 192f; *Theoretical Writings* 114e). I am intrigued, however, by Žižek's idea that a kind of formalization, as an approach to the real, might allow Badiou to surpass the "Kantian" impasse that Žižek sees in the way Badiou manages the gap between situational knowledge and real truth and between finite animal and immortal subject (Hallward 174, 178). Regarding Žižek's critique of Badiou's Kantianism, see Adrian Johnston's fine "There is Truth, and then there are truths—or, Slavoj Žižek as a Reader of Alain Badiou."

38. Badiou's examples in the *Ethics* book include a range of contemporary moral discourses, from multiculturalism to Western humanitarianism to a certain formation of human rights discourse. Briefly put, Badiou's philosophical

objections to these moral discourses are fourfold. First, the centrality of the image of victimhood poses evil as primary and poses good as merely reactive and remediary. Second, the *image* of suffering (with the emotion of horror it produces) cripples thought and reason, including any truly progressive analysis of oppression. Third, in making a fetish of human suffering, such discourses take as their object only the most animal aspect of humanity and do not recognize the human being defined by his or her potential for situation-transcending thought and action. Fourth and finally, the set-apartness of any group under the exceptional name of "victim" participates in the anti-universalist gesture that (as in the case of the European Jews) made possible their oppression to begin with. This fourth objection, or rather its example of the European and Israeli Jews in the twentieth and twenty-first centuries, has inspired a rather spirited public exchange in *Les temps modernes* (Dec. 2005 to Feb. 2006), where Badiou was accused of anti-Semitism. Eric Marty subsequently published his polemic as *Une querelle avec Alain Badiou, philosophe* (Gallimard, 2007).

In the short interview with Nicolas Weill appearing in *Le Monde*, 15 July 2007, Badiou defends himself concisely against the anti-Semitism charge and presents to a general reader his defense of universalism as emancipatory. To be brief, Badiou's philosophical claim is that, in an event, the ethical subject identifies the void of the existing situation as pertaining universally within that situation, informing its every aspect. Truth, we recall, is always universal for Badiou: a truth is true for all. In a pseudo-event, as in the revolutionary break claimed by the Nazis, the universality of the void is disavowed and the void itself displaced onto an exceptional set of particular elements (*L'éthique* 99–100f, 74e). For the Nazis, the Jews (and others) filled this function and were subsequently, brutally, "voided" to speciously assert plenitude (rather than a void) in a situation that named German Jews as exceptions to the "German people." Badiou sees a contemporary moral plenitude or prestige attached to the word *Jew*, and insofar as it refers to the sufferings of the Jews in the Holocaust, it participates in that same gesture of setting apart a subset of elements as exceptional and subject to its own moral "truth." Badiou is not at all dismissive of man's "animal" suffering or making a general, philosophical objection to collective action in pursuit of justice or, for that matter, contesting the historical suffering of the Jewish people or their rights to live in Israel. He is arguing that brutality and oppression are often banal cruelties "beneath" good and evil, having no relation to any situation-transcending event. He is arguing that any true political good proceeds from a universalist avowal of the real of a situational void, not a particularist displacement of the void. And, he is arguing that a properly human politics proceeds out of an ethical fidelity to a singular, radical truth that inventively addresses the state of the situation and holds forth the promise of producing something new in relation to that situation.

Works Cited

Anna. "An Account of a Murder committed by Mr. J— Y— upon his Family, in December, A.D. 1781." *New-York Weekly Magazine; or Miscellaneous Repository.* 20 and 27 July 1796: 20, 28. Rpt. in *Philadelphia Minerva.* 20 and 27 Aug. 1796.

Apollon, Willy. "The Letter of the Body." 1989. *After Lacan: Clinical Practice and the Subject of the Unconscious.* Ed. Robert Hughes and Kareen Malone. Albany: State University of New York Press, 2002. 103–15.

Aristotle. *Physics, Books III and IV.* c. 340 BCE. Trans. Edward Hussey. New York: Oxford University Press, 1993.

———. *Poetics.* 335 BCE. Ed. and Trans. Stephen Halliwell. Cambridge: Harvard University Press, 1995.

Augustinus, Aurelius. *Confessions.* c. 400 CE. Trans. William Watts. Cambridge: Harvard University Press, 1979.

Badiou, Alain. *Abrégé de métapolitique.* Paris: Éditions du Seuil, 1998. Trans. as *Metapolitics.* Trans. Jason Barker. London: Verso, 2006.

———. "Being by Numbers: Lauren Sedofsky Talks with Alain Badiou." *Artforum* (October 1994): 84–87, 118, 123–24.

———. *Conditions.* Paris: Éditions du Seuil, 1992.

———. *Deleuze: « La clameur de l'Etre ».* Paris: Hachette, 1997. Trans. as *Deleuze: The Clamor of Being.* Trans. Louise Burchill. Minneapolis: University of Minnesota Press, 1999.

———. "L'écriture du générique: Samuel Beckett." 1989. *Conditions.* 329–66. Trans. as "The Writing of the Generic." *On Beckett.* Ed. by Alberto Toscano and Nina Power. Manchester, England: Clinamen Press, 2003. 1–36.

———. *L'éthique: Essai sur la conscience du Mal.* Paris: Éditions Hatier, 1993. Trans. as *Ethics: An Essay on the Understanding of Evil.* Trans. Peter Hallward. London: Verso, 2001.

———. *L'être et l'événement.* Paris: Éditions du Seuil, 1988. Trans. as *Being and Event.* Trans. Oliver Feltham. London: Continuum, 2005.

———. *Manifeste pour la philosophie.* Paris: Éditions du Seuil, 1989. Trans. as *Manifesto for Philosophy.* Trans. Norman Madarasz. Albany: State University of New York Press, 1999.

———. *Petit Manuel d'Inesthetique*. Paris: Éditions du Seuil, 1998. Trans. as *Handbook of Inaesthetics*. Trans. Alberto Toscano. Stanford: Stanford University Press, 2005.

———. "Qu'est-ce que l'amour?" *Conditions*. 253–73. Trans. as "What is Love?" Trans. Justin Clemens. *Sexuation*. Ed. Renata Salecl. Durham: Duke University Press, 2000. 263–81.

———. "Le Recours philosophique au poème." *Conditions*. 93–107. Trans. as "Philosophy and Art." In *Infinite Thought*. Ed. Oliver Feltham and Justin Clemens. London: Continuum, 2003. 69–82.

———. *Saint Paul: La fondation de l'universalisme*. Paris: Presses Universitaires de France, 1997. Trans. as *Saint Paul: The Foundation of Universalism*. Trans. Ray Brassier. Stanford: Stanford University Press, 2003.

———. *Le Siècle*. Paris: Éditions du Seuil, 2005. Trans. as *The Century*. Trans. Alberto Toscano. Cambridge: Polity Press, 2007.

———. *Theoretical Writings*. Trans. Ray Brassier and Alberto Toscano. London: Continuum, 2004.

Bambach, Charles. *Heidegger's Roots: Nietzsche, National Socialism, and the Greeks*. Ithaca: Cornell University Press, 2003.

Bergeron, Danielle. "Violence in Works of Art, or, Mishima, from the Pen to the Sword." 1997. *After Lacan: Clinical Practice and the Subject of the Unconscious*. Ed. Robert Hughes and Kareen Malone. Albany: State University of New York Press, 2002. 181–92.

Bernstein, Susan. "It Walks: The Ambulatory Uncanny." *MLN* 118 (2004): 1111–39.

Bosteels, Bruno. "Alain Badiou's Theory of the Subject: Part I. The Recommencement of Dialectical Materialism?" *Pli* 12 (2001): 200–29.

———. "Alain Badiou's Theory of the Subject: The Recommencement of Dialectical Materialism? (Part II)" *Pli* 13 (2002): 172–208.

Brobjer, Thomas. *Nietzsche's Philosophical Context: An Intellectual Biography*. Urbana: University of Illinois Press, 2008.

Brooks, Van Wyck. *The World of Washington Irving*. New York: E. P. Dutton, 1944.

Brown, Charles Brockden. *Literary Essays and Reviews*. Ed. Alfred Weber and Wolfgang Schäfer. Frankfurt am Main: Peter Lang, 1992.

———. *Three Gothic Novels: Wieland, or, The Transformation; Arthur Mervyn, or, Memoirs of the Year 1793; Edgar Huntly, or, Memoirs of a Sleep-Walker*. New York: The Library of America, 1998.

———. *Wieland oder die Verwandlung*. Trans. Friedrich Polakovics. Munich: Deutscher Taschenbuch Verlag, 1977.

———. *Wieland, ou la Voix mystérieuse*. Trans. Auguste Callet and Javelin Pagnon. Two vols. in 8 numbers. Paris: W. Coquebert, 1841.

Burton, Tim, dir. *Sleepy Hollow*. Adapt. Andrew Kevin Walker. Paramount Pictures, 1999. DVD. Paramount Pictures, 2000.

Cantin, Lucie. "The Trauma of Language." 1993. *After Lacan: Clinical Practice and the Subject of the Unconscious*. Ed. Robert Hughes and Kareen Malone. Albany: State University of New York Press, 2002. 35–47.

Caruth, Cathy, ed. *Trauma: Explorations in Memory.* Baltimore: Johns Hopkins University Press, 1995.

Chase, Richard. *The American Novel and its Tradition.* 1957. Baltimore: Johns Hopkins University Press, 1980.

Clemens, Justin. *The Romanticism of Contemporary Theory: Institution, Aesthetics, Nihilism.* London: Ashgate, 2003.

Cornell, Drucilla. "Rethinking the Beyond of the Real." *Levinas and Lacan: The Missed Encounter.* Ed. Sarah Harasym. Albany: State University of New York Press, 1998. 139–81.

Cowie, Alexander. Historical Essay. *Wieland; or The Transformation. An American Tale.* By Charles Brockden Brown. Bicentennial Edition. Kent, Ohio: Kent State University Press, 1977. 311–48.

Crane, Stephen. "Should the Wide World Roll Away." 1895. *Prose and Poetry: Maggie: A Girl of the Streets; The Red Badge of Courage; Stories, Sketches, and Journalism; Poetry.* New York: The Library of America, 1984.

Cray, Robert E. Jr. "Major John André and the Three Captors: Class Dynamics and Revolutionary Memory Wars in the Early Republic, 1780–1831." *Journal of the Early Republic* 17, no. 3 (Fall 1997): 371–97.

Critchley, Simon. "The Original Traumatism: Levinas and Psychoanalysis." *Questioning Ethics: Contemporary Debates in Philosophy.* Ed. Richard Kearney and Mark Dooley. London: Routledge, 1999. 230–42.

Davies, Paul. "A Fine Risk: Reading Blanchot Reading Levinas." *Re-Reading Levinas.* Ed. Robert Bernasconi and Simon Critchley. Bloomington: Indiana University Press, 1991.

De Man, Paul. "Heidegger's Exegeses of Hölderlin." 1955. *Blindness and Insight: Essays in the Rhetoric of Contemporary Criticism.* Second Edition. Minneapolis: University of Minnesota Press, 1983.

Derrida, Jacques. "Adieu." 1997. *Adieu to Emmanuel Levinas.* Trans. Pascale-Anne Brault and Michael Naas. Stanford: Stanford University Press, 1999.

———. *Donner la mort; L'éthique du don: Jacques Derrida et la pensée du don.* Ed. Jean-Michel Rabaté and Michael Wetzel. Paris: Métailié-Transition, 1992. *Donner la mort* trans. as *The Gift of Death.* Trans. David Wills. Chicago: University of Chicago Press, 1995.

———. *The Truth in Painting.* 1978. Trans. Geoff Bennington and Ian McLeod. Chicago: University of Chicago Press, 1987.

———. "Violence et métaphysique: Essai sur la pensée d'Emmanuel Lévinas." 1964. *L'écriture et la différence.* Paris: Éditions du Seuil, 1967. Trans. as "Violence and Metaphysics: An Essay on the Thought of Emmanuel Levinas." *Writing and Difference.* Trans. Alan Bass. Chicago: University of Chicago Press, 1978.

Disney Productions. *The Adventures of Ichabod and Mr. Toad.* Narr. Bing Crosby. Walt Disney Productions, 1949. DVD. Walt Disney Home Video, 2000.

Dunlap, William. *The Life of Charles Brockden Brown: Together With Selections from the Rarest of his Printed Works, from his Original Letters, and from his Manuscripts Before Unpublished. Volume II.* Philadelphia: James P. Parke, 1815.

Emerson, Ralph Waldo. "The Poet." 1844. *Essays and Lectures.* New York: The Library of America, 1983.

Feidelson, Charles. *Symbolism and American Literature.* Chicago: University of Chicago Press, 1953.

Foucault, Michel. "Le langage à l'infini." 1963. *Dits et écrits 1954–1988. Vol I, 1954–1969.* Ed. Daniel Defert and François Ewald, with Jacques Lagrange. Paris: Gallimard, 1994. 250–61. Trans. as "Language to Infinity." *Aesthetics, Method, and Epistemology. Essential Works of Foucault 1954–1984. Volume Two.* Ed. James D. Faubion. Trans. Robert Hurley and others. New York: The New Press, 1998. 89–101.

Freud, Sigmund. "Das Unbehagen in der Kultur." 1930. *Gesammelte Werke. XIV.* Ed. Anna Freud et al. Frankfurt am Main: Fischer Taschenbuch Verlag, 1999. 419–506. Trans. as *Civilization and Its Discontents. The Standard Edition of the Complete Psychological Works of Sigmund Freud. Volume XXI.* Ed. James Strachey. London: The Hogarth Press, 1961. 57–145.

———. "Das Unheimliche." 1919. *Gesammelte Werke. XII.* Ed. Anna Freud et al. Frankfurt am Main: Fischer Taschenbuch Verlag, 1999. Trans. as "The Uncanny." *The Standard Edition of the Complete Psychological Works of Sigmund Freud. Volume XVII.* Ed. James Strachey. London: The Hogarth Press, 1955.

Gilmore, Michael T. *Surface and Depth: The Quest for Legibility in American Culture.* Oxford: Oxford University Press, 2003.

Gratton, Peter. "Heidegger and Levinas on the Question of Temporality." *Journal of Philosophical Research* 30 (2005): 157–68.

Hallward, Peter, ed. *Think Again: Alain Badiou and the Future of Philosophy.* New York: Continuum, 2004.

Harding, Walter. *Emerson's Library.* Charlottesville: The University Press of Virginia, 1967.

Hawthorne, Nathaniel. *Collected Novels: Fanshawe; The Scarlet Letter; The House of the Seven Gables; The Blithedale Romance; The Marble Faun.* New York: The Library of America, 1983.

———. *The French and Italian Notebooks.* Ed. Thomas Woodson. Columbus: Ohio State University Press, 1980.

Hegel, G. W. F. *Aesthetics: Lectures on Fine Art. Volume 1.* 1835. Trans. T. M. Knox. Oxford: Clarendon Press, 1998.

Heidegger, Martin. "Brief über den Humanismus." 1946. *Wegmarken.* Dritte Aufl. Ed. Friedrich-Wilhelm von Herrmann. Frankfurt am Main: Vittorio Klostermann, 1996. Trans. as "Letter on Humanism." *Basic Writings.* Revised and Expanded Edition. Ed. David Farrell Krell. San Francisco: HarperCollins Publishers, 1993.

———. *Einführung in die Metaphysik.* 1935. Tübingen: Max Niemeyer Verlag, 1953. Trans. as *Introduction to Metaphysics.* Trans. Gregory Fried and Richard Polt. New Haven: Yale University Press, 2000.

———. *Erläuterungen zu Hölderlins Dichtung.* 1944. Sechste Aufl. Ed. Friedrich-Wilhelm von Herrmann. Frankfurt am Main: Vittorio Klostermann, 1996. Trans. as *Elucidations of Hölderlin's Poetry.* Trans. Keith Hoeller. Amherst, NY: Humanity Books, 2000.

———. *Hölderlins Hymne »Der Ister«.* 1942. Ed. Walter Biemel. Frankfurt am Main: Vittorio Klostermann, 1984. Trans. as *Hölderlin's Hymn "The Ister."* Trans. William McNeill and Julia Davis. Bloomington: Indiana University Press, 1996.

———. *Holzwege.* 1950. Siebte Aufl. Ed. Friedrich-Wilhelm von Herrmann. Frankfurt am Main: Vittorio Klostermann, 1994. Trans. as *Off the Beaten Track.* Ed. and Trans. Julian Young and Kenneth Haynes. Cambridge: Cambridge University Press, 2002.

———. "Logos (Heraclitus, Fragment B 50)." 1954. *Early Greek Thinking.* Trans. David Farrell Krell and Frank A. Capuzzi. San Francisco: Harper and Row, Publishers, 1984. 59–78. Original essay appeared in *Vorträge und Aufsätze.*

———. *Poetry, Language, Thought.* Trans. Albert Hofstadter. New York: Perennial Classics, 2001.

———. *Prolegomena zur Geschichte des Zeitbegriffs.* 1925. Ed. Petra Jaeger. Frankfurt am Main: Vittorio Klostermann, 1979. Trans. as *History of the Concept of Time: Prolegomena.* Trans. Theodore Kisiel. Bloomington: Indiana University Press, 1985.

———. *Sein und Zeit.* 1927. Tübingen: Niemeyer, 1953. Trans. as *Being and Time.* Trans. John Maquarrie and Edward Robinson. New York: Harper and Row, 1962.

———. *Unterwegs zur Sprache.* 1959. Elfte Aufl. Stuttgart: Verlag Günther Neske, 1997. Partially trans. as *On the Way to Language.* Trans. Peter D. Hertz. San Francisco: HarperCollins Publishers, 1982.

———. *Vorträge und Aufsätze.* 1954. Achte Aufl. Stuttgart: Neske, 1997.

Herder, Johann Gottfried von. "Treatise on the Origin of Language." 1772. *Philosophical Writings.* Trans. and Ed. Michael N. Forster. Cambridge: Cambridge University Press, 2002. 65–164.

Hoog, Michel. *Cézanne: Father of Twentieth Century Art.* 1989. Trans. Rosemary Stonehewer. New York: Harry N. Abrams, 1994.

Horace. *Ars Poetica.* c. 15 BCE. *Satires, Epistles, and Ars Poetica.* Trans. H. R. Fairclough. Cambridge: Harvard University Press, 1999.

Hutner, Gordon. *Secrets and Sympathy: Forms of Disclosure in Hawthorne's Novels.* Athens: University of Georgia Press, 1988.

Irving, Washington. *Bracebridge Hall, Tales of a Traveller, The Alhambra.* New York: The Library of America, 1983.

———. *History, Tales and Sketches: Letters of Jonathan Oldstyle, Gent.; Salmagundi; A History of New York; The Sketch Book of Geoffrey Crayon, Gent.* New York: The Library of America, 1983.

———. "Sleepy Hollow: An Essay by Geoffrey Crayon." *The Knickerbocker Magazine*, May 1839. *The Sleepy Hollow Home Page.* Ed. Henry Steiner. 08 May 2001 <http://members.aol.com/sleepy129/sh/sh-artic.htm>.

Jaanus, Maire. "The Ethics of the Real in Lacan's Seminar VII." *Literature and Psychology* 43, no. 1–2 (1997): 1–18.

James, Henry. *Literary Criticism: Essays on Literature, American Writers, English Writers.* New York: The Library of America, 1984.

Johnston, Adrian. "Addendum: Let a thousand flowers bloom!—Some Brief Remarks on and Responses to Žižek's 'Badiou: Notes from an Ongoing Debate.'" *International Journal of Žižek Studies* 1, no. 2 (2007): 1–18.

———. "The Quick and the Dead: Alain Badiou and the Split Speeds of Transformation." *International Journal of Žižek Studies* 1, no. 2 (2007): 1–32.

———. "There Is Truth, and Then There Are Truths—or, Slavoj Žižek as a Reader of Alain Badiou." *International Journal of Žižek Studies* 1, no. 0 (2007): 141–85.

Kant, Immanuel. *Kritik der Urteilskraft.* 1790. Ed. Gerhard Lehmann. Stuttgart: Philipp Reclam, 1963. Trans. as *Critique of Judgment.* Trans. Werner Pluhar. Cambridge: Hackett, 1987.

Kierkegaard, Søren. *Fear and Trembling; Repetition.* 1843. Ed. and Trans. Howard V. Hong and Edna H. Hong. *Kierkegaard's Writings, Volume VI.* Princeton: Princeton University Press, 1983.

Lacan, Jacques. *Autres écrits.* Paris: Éditions du Seuil, 2001. Partially trans. in *Television; A Challenge to the Psychoanalytic Establishment.* Ed. Joan Copjec. New York: W. W. Norton, 1990.

———. *Écrits.* Paris: Éditions du Seuil, 1966. Partially trans. in *Écrits: A Selection.* Ed. Alan Sheridan. New York: W. W. Norton, 1977.

———. *Le Séminaire, Livre VII: L'éthique de la psychanalyse, 1959–1960.* Ed. Jacques-Alain Miller. Paris: Éditions du Seuil, 1986. Trans. as *The Seminar of Jacques Lacan. Book VII: The Ethics of Psychoanalysis, 1959–1960.* Ed. Jacques-Alain Miller. Trans. Dennis Porter. New York: W. W. Norton, 1992.

———. *Le Séminaire, Livre XI: Les quatre concepts fondamentaux de la psychanalyse*, 1964. Ed. Jacques-Alain Miller. Paris: Éditions du Seuil, 1973. Trans. as *The Seminar of Jacques Lacan. Book XI: The Four Fundamental Concepts of Psycho-Analysis.* Ed. Jacques-Alain Miller. Trans. Alan Sheridan. New York: W. W. Norton, 1978.

———. *Le Séminaire, Livre XX: Encore, 1972–1973.* Ed. Jacques-Alain Miller. Paris: Éditions du Seuil, 1975. Trans. as *The Seminar of Jacques Lacan. Book XX: Encore: On Feminine Sexuality, The Limits of Love and Knowledge, 1972–1973.* Ed. Jacques-Alain Miller. Trans. Bruce Fink. New York: W. W. Norton, 1998.

Lawrence, David Herbert. *Studies in Classic American Literature.* 1923. Harmondsworth: Penguin, 1977.

Lessing, Gotthold Ephraim. *Laokoon, oder, Über die Grenzen der Malerei und Poesie.* 1766. Stuttgart: Philipp Reclam, 2001. Trans. as *Laocoon: An Essay Upon the Limits of Painting and Poetry.* Trans. Ellen Frothingham. New York: Farrar Straus Cudahy, 1961.

Levinas, Emmanuel. *Autrement qu'être ou au-delà de l'essence.* 1974. Paris: Kluwer Academic/Le Livre de Poche, [1996?]. Trans. as *Otherwise than*

Being or Beyond Essence. Trans. Alphonso Lingis. Boston: Kluwer Academic Publishers, 1991.

———. *De l'existence à l'existant*. 1947. Seconde édition augmentée. Paris: J. Vrin, 1998. Trans. as *Existence and Existents*. Trans. Alphonso Lingis. Pittsburgh: Duquesne University Press, 2001.

———. *Dieu, la mort, et le temps*. 1975–1976. Ed. Jacques Rolland. Paris: Éditions Grasset & Fasquelle, 1993. Trans. as *God, Death, and Time*. Trans. Bettina Bergo. Stanford: Stanford University Press, 2000.

———. *Éthique et infini: Dialogues avec Philippe Nemo*. 1982. Paris: Fayard/Le Livre de Poche. Trans. as *Ethics and Infinity: Conversations with Philippe Nemo*. Trans. Richard A. Cohen. Pittsburgh: Duquesne University Press, 1985.

———. *Noms propres*. Montpellier, France: Fata Morgana, 1976. Trans in *Proper Names*. Trans. Michael B. Smith. Stanford: Stanford University Press, 1996. 1–123, 171–82.

———. "La réalité et son ombre." 1948. *Les imprévus de l'histoire*. Montpellier, France: Fata Morgana, 1975. Trans. as "Reality and Its Shadow." *Collected Philosophical Papers*. Trans. Alphonso Lingis. Pittsburgh: Duquesne University Press, 1998.

———. *Sur Maurice Blanchot*. 1975. Montpellier, France: Fata Morgana, 2004. Trans. in *Proper Names*. Trans. Michael B. Smith. Stanford: Stanford University Press, 1996. 125–70, 183–87.

———. *Le temps et l'autre*. 1947. Paris: Quadrige/PUF, 2001. Trans. as *Time and the Other*. Trans. Richard A. Cohen. Pittsburgh: Duquesne University Press, 1987.

———. *Totalité et infini: Essai sur l'extériorité*. 1961. Paris: Kluwer Academic/Le Livre de Poche, [1988?]. Trans. as *Totality and Infinity: An Essay on Exteriority*. Trans. Alphonso Lingis. Pittsburgh: Duquesne University Press, 1998.

———. "The Transcendence of Words." 1949. *The Levinas Reader*. Ed. Seán Hand. Oxford: Blackwell, 1989.

Lyotard, Jean-François. *Le différend*. Paris: Les éditions de minuit, 1983. Trans. as *The Differend: Phrases in Dispute*. Trans. Georges Van Den Abbeele. Minneapolis: University of Minnesota Press, 1988.

———. "Levinas's Logic." 1980. *The Lyotard Reader*. Ed. Andrew Benjamin. Oxford: Blackwell, 1989.

———. "Prescription." 1991. Trans. Christopher Fynsk. *Toward the Postmodern*. Ed. Robert Harvey and Mark S. Roberts. New Jersey: Humanities Press, 1992.

MacCannell, Juliet Flower. "Alain Badiou: Philosophical Outlaw." *Alain Badiou: Philosophy and its Conditions*. Ed. Gabriel Riera. Albany: State University of New York Press, 2005. 137–84.

Matthiessen, F. O. *American Renaissance: Art and Expression in the Age of Emerson and Whitman*. London: Oxford University Press, 1941.

Melville, Herman. *Journals*. Ed. Howard C. Horsford and Lynn Horth. Chicago: Northwestern University Press and The Newberry Library, 1989.

———. *Pierre; Israel Potter; The Piazza Tales; The Confidence-Man; Uncollected Prose; Billy Budd, Sailor*. New York: The Library of America, 1984.

Merleau-Ponty, Maurice. *L'Œil et l'Esprit*. 1961. Paris: Éditions Gallimard, 1964. Trans. as "Eye and Mind." *The Merleau-Ponty Aesthetics Reader: Philosophy and Painting*. Ed. Galen A. Johnson. Trans. Michael B. Smith. Evanston: Northwestern University Press, 1993. 121–60.

Nicholl, Charles. "Screaming in the Castle." *London Review of Books* 20, no. 13 (2 July 1998).

Nietzsche, Friedrich. *The Birth of Tragedy*. 1872. *Basic Writings of Nietzsche*. Ed. and trans. Walter Kaufmann. New York: The Modern Library, 1968.

———. *On the Genealogy of Morals*. 1887. *Basic Writings of Nietzsche*. Ed. and trans. Walter Kaufmann. New York: The Modern Library, 1968.

———. "On the Uses and Disadvantages of History for Life." 1874. *Untimely Meditations*. Trans. R. J. Hollingdale. Cambridge: Cambridge University Press, 1983.

Pease, Donald. *Visionary Compacts: American Renaissance Writings in Cultural Context*. Madison: University of Wisconsin Press, 1987.

Plato. *Euthydemus*. c. 385 BCE. *The Collected Dialogues*. Ed. Edith Hamilton and Huntington Cairns. Princeton: Princeton University Press, 1963.

———. *Republic*. c. 375 BCE. *The Collected Dialogues*. Ed. Edith Hamilton and Huntington Cairns. Princeton: Princeton University Press, 1963.

Plotnitsky, Arkady. "Badiou's Equations—and Inequalities: A Response to Robert Hughes's 'Riven.' " *Postmodern Culture* 17, no. 3 (May 2007). <http://muse.jhu.edu/journals/postmodern_culture/toc/pmc17.3.html>.

Poe, Edgar Allan. *Essays and Reviews*. New York: The Library of America, 1984.

———. "The Purloined Letter." 1844. *Poetry and Tales*. New York: The Library of America, 1984. 680–98.

Rabaté, Jean-Michel. *Jacques Lacan: Psychoanalysis and the Subject of Literature*. New York: Palgrave, 2001.

Riera, Gabriel. "For an 'Ethics of Mystery': Philosophy and the Poem." *Alain Badiou: Philosophy and its Conditions*. Ed. Gabriel Riera. Albany: State University of New York Press, 2005. 61–85.

———. " 'The *Possibility* of the Poetic *Said*' in *Otherwise than Being* (Allusion, or Blanchot in Lévinas)." *Diacritics* 34, no. 2 (Summer 2004): 14–36.

Robbins, Jill. *Altered Reading: Levinas and Literature*. Chicago: University of Chicago Press, 1999.

Roudinesco, Elisabeth. *Jacques Lacan*. 1993. Trans. Barbara Bray. New York: Columbia University Press, 1997.

Sartre, Jean-Paul. *The Psychology of the Imagination*. 1940. New York: Citadel Press, 1991.

———. *Qu'est-ce que la littérature?* 1947. Paris: Éditions Gallimard, 1985. Trans. as *What is Literature? And Other Essays*. Cambridge: Harvard University Press, 1988.

Schiller, Friedrich. *Über die ästhetische Erziehung des Menschen in einer Reihe von Briefen*. 1795. *Sämtliche Werke. Band V: Erzählungen; Theoretische Schriften*. Herausgegeben von Wolfgang Riedel. München, Germany: Deutscher

Taschenbuch Verlag, 2004. 570–669. Trans. as *On the Aesthetic Education of Man*. Trans. Reginald Snell. Mineola, NY: Dover Publications, 2004.

Schlegel, Friedrich. *Athenäums-Fragmente*. 1798. *Kritische Schriften und Fragmente [1798–1801]. Studienausgabe. Band 2*. Herausgegeben von Ernst Behler und Hans Eichner. Paderborn, Germany: Ferdinand Schöningh, 1988. 105–56. Trans. as *Athenaeum Fragments*. In *Philosophical Fragments*. Trans. Peter Firchow. Minneapolis: University of Minnesota Press, 1991. 18–93.

Shakespeare, William. *The Tragedy of Macbeth*. 1606. *The Riverside Shakespeare*. Second Edition. Boston: Houghton Mifflin, 1997.

Sophocles. *The Three Theban Plays: Antigone, Oedipus the King, Oedipus at Colonus*. Trans. Robert Fagles. New York: Penguin Books, 1984.

Stambaugh, Joan. Translator's Preface. *Being and Time*. By Martin Heidegger. Albany: State University of New York Press, 1996. xiii–xvi.

Steiner, Henry. "Re: Question: Sleepy Hollow during the revolution." E-mail to Robert Hughes. 13 June 2001.

Stendhal. "Les Cenci." 1837. *L'Abbesse de Castro et autres chroniques italiennes*. Ed. Pierre-Louis Rey. Paris: Pocket Classiques, 1999. Trans. as "The Cenci." *Three Italian Chronicles*. Trans. C. K. Scott-Moncrieff. New York: New Directions Paperbook, 1991.

Van Haute, Philippe. "Death and Sublimation in Lacan's Reading of Antigone." *Levinas and Lacan: The Missed Encounter*. Ed. Sarah Harasym. Albany: State University of New York Press, 1998.

Vandenbogaerde, F. "Analyse de 'Nomos Alpha' de I. Xenakis." *Mathématiques et Sciences Humaines* 24 (1968): 35–50.

Wieland, Christoph Martin. *Der geprüfte Abraham*. 1753. Trans. as *The Trial of Abraham in Four Cantos*. [Boston] 1764.

Williams, Susan S. *Confounding Images: Photography and Portraiture in Antebellum American Fiction*. Philadelphia: University of Pennsylvania Press, 1997.

Xenakis, Iannis. *Nomos Alpha: Violoncello Solo*. London: Boosey and Hawkes, 1965.

———. "Nomos Alpha." 1965. Perf. Siegfried Palm. Rec. 1974. *Intercommunicazione*. Deutsche Grammophon, 2002.

———. "Towards a Philosophy of Music." 1966. *Formalized Music: Thought and Mathematics in Music*. Ed. and Trans. Sharon Kanach. Stuyvesant, NY: Pendragon Press, 1992.

Young, Julian. *Heidegger's Philosophy of Art*. Cambridge: Cambridge University Press, 2001.

Žižek, Slavoj. "Badiou: Notes from an Ongoing Debate." *International Journal of Žižek Studies* 1, no. 2 (2007): 1–15.

———. *Looking Awry: An Introduction to Jacques Lacan through Popular Culture*. Cambridge: The MIT Press, 1992.

———. *The Ticklish Subject: The Absent Centre of Political Ontology*. London: Verso, 2000.

Zupančič, Alenka. *Ethics of the Real: Kant, Lacan*. 1994. London: Verso, 2000.

Index